Ellis Island

Ivan Chermayeff
Designer

Fred Wasserman
Editor

Mary J. Shapiro
Writer

Ellis Island

*An Illustrated History
of the Immigrant Experience*

Macmillan Publishing Company
New York

Maxwell Macmillan Canada
Toronto

Maxwell Macmillan International
New York Oxford Singapore Sydney

Photographs of the Ellis Island
Immigration Museum Collection by
Karen Yamauchi

Pages 2–3
View of Ellis Island, 1905.

Page 4
Women from Guadeloupe, French West Indies, at Ellis Island, April 6, 1911, after arrival on S.S. Korona.

Pages 8–9
Immigrants arriving at Ellis Island, June 1, 1920.

Pages 10–11
Immigrants waiting to enter Ellis Island's main building for inspection.

Macmillan Publishing Company
866 Third Avenue
New York, NY 10022

Maxwell Macmillan Canada, Inc.
1200 Eglinton Avenue East
Suite 200
Don Mills, Ontario M3C 3N1

Macmillan Publishing Company is part of the Maxwell Communication Group of Companies.

Library of Congress Cataloging-in-Publication Data

Chermayeff, Ivan.
    Ellis Island : an illustrated history of the immigrant experience / by Ivan Chermayeff, Fred Wasserman, and Mary J. Shapiro.
        p.   cm.
    ISBN 0–02–584441–5
    1. Ellis Island Immigration Station (New York, N.Y.)—History—Pictorial works. 2. Immigrants—United States—History—Pictorial works.
    3. United States—Emigration and immigration—History—Pictorial works.
    I. Wasserman, Fred. II. Shapiro, Mary J. III. Title.
    JV6484.C46 1991
    325'.1'0973—dc20   91–11376
                                                            CIP

Macmillan books are available at special discounts for bulk purchases for sales promotions, premiums, fund-raising, or educational use. For details contact:

Special Sales
Macmillan Publishing Company
866 Third Avenue
New York, NY 10022

Color separations by Hong Kong Scanner Craft Co., Ltd.

Printed and bound by Horowitz/Rae Book Manufacturers

Printed in the United States of America

10 9 8 7 6 5 4 3 2

Contents

Acknowledgments

This book has evolved from the work of MetaForm Incorporated in designing the Ellis Island Immigration Museum, which opened to the public on September 10, 1990. The exhibits in the museum were produced by The Liberty/Ellis Island Collaborative for the United States Department of the Interior, National Park Service. As the design arm of the Collaborative, MetaForm conceptualized, planned, researched, curated, and designed the exhibits in the museum. MetaForm also played a key role in identifying and procuring all the artifacts, photographs, and video and audio tapes that comprise the museum experience. All the artifacts, photographs, and oral history quotations from the museum exhibits that MetaForm has included in this book were created, developed, researched, or procured under contract with the National Park Service.

A project of this magnitude necessarily owes a great deal to the efforts and generosity of many organizations and individuals. We would like to thank Jack Masey, Project Manager for the Ellis Island Immigration Museum, who kept the various aspects of this enormous undertaking on course; and Principal Designers Ivan Chermayeff, Thomas H. Geismar, and John P. Grady, partners of MetaForm and Chermayeff & Geismar, Inc., who directed the exhibition design process, and through their designs brought the immigration epic to life within the museum's walls.

Our research and curatorial team uncovered and developed the content of the exhibits that forms the basis for this book. Phyllis Montgomery, Director of Research and Chief Curator, guided the effort to build a collection and interpret the immigrant experience, infusing the enterprise with her vision, knowledge, and humanity; Senior Researchers and Curators Mary-Angela E. Hardwick and Fred Wasserman were unrelenting in their dedication to uncover the words, images, and objects that would bring fresh insight into the immigration story. Mary J. Shapiro brought a keen sensitivity and understanding of Ellis Island and immigration to her exhibit texts. Registrar Elizabeth G. Wilmerding miraculously kept track of the collection, obtained rights and releases, and assisted in diverse aspects of the research; Researchers Suzanne Considine, Silvia Koner, Gerry Raker, Evelyn Silberman, and Anne Stovell diligently pursued potential sources for artifacts and photographs.

Senior Designers Robin Parkinson, Christopher W. Farley, and Gina Russell devoted long hours of painstaking effort to the exhibit design; Project Coordinator Christina Trimble skillfully managed an exceedingly complicated venture; Assistant Designers Eugenie

Anderson, Stephen Bamonte, Jane Bocker, Raymond C. Short, and Lorri Shundich contributed to the design and production process; Barbara Gertzen provided impressive secretarial skills; and Betsy Friedman carefully handled the cash flow.

Over a six-year period, MetaForm's researchers and designers worked closely with National Park Service project manager Gary G. Roth. Several branches of the National Park Service assisted in the creation of the museum, including the Washington Office, the North Atlantic Regional Office, the Harpers Ferry Center, and the Statue of Liberty National Monument. The Statue of Liberty-Ellis Island Foundation, Inc., raised the funds for the project and generated national interest in the restoration of Ellis Island. Architects Beyer Blinder Belle/Notter Finegold & Alexander, Inc., restored Ellis Island's main building. Rathe Productions Incorporated and Design and Production Incorporated, the other members of the Collaborative, fabricated the exhibits.

MetaForm appreciates the scholarly advice of the History Committee of the Statue of Liberty-Ellis Island Centennial Commission: Chairman Rudolph Vecoli, Kathleen Neils Conzen, Roger Daniels, Jay P. Dolan, Angier Biddle Duke, Victor R. Greene, William H. Harris, F. Ross Holland, Jr., Alfred Horowitz, Joan M. Jensen, Louise Año Nuevo Kerr, Alan M. Kraut, Bara Levin, Dwight T. Pitcaithley, Moses Rischin, and Virginia Yans-McLaughlin. Additional imput was provided by our own historical consultants, Nathan Glazer, Neil Harris, John Higham, and Thomas Kessner.

Hundreds of individuals and archives, libraries, and museums assisted in the research effort. Of particular note are M. Mark Stolarik, Gail F. Stern, and Pat Proscino of the Balch Institute for Ethnic Studies; Joel Wurl of the Immigration History Research Center at the University of Minnesota; Esther Brumberg of the Museum of Jewish Heritage, New York; Laurie Winfrey of Carousel; and Sam Holmes.

MetaForm is indebted to those who conducted oral histories: Nancy Dallett of AKRF, Inc., who directed the Ellis Island Oral History Project; Joan Morrison and Charlotte Fox Zabusky, who wrote *American Mosaic*; and Charles Guggenheim and Cynthia Coppage of Guggenheim Productions, Inc., who shared oral histories as well as photographic research. Steve Rathe, Lauren Krenzel, Donna Gallers, Ginger Miles, and Lutz Rath of Murray Street Enterprise created audio and music programs for the museum.

Louis Alvarez and Andrew Kolker of the Center for New American Media produced video programs, Burns Connacher Waldron Design Associates created an interactive citizenship test, and Lester Associates designed models of Ellis Island.

Many people assisted in the translation of documents and archival material, particularly Gihan M. Aboulezz, M.G. Carter, Rev. Joseph A. Cogo, Rev. Vartan Hartunian, Denise Heller, Elizabeth Johannsen, Gabriel Lyon, Grazina Noreen, Rabbi and Mrs. J. Howard Ralbag, Anita Rasmussen, Bard Schjolberg, Audrey Slighton, Irena and Carl Stolarik, Simoni Zafiropoulos, and Nina Zucker.

Photographer Karen Yamauchi gave of herself tirelessly in traveling to several conservation laboratories to shoot the artifacts; especially helpful at these facilities were Glen Ruzicka and Mike Jehle of the Conservation Center for Art & Historic Artifacts and Patsy Orlofsky of the Textile Conservation Workshop. Installation photographs of the museum exhibits were taken by Norman McGrath, James Nubile, and Gilles Peress of Magnum Photos.

Transforming the subject matter of an enormous exhibition into a book was a challenge. MetaForm owes special thanks to Ivan Chermayeff, Fred Wasserman, and Mary J. Shapiro, who were assisted by a talented and dedicated staff: Assistant Designer Pamela White oversaw the layout and production of the book with great care; Editorial Assistant Lori Hanley Moody efficiently negotiated rights and releases and helped on innumerable aspects of the project; computer specialist Kate Abell perceptively organized and formatted the manuscript; Lou Vallejo capably assisted with production; and editorial consultant William Zeisel offered many suggestions that greatly improved our manuscript. Phyllis Montgomery and Mary-Angela E. Hardwick graciously responded to frequent requests for information about research materials.

Many avid supporters helped bring the book to fruition: Catherine Chermayeff of Umbra Editions, Inc., and Peter Matson of Sterling Lord Literistic, Inc., were enthusiastic about the book from the beginning. At Macmillan, Senior Editor Wendy G. Batteau made many important recommendations, Editorial Assistant Patrick Groom handled numerous details, and Production Manager Camillo Lo Giudice took a special interest in the book.

Finally, we would like to thank the hundreds of immigrants and their families who shared their stories, photographs, and artifacts with us. They provided the heart of this book.

Foreword

On an overcast, drizzly day several summers ago, I took the boat from Manhattan to Ellis Island and joined one of the National Park Service tours that were offered in the days before the restoration of the island's main building and its transformation into the Ellis Island Immigration Museum. I had just been appointed to guide the planning, design, and installation of the new museum, and among my tour companions were several designers from the firm that would do the work.

The gray sky intensified the bleakness of the island's deteriorated buildings. By a stroke of luck, two members of the tour group were a man and a woman (brother and sister, it turned out) who had come through Ellis Island as children. In his pocket the man carried an old photograph that he willingly shared once inside the building. The photograph showed two adults, his parents, now deceased, and two children, his sister and himself. While a Park Service ranger deftly guided us through the damp interior of the main building, with its flaking paint, fallen plaster, and rotted doors, the two former immigrants, now something of celebrities, each volunteered recollections of the family's experiences.

Mostly they talked of hardship, of life in the old country, a midnight escape, the long transatlantic trip, and then a brief, unexplained detention on the island. Sometimes, as in the dining room, they disagreed (he liked the food, she did not). Finally, they spoke of their parents' fear of rejection and their subsequent elation when they were pronounced free to land in America.

I remember thinking on that day how their words had made the old building live. Ellis Island might be able to do that again, for all Americans, I thought, if only we could bring to the new museum some of what we had just experienced.

I also reflected on the island's ability to elicit sharply contrasting feelings and recollections. Far from being a welcoming symbol, like the nearby Statue of Liberty, the island was intended to control, limit, and channel the huge immigrant flow into the United States. It was a massive, intimidating government facility, the scene of many personal disappointments and even tragedies. Yet, as our two tour companions made clear, Ellis Island could also be the focus of hopes and aspirations and, at least in retrospect, a place to hold close to the heart.

Today's restored Ellis Island captures that dual character. Through the museum, and now through this book, we glimpse the personal reality and the complex historical factors that led a Polish woman to dream of a new life in America, or a man from Barbados to leave all that was familiar and strike out for an uncertain future on a different shore. We share the joy of an Irish woman at her first sight of the Statue of Liberty and the New World. We feel the deep anxiety of a Russian youth as he waited his turn for inspection.

For most of these people, Ellis Island was merely an interlude on their great journey. Yet the significance of those moments for tens of millions of their descendants has permanently etched the island deep into American history and culture. Though the island has an ambiguous reputation as both gateway and barrier, it was a common rite of passage for those who came this way. Through good fortune, virtue, and in some cases quick thinking, these people were allowed into the promised land.

What happened to them after they passed through Ellis Island and took the ferries to the mainland? The museum and the book follow immigrants to their new lives in the new land. With an Italian family we take the train across America, en route to a new home in an alien, uncertain place. We peer over the shoulders of Jewish garment workers in a New York sweatshop. We listen to Swedish brothers who describe their new life in Texas.

As we read their words, see their faces, and look at their treasured possessions, we better understand what it meant to leave the familiar and travel far away, and also what the fact of immigration has meant for this country. Like the brother and sister on the Ellis Island tour several summers ago, we can see the immigrants not only as people of another time but as part of our heritage, part of who we are.

Gary G. Roth
National Park Service

Opposite: Italian girl at Ellis Island holding her first U.S. penny, 1926.

Introduction

"Well, we're off for America. Where it is, I don't know. I only know it's far." Thus spoke Sholom Aleichem's quintessential immigrant, who, like legions of men, women, and children before him, packed up his belongings, trekked overland to the nearest seaport, and then sailed to the New World. He was following in a long procession of immigrants that began shortly after the first European explorations of the Western Hemisphere. The influx of newcomers started as a trickle but, by the nineteenth century, had grown into a torrent. Since 1600, over 60 million people from all over the world have come to the land now known as the United States. This mass migration of humankind, epic in scale, is remarkable not only for its volume but also for its diversity. The settlers came from every corner of the earth and together created a multiethnic, multiracial society unparalleled in history.

Early voyagers, mostly from Spain, England, and France, found a continent sparsely populated by some 200 distinct groups of Native Americans (an estimated 5 million people) who had been here since prehistoric times. The newcomers pushed their way into the land, established trading outposts, and imported enslaved Africans to work on vast plantations. By the end of the colonial period, about 20% of the American population was African or descended from Africans. The remainder was primarily English, with significant numbers of Germans and Scots-Irish and sprinklings of other northern Europeans, including Dutch, French, Swedes, Welsh, and Finns.

The great tide of European immigration began in earnest following the Napoleonic Wars. During the 1820s and 1830s, 600,000 newcomers, primarily English and Irish, entered the United States. Then, over the next two decades, immigration exceeded three million. Disastrous circumstances in Ireland and Germany caused this tremendous surge in numbers. The first of several potato famines occurred in Ireland in 1845. Over the next decade, nearly two million Irish fled their stricken homeland, the majority of them bound for America. In Germany, the brutal suppression of the 1848 revolution prompted political dissidents to emigrate; they were joined by others seeking economic opportunity. During the next ten years, nearly one million Germans came to the United States.

The Civil War brought about a temporary decline in immigration, but by the late 1860s and 1870s, French Canadians were flocking to New England, while 200,000 Chinese had settled on the West

Opposite: Slovak mother and children, Ellis Island.

Coast. Scandinavians, who had been immigrating in small numbers in previous decades, were now arriving in the hundreds of thousands, moving into America's western lands and establishing farms.

By the 1880s, millions of immigrants had made the journey, and the annual rate of arrivals continued to rise. The sheer magnitude and diversity of the incoming stream, with southern and eastern Europeans joining the flow, caused Americans to reconsider the country's open-door immigration policies. At the very least, critics said, the country ought to make sure all of the immigrants were desirable additions to society. The outcry was such that the federal government took over the regulation of immigration from the states and established inspection depots at various ports, including New York's Ellis Island, which opened on January 1, 1892. On Ellis Island, newcomers encountered an American bureaucracy charged with inspecting arrivals, weighing their merits, and deciding whether they were entitled to enter the promised land. Though only 2% of the immigrants were turned away, fear and confusion seemed to pervade and characterize the island's proceedings.

Since the early part of the nineteenth century, New York had been America's chief port of entry, receiving over 70% of the immigrants. This remained true during Ellis Island's busiest years of operation, 1892 to 1924, when over 12 million newcomers passed through the island's narrow portal on their way to new lives. As the Plymouth Rock of its day, Ellis Island provides a fixed point in the vast and sprawling narrative of the immigrant experience. The uncelebrated men, women, and children who crossed this island on pilgrimages of hope entered American life, set down roots, found work, married, and raised their families. Today, over 100 million Americans can trace their ancestry through Ellis Island: a place that had once aroused so much fear but now suggests the fulfillment of millions of dreams.

The Ellis Island Immigration Museum, which opened in 1990, fulfills another dream. "By preserving their stories for the future," wrote the daughter of one immigrant, "the museum has validated their past and given these wonderful people a new sense of who they are. And they are, of course, America."

In a sense, the museum was created by the immigrants themselves. They and their descendants contributed photographs, mementos from the old country, and souvenirs of long journeys. Many donors sent in letters or recorded oral histories recounting their experiences. "My father left first, and then sent for us." "I went to join my brother who found a job for me." "As soon as I had saved enough money I sent for my parents." Most newcomers were of modest means but had at least the money to buy a ticket and were strong enough to make the journey. They came primarily from the working classes. They were domestics, carpenters, masons, farmers, tailors, laborers—as one immigrant said, "I'll do anything!" Willing to risk the little they had, they came to a new place to start again.

Their memories of the day of arrival in New York are often vivid. "You come to America," recalled Alexander Alland, a Jewish immigrant who came from Russia in 1923. "You should have come to a small, little place. But no—the boat stopped right in front of the most impressive sight in the United States, downtown New York." Others remember the Statue of Liberty. "Everybody clapped and yelled when they saw the statue because they knew that was America," said Dolores Martin, a Spanish immigrant in 1913. "Everybody was so happy. 'We're in America. We finally got to America.'" People waved to her as if she were an old friend. "The thrill was unbelievable," said Joseph Talese, an Italian immigrant in 1920. "But always the fear, you know, because you have to go through Ellis Island. I heard all kinds of things that they would tell you on the boat. 'My God,' I said, 'I hope they're not going to send me back.'"

"You'll be sorry when you get to Ellis Island," friends of Mary Dunn told her in 1923, before she made her journey from Scotland. She wasn't sorry, she said later, just bothered by all the handling by strangers. "You just did whatever you were told," said Emanuel Steen, an Irish immigrant in 1925. "The guards, I guess, had no time to explain matters. Wherever you were pushed, there's where you went. The only thing that kept me going, I guess all of the other immigrants too, was that right across the water you could see the land of golden opportunity."

Other immigrants remember the chaos, confusion, and noise. "The echo of all those different languages," said Anna Vida, who arrived from Hungary in 1921. "The fright, you know, the voices rise with fright." Nearly all passed the inspection process and were admitted, but about 20% of the arrivals were detained for days or weeks before they were cleared to enter the country. Inga Nastke, a German immigrant in 1922, spent two weeks on Ellis Island before her release. "I took a last look at the Statue of Liberty," she said, "and then I looked at Ellis Island. I thought, oh, how many tears I had to shed there." But not all memories were sad. "I remember joy in Ellis Island," said Vartan Hartunian, an Armenian immigrant who had escaped violent persecution in Turkey in 1922. "I was a kid of seven, and in contrast to what I had gone through, Ellis Island was like not a haven but a heaven."

Within the museum exhibits, America's immigration epic resonates with the personal recollections of the immigrants themselves. Their stories of survival and continuity reveal the profound human issues that were at stake in making the long journey. Most left their homelands because of economic necessity, while others were driven out by wars and persecution. They were drawn by the hope of finding freedom, work, and a chance to succeed. Each of their stories is unique and bears witness to the courage, ingenuity, and determination that enabled men and women to leave the homes of their youth to seek new opportunities in an unknown land.

This book is based on the exhibits and collections of the Ellis Island Immigration Museum. Like the museum, the book concentrates on America's busiest years of immigration, the decades surrounding the turn of the twentieth century, when Ellis Island was central to the immigration experience. A broad historical survey portrays the "Peak Immigration Years: 1880–1924," from the uprooting from the homeland to the often painful experience of adjusting to American life. The following chapter, "Through America's Gate," offers a detailed description of what happened to immigrants on Ellis Island, the various inspections as well as services related to caring for hundreds, sometimes thousands, of detainees held on the island. "Treasures from Home" presents a look at the things the immigrants carried with them and recounts personal histories and anecdotes of their journeys to and into America. And "Island Chronicles" relates the story of the island itself, from its early Native American and colonial days to its rebirth as a national museum.

Opposite: Ruthenian immigrant, Ellis Island.

Overleaf: Market day in Strij, Galicia, 1905. Between 1880 and 1924, more than one million immigrants, predominantly Poles, Ukrainians, and Jews, came to the United States from this poor region of the Austro-Hungarian Empire.

"I left Barbados because the jobs were scarce. I decided to take a chance and come to this new country. There were a lot of us from the West Indies. We heard this was a good, new country where you had the opportunity to better your circumstances."

Lyle Small, a Barbadian immigrant in 1921

"As a child, I witnessed 2,000 or so Armenians burned alive in a church. We even heard their cries from where we were. And one woman tried to escape from that burning church. And of course, there were Turkish soldiers outside who shot her. You know, sometimes I hear their screaming and shouting even now."

Vartan Hartunian, an Armenian immigrant in 1922

Top: Jamaican marketplace. Approximately 350,000 West Indians immigrated to the United States between 1880 and 1924.

Bottom: Mexican family. Between 1900 and 1924, 475,000 Mexicans, some fleeing the Mexican Revolution and many others drawn by the expanding U.S. economy, officially entered the country. Since most of the border was unregulated, the actual number was probably far greater.

Top: One of the public executions of Armenians that took place in Ottoman Turkey during 1915–16. By 1924, nearly 100,000 Armenians had come to the United States, many fleeing periodic Turkish massacres and deportations in which over one million Armenians died.

Bottom: Irish peasants, ca. 1880. During the peak immigration years, desperate economic necessity drove 1.5 million Irish to leave for America.

Peak Immigration Years: 1880–1924

"Once there was a pogrom in our town and we had to run. I said to my mother, 'Ma, we are such good people. Why are they killing us?'"

Fannie Friedman, a Ukrainian Jewish immigrant in 1921

By the late nineteenth century, the migration phenomenon had shifted into high gear. Beginning around 1880 and continuing for the next four and a half decades, millions of men and women packed up their belongings and traveled thousands of miles to seek new opportunities in new lands or to find political or religious freedom. It was an era of mass migrations, the largest recorded in world history. Not all the emigrants came to the United States; Australia, New Zealand, Argentina, Brazil, and Canada were all popular destinations. But for the overwhelming majority, the United States was the land of choice. Between 1880 and 1924, the peak immigration years, over 26 million people arrived at America's shores.

This period saw not only a dramatic surge in numbers but also a far more diverse immigrant population. For much of the nineteenth century, arrivals had been mostly from the northern European countries, primarily England, Ireland, Germany, and Scandinavia. During the 1880s, however, this pattern gradually began to change, with more and more immigrants from Italy, Russia, and Austria-Hungary. The shift in incoming nationalities continued, and by 1907, a record-breaking year for immigration, the new groups accounted for 75% of America's arrivals. Though the remainder hailed mostly from northern Europe, they also included significant numbers from countries all over the world, including Canada, Mexico, the West Indies, China, and Japan.

This great migration arose from conditions that had been troubling Europe since the early decades of the nineteenth century. A steady growth in population, a serious shortage of farmland, primitive economies, and oppressive taxes created severe economic burdens. Military conscription menaced young men and legalized persecution threatened ethnic and religious minorities. Many of the eastern European Jews who emigrated were fleeing not only the outright violence of pogroms but also discriminatory czarist laws that impoverished Jewish communities. Confined by law to the Pale of Settlement (an area along the western Russian frontier), Russian Jews could not practice certain trades, own land, or attend most secondary schools or universities. Other groups also felt the sting of discrimination: centuries of British rule had left many Irish without land, capital, or education; ethnic minorities living in Austria-Hungary could not speak or publish newspapers in their own languages; and Armenians in Turkey suffered violent persecutions.

Hardship and a deep desire for change led many to think seriously about breaking with the past and starting over in the New

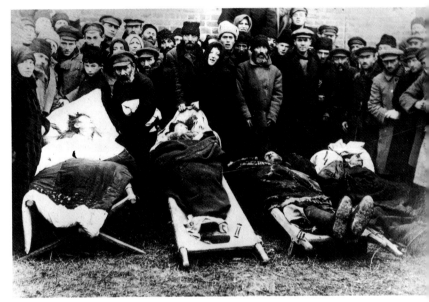

First victims of the Proskurov pogrom on February 15, 1919, in which 1,500 Jews were murdered and thousands injured. This was one of 1,200 pogroms that occurred in the Ukraine during 1918–19. Four decades of violence against Russian Jews followed the assassination of the liberal Czar Alexander II in 1881. In that year alone, over 200 Jewish communities suffered attacks by mobs acting with apparent government approval. Between 1880 and 1924, poverty and persecution drove around 2.3 million eastern European Jews to immigrate to America.

"That's all you heard. Gold on the streets of America. There's no North America and no South America, not United States, just America. It was all good things. You could be anything you want here and make a lot of money, even if it was a dollar a day."

Louise Nagy, a Polish immigrant in 1913

"My boyish imagination was aflame with America....At that time I accepted as truth nearly everything I heard about America. I believed that a single cattleman in Texas owned more cattle than there were in the entire Balkans. And my credulity was not strained when I heard that there were gold mines in California, and trees more than a thousand years old....In America everything was possible."

Louis Adamic, a Slovenian immigrant in 1913

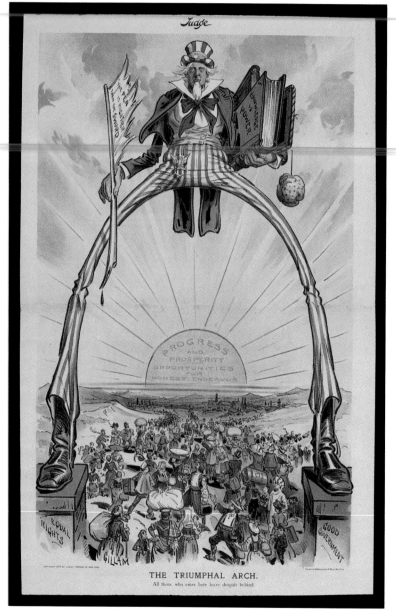

Above: A 1903 perspective on why the United States was attracting so many immigrants. "All those who enter here leave despair behind," reads the caption. Indeed, the United States developed a mythical reputation: to eastern European Jews it was the "golden land," to Finns the "golden nest," and to the Chinese it was known as "golden mountain."

Right: Published in 1919, this poster depicts a somewhat simplistic version of factors that motivated immigration.

World. These latter-day pioneers had not only the will to uproot themselves but also the way. The introduction of the railroad and the steamship made the journey faster, easier, and cheaper than ever before. In 1910, a year that counted a million immigrant arrivals, the *New York Times* commented, "There was never a period when the spirit of restlessness was so generally abroad over the world as it is now." The article added, "This very restlessness, combined with the ease with which human beings can now travel, suggests that this may soon be a very different world than it has ever been."

These migrations, however, cannot be understood solely in terms of historical trends; the decision to leave was ultimately a matter of personal choice. Each traveler had his or her own reasons, ambitions, and dreams—a set of personal goals that made the difficult and risky voyage a deed worth doing. It was, above all, a courageous decision that meant giving up all that was familiar for an adventure into unknown territory. The prospective immigrant had to be willing to endure the emotional pain of leaving family, friends, and home, to pursue the hope that life in America would somehow be better. Rocco Morelli, an Italian immigrant in 1920, remembered his mother's words, "I do not want to raise my children in this country any longer. I don't want no wars. I don't want no poverty. I want to go to the United States. You work over there. The children

Opposite: "Emigrants!" announced this German poster, ca. 1920, "Look at the victims of unscrupulous agents! In foreign countries no one will look after your needs! Get advice and information at the Office of Immigration." Many countries established agencies to assist emigrants.

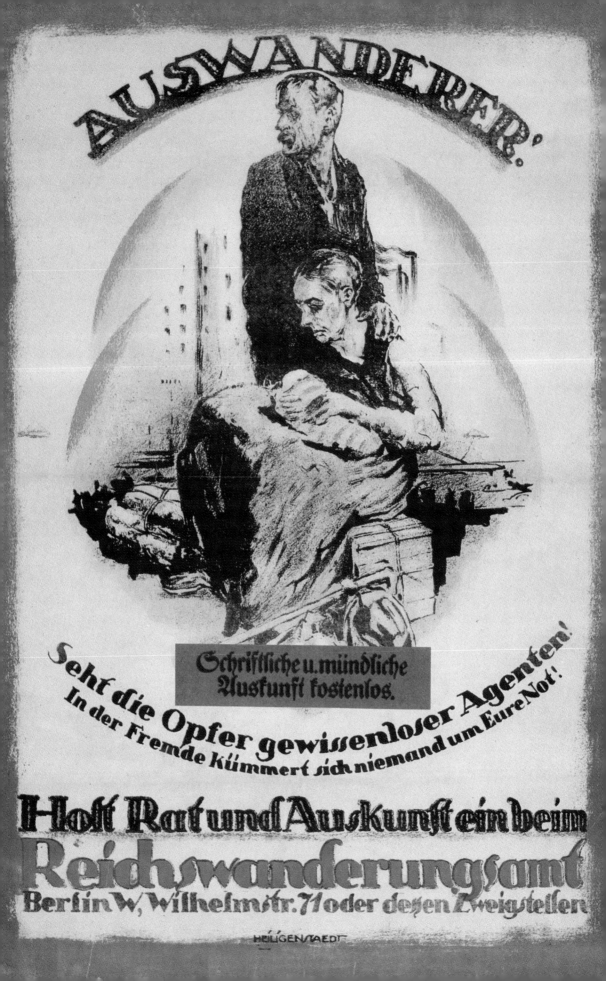

"Well, we didn't have anything to do in Ireland, there was no work. And you didn't want to be poor all your life. You could have married an old farmer if you wanted to and stay there for the rest of your life and work on that old farm. But I wasn't about to do that. So I said, 'Goodbye, I'll see you later.'"

Bertha Devlin, an Irish immigrant in 1923

"I can remember only the hustle and bustle of those last weeks in Pinsk, the farewells from the family, the embraces and the tears. Going to America then was almost like going to the moon."

Golda Meir, a Russian Jewish immigrant in 1906

Top: Norwegian emigrants begin their journey to America. Over 500,000 Norwegians came to the United States between 1880 and 1924.

Bottom: Passengers on train to port of Gdansk in Poland.

will work over there. And at least we'll eat."

America's booming economy and its demand for workers held out favorable prospects for Europe's masses of unemployed and underemployed. Letters from those who had already emigrated to the United States often gave glowing reports of the opportunities enjoyed by the newcomers. "I wish you to come to America," wrote Adam Raczkowski in 1906 to a relative in Poland. "Up to the present I am doing very well here, and I have no intention of going to our country, because [there] I experienced only misery and poverty, and now I live better than a lord." Letters like this, filled with enthusiastic, often exaggerated claims, were read aloud in homes all over Europe. Emigrants who came back to the old country were able to tell their stories first-hand. "When someone returns from America to tell us that the wages are superior and that there are fewer discomforts," said Adolfo Rossi in 1908, "many of the men cannot resist the temptation to go and find out for themselves." Though many returned to Europe broken in body and spirit from working in American industries, their cautionary tales were less influential than the stories of success.

Emigrant guidebooks, newspaper articles, and promotional brochures from railway and steamship companies also spread the good word about America as a new promised land. After an initial few from a village had been persuaded to embark for America, it was only a matter of time before others followed. Perhaps a father or older brother would emigrate first, find a job, and save to buy tickets for other family members. This was a regimen that demanded both patience and frugality. Around the turn of the century, the lowest cost of a steamship ticket was about $25 to $35, depending on the port of embarkation. An immigrant miner working in Pennsylvania's coalfields, for example, would find the price of one ticket equivalent to two or three weeks' wages. After paying his room and board, he could save perhaps 50 cents each week to buy his family's passage. By 1900, the majority of immigrants were traveling on prepaid tickets sent from America, indicating the remarkable strength of family ties and the human desire for roots and continuity.

Opposite: Italians arriving at the Emigrant Aid Society in Naples before embarking for the United States. Many Italians, as well as Greeks, Slavs, and British, followed a pattern of migration that brought them to the United States in the spring and returned them home in time for Christmas. Immigration officials called them "birds of passage."

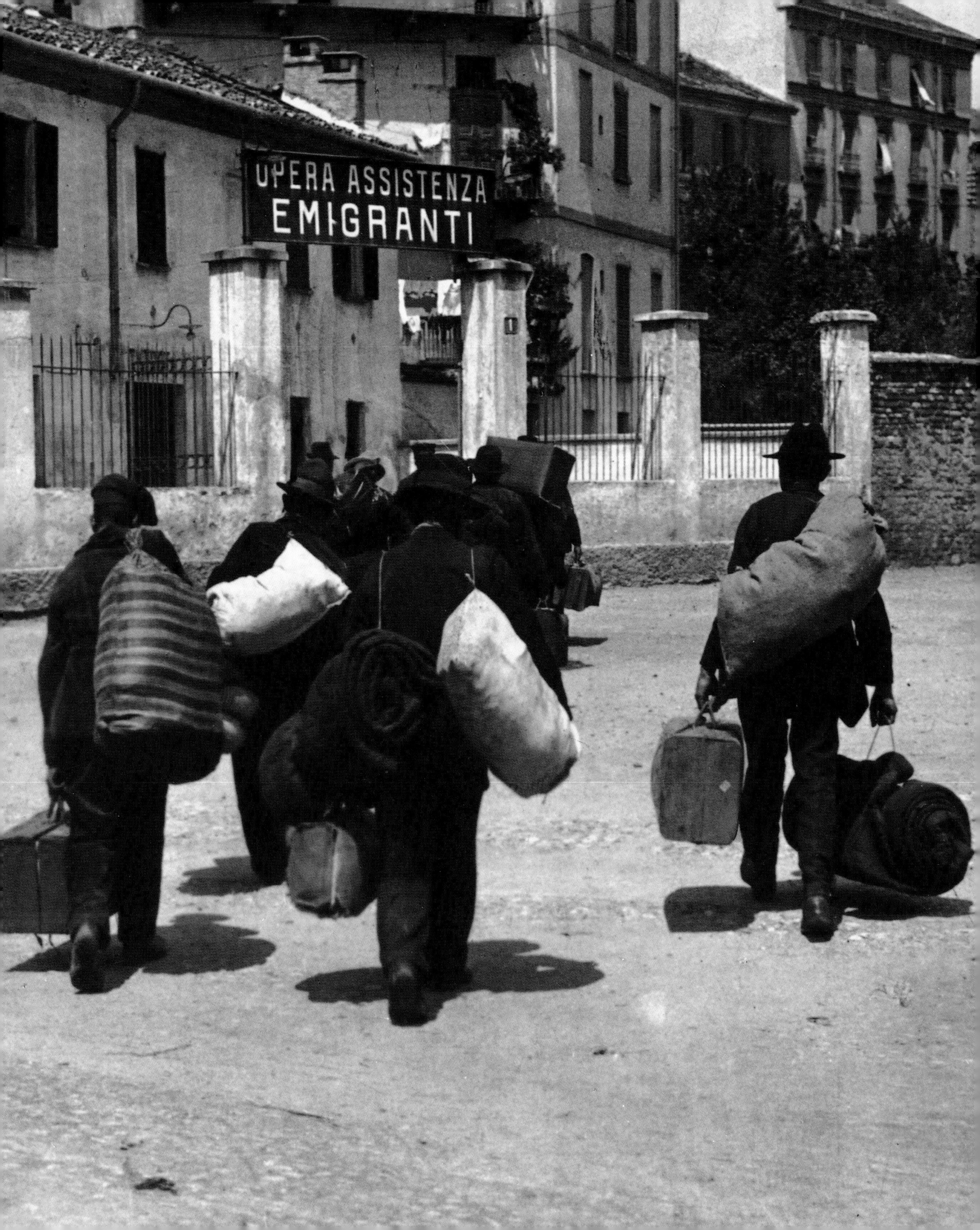
OPERA ASSISTENZA
EMIGRANTI

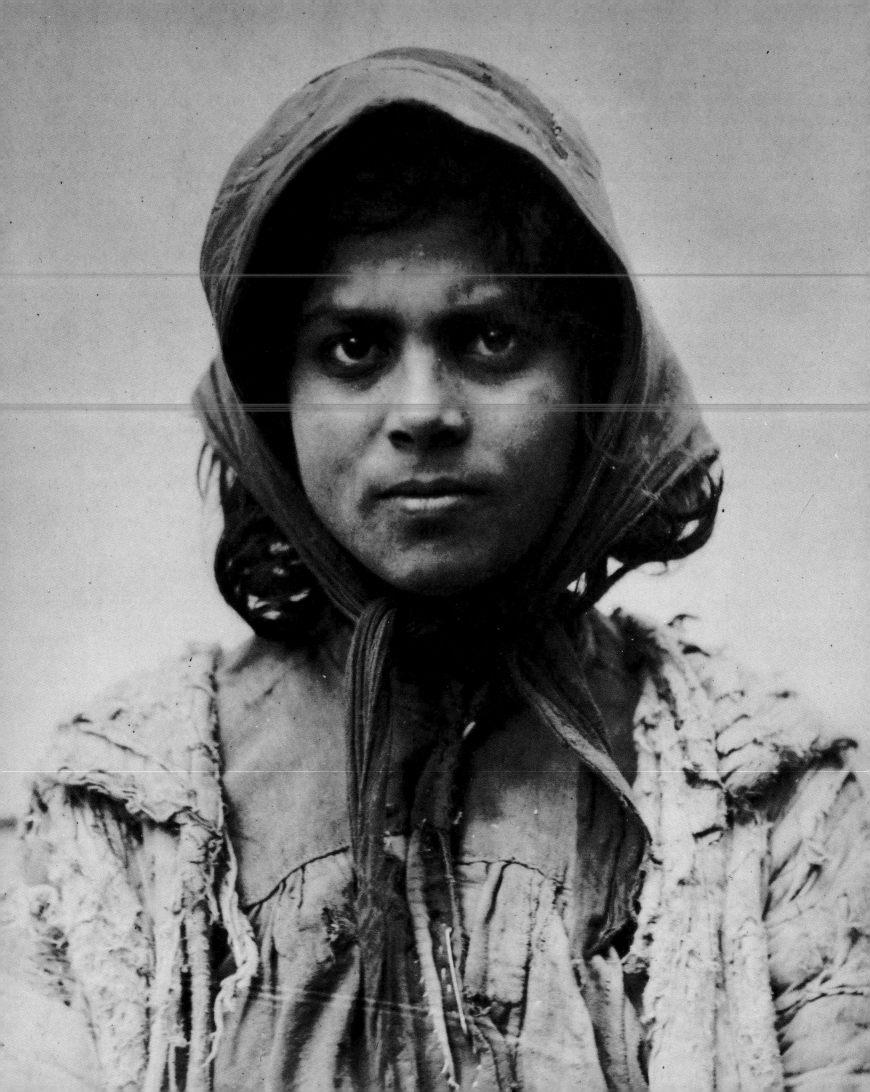

"The day I left home, my mother came with me to the railroad station. When we said goodbye, she said it was just like seeing me go into my casket. I never saw her again."

Julia Goniprow, a Lithuanian immigrant in 1899

"I felt lost, as if there was nothing to hold onto ahead of us. But having my mother and my two brothers with me, we felt we were still a family, though our life would never be the same."

Maria Oogjen, a Russian immigrant in 1923

Above: Bulgarian refugees leaving for America.

Opposite: Gypsy refugee, Salonika, Greece, 1918.

World War I caused a sharp decline in immigration. But soon after the war, the reopening of the Atlantic shipping lanes to civilian travel brought hundreds of thousands of refugees from Europe's war-stricken regions. In 1921, immigrants numbered over 800,000, close to the annual, record figures of the early 1900s.

immigrants' passports. Before the 1910s, many countries did not require passports, but carrying one generally made travel more convenient, especially for immigrants who had to cross several borders within Europe to get to a seaport. Other countries, such as Russia, Hungary, and Romania, required passports for citizens who were planning to leave the country. In this way governments controlled the outward flow of professionals, skilled workers, and young men of military age.

With the outbreak of World War I, nations attempting to protect their borders required travelers to carry passports. In 1918, the United States also instituted a wartime policy (made permanent in 1921) that required arriving aliens to show their passports.

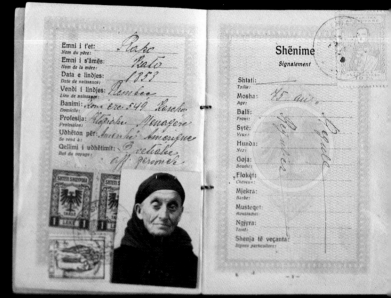

Passports, left to right.

Top row:
Kalotina Kakias Fatolitis and daughter Eleni, Greece, 1923.
Celesta Ciavarella DelForno, Italy, 1918.
Felix D. Lowenfish, Poland, 1923.
Vilhelm Ragnar Hedman, Sweden, 1923.

Middle row:
Arie A. Sablerolle, Netherlands, 1920.
Manny Joe Marcus, Poland, 1923.
Manuel and Buena Sarfatti and children Hyman, Sam, Regina, and Victoria, Greece, 1916.
Konino Leko Pojani, Albania, 1928.

Bottom Row:
Henriette Herz, Saarland (now part of Germany), 1928.

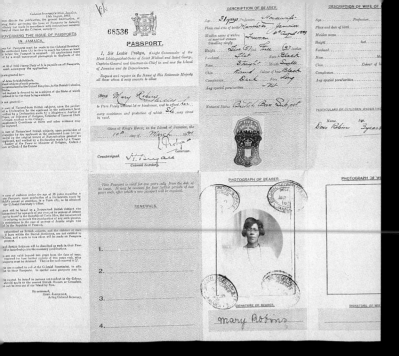

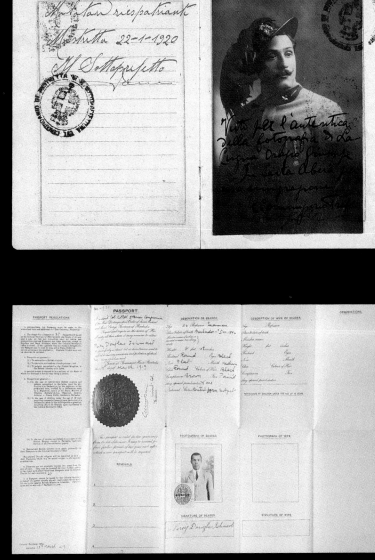

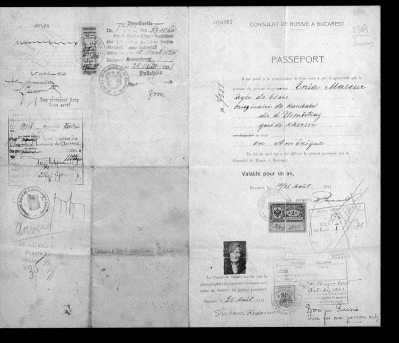

Passports, left to right.

Top row:

Mary Robins and daughter Doris, Jamaica, 1921.

Eric and Hilda Flinck and children Margaret and Anton, Sweden, 1923.

Ana Suknaich and son Peter, Yugoslavia, 1920.

Orazio Giuseppe LaCugna, Italy, 1920.

Middle row:

Mehar Singh, India, 1922.

Percy D. Ishmael, Barbados, 1919.

Bottom row:

Chiyoto Sakai, Japan, 1919.

Esther Pivirotto, Italy, 1922.

Enia Masour, Russia, 1921.

"We were stationed in Hamburg in a tremendous big place. It was sort of an assembly building where you got processed. There was an exodus from Europe at that time, and they had all races in this place. You could see people from Russia, Poland, Lithuania, you name it. I can't describe the way I felt—it was part fear, it was exciting. It's something I'll never forget."

Ludwig Hofmeister, a German immigrant in 1925

Passage to America

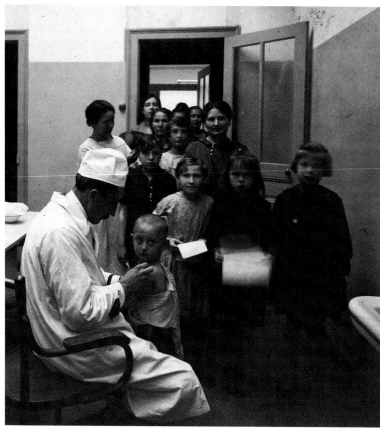

By the 1880s, the great age of sail was over, and a new era of giant steam-powered ships was underway. An Atlantic crossing on these iron-hulled leviathans lasted eight to fourteen days, mercifully short when compared to earlier voyages in sailing ships that took one to three months to tack their way across the ocean. The introduction of steam power modernized the entire business of ocean travel. Cunard, White Star, Hamburg-America, and other major lines competed not only for the luxury trade but also for emigrant passengers, who were considered a highly profitable, self-loading cargo. Ships could accommodate a thousand or more emigrants in steerage—so-called because it was on the lower decks, where the steering mechanism was once located.

During the 1890s, when more emigrants were coming from eastern and southern Europe, Naples and Bremen were the two top seaports for embarkation to America, with Liverpool and Hamburg ranking third and fourth. Other busy ports were Rotterdam, Gdansk, Trieste, and Fiume.

As the emigrant business grew, major shipping lines built extensive seaport hotels where steerage passengers could stay until their ships were ready to sail. The Hamburg-America Line, for example, maintained an entire village that had two churches, a synagogue, a kosher kitchen, and accommodations for 5,000 passengers. In the town square, afternoon concerts were held regularly. At the Holland-America Line's emigrant complex at Rotterdam, the

Top: Hamburg-America Line clerks register emigrants, 1909. The sign above them says, "My field is the world."

Bottom: Vaccinating emigrants at Cherbourg, France.

Opposite top: Italian family in port of Naples, ca. 1900, part of a large exodus from southern Italy. More passengers left from Naples than from all other Italian ports combined, and typically 2,000 to 3,000 emigrants were examined on a busy afternoon. Four million Italians emigrated to the United States between 1880 and 1924.

Opposite bottom left: Certificate issued to emigrant after being vaccinated and "unloused," 1921.

Opposite bottom right: Steamship ticket for Sore Judin and her two children, who emigrated from Russia in 1910.

NAME *Awlawski Samuel*

DATE *Aug 16 1921*

HAS BEEN **VACCINATED** AND

UNLOUSED

AND IS PASSED AS VERMIN-FREE THIS DATE AT THE

DESINFECTION MARITIME CHERBOURG

SUBSEQUENT EXPOSURE TO VERMINOUS REINFESTA-
TION RENDERS THIS CERTIFICATE INVALID, AND NECESSITATES
ANOTHER UNLOUSING OF THE PERSON AND DISINFECTION AND
DELOUSING OF HIS CLOTHING, PERSONAL EFFECTS AND BAGGAGE
BEFORE EMBARKATION TO THE UNITED STATES OF AMERICA.

A. A. SURGEON,
UNITED STATES PUBLIC HEALTH SERVICE

Листъ 9
№ 4-6

С.
№ 7904

РУССКОЕ ВОСТОЧНО-АЗІАТСКОЕ ПАРОХОДСТВО.

ПАССАЖИРСКІЙ — Passenger / БИЛЕТЪ — Ticket.

THE RUSSIAN EAST-ASIATIC STEAMSHIP COMPANY LD.

АТЛАНТИЧЕСКАЯ ЛИНІЯ
ATLANTIC LINE.

§ 1. Русское Восточно-Азіатское Пароходство обя-
зался принять на пароходъ ...
доставить на эмигрантскомъ помещеніи изъ Либавы
въ Нью-Іоркъ и изъ Нью-Іорка далее въ III классѣ
эмигрантскаго поѣзда въ ...
штата ... слѣдующихъ лицъ:

§ 1. The Russian East-Asiatic Steamship Co. Ld.
hereby agrees to take on board the steamship ...
and carry in the accommodation provided for emigrants
from Libau to New-York and further by emigrants'train from
New-York to
in the State of
following persons:

№	Имя и фамилія пассажира. Name of passenger.	Возрастъ. Age.	Наименованіе членовъ семьи. Family relationship.	Прежнее жите- льство. Former residence.	Плата за пере- ѣздъ по морю. Passage freight. by sea.	по жел. дор. per. rs. Aussgezf. by railway.
1	Sore Yardin	48		Dwinsa		
2	Sheine ,,	13			6393	
3	Schmeril ,,	10				
4					23046	
5						
6						
7						
8						

"Many immigrants had brought on board balls of yarn, leaving one end of the line with someone on land. As the ship slowly cleared the dock, the balls unwound amid the farewell shouts of the women, the fluttering of the handkerchiefs, and the infants held high. After the yarn ran out, the long strips remained airborne, sustained by the wind, long after those on land and those at sea had lost sight of each other."

Luciano De Crescenzo, "The Ball of Yarn"

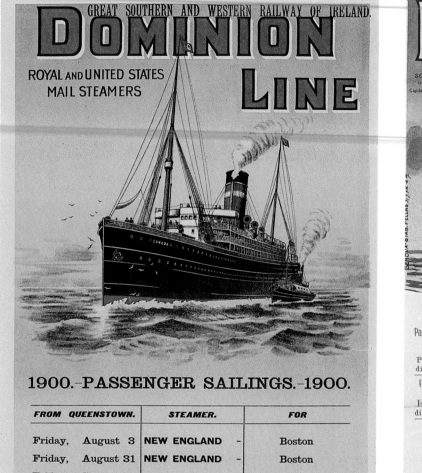

The Great Southern and Western Railway of Ireland posted this announcement at the station in Midleton, County Cork, in 1900. Queenstown (today's Cobh) was a popular port of departure for Irish emigrants.

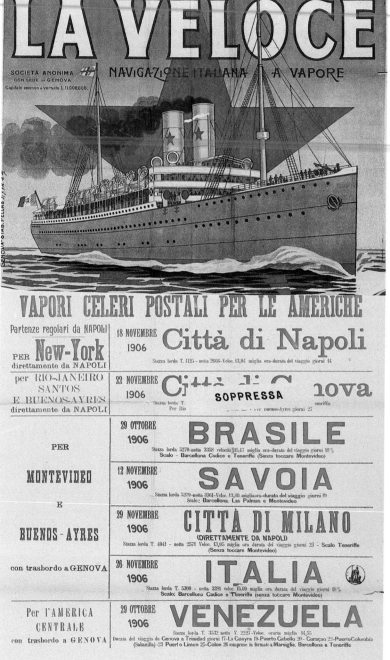

Italian poster advertising sailings to the United States, Brazil, Uruguay, Argentina, and Central America, 1906.

"Oh God, I was sick. Everybody was sick. I don't ever want to remember anything about that old boat. One night I prayed to God that it would go down because the waves were washing over it. I was that sick, I didn't care if it went down or not. And everybody else was the same way."

Bertha Devlin, an Irish immigrant in 1923

"Time between meals was spent on the deck if the weather was good. Some immigrant would always come out with a harmonica or some musical instrument and the dance would follow. And during the day, of course, there were always acquaintances to be made, discussions about America, the conditions in America, and preparation for life in America."

Paul Sturman, a Czechoslovakian immigrant in 1920

Above: The French Line's S.S. Paris *could accommodate 563 first-class, 460 second-class, and 1,092 third-class passengers. It made its maiden voyage between Le Havre and New York in 1921.*

Left: This 1906 steamship poster advertises travel advantages: medical care, comfort against seasickness, electric light, and ventilation. Trieste was the largest port in the Austro-Hungarian Empire at that time, although over two-thirds of the residents were Italian. The city became part of Italy after World War I.

"We naturally were in steerage. Everyone had smelly food, and the atmosphere was so thick and dense with smoke and bodily odors that your head itched, and when you went to scratch your head you got lice in your hands. We had six weeks of that."

Sophia Kreitzberg, a Russian Jewish immigrant in 1908

Above: Third-class cabin on S.S. Hellig Olav, *August 25, 1904. The typical steerage compartment was a large open dormitory with hundreds of bunk beds. Women and children stayed in one section of steerage, men in another.*

Opposite top: R.M.S. Mauretania, *one of the most famous ocean liners, made its maiden voyage between Liverpool, England, and New York on November 16, 1907. The ship held the transatlantic speed record for a number of years, having made the eastward journey in 4 days, 17 hours, and 21 minutes in June 1909.*

"Neither cleanliness, decency, nor comfort, is possible...sometimes two to three thousand persons are crowded into a space hardly sufficient to accommodate 1,200. Steerage passengers can not, with any degree of truth or justice, be said to be humanely or properly treated at any stage of their long and painful journey."

Report of Conditions Existing in Europe and Mexico Affecting Emigration and Immigration, ca. 1907

dormitories were arranged like steerage to help travelers adjust to conditions on board ship. The average stay in these villages was four days. Emigrants had to pay for room and board, but most lines offered these services at cost.

Before allowing steerage passengers on board, shipping companies required them to take an antiseptic bath, have their baggage fumigated, and be examined by company doctors. Anna Salvia, who emigrated from the Ukraine in 1923, recalled her brother wondering at all the fuss. "Gee," he exclaimed, "everyone in America must be so healthy." Since steamship companies could be fined $100 for each prospective immigrant rejected by the U.S. Immigration Service, most lines refused to carry anyone who appeared sick or disabled. To increase their efficiency in screening out potential rejects, Hamburg-America's doctors actually visited Ellis Island to study American methods of examination.

The ocean voyage and conditions on board ship varied, depending on the line, the captain, and the crew. But, even on the great liners, steerage most often meant inadequate ventilation, little privacy, and cramped bunk rooms that became more stuffy and noisome as the journey progressed. Edward Steiner, a veteran traveler who championed the rights of immigrants, made several journeys in steerage. In his book *On the Trail of the Immigrant*, Steiner described steerage conditions on one of the world's most luxurious ships, the *Kaiser Wilhelm II*: "There is neither breathing space below nor deck room above, and the 900 steerage passengers...are positively packed like cattle, making a walk on deck when the weather is good absolutely impossible, while to breathe clean air below in rough weather, when the hatches are down, is an equal impossibility." Steiner concluded, "On the whole, the steerage of the modern ship ought to be condemned as unfit for the transportation of human beings."

Conditions were even worse aboard the majority of vessels that

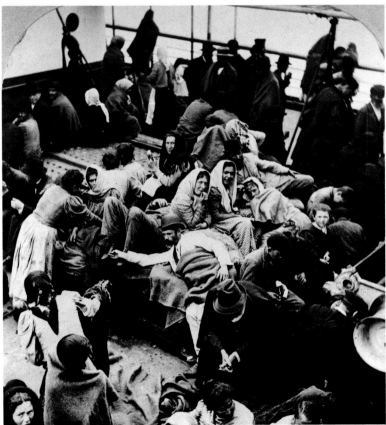

Top right: Immigrants aboard S.S. Prinz Friedrich Wilhelm, *1915. This ship could carry 1,700 steerage passengers.*

Bottom right: "Emigrants Coming to the 'Land of Promise,'" 1902.

Overleaf: Postcards of steamships that transported immigrants to the United States during the peak immigration years.

The Gigantic Leviathan   C. UNDERWOOD & UNDERWOOD

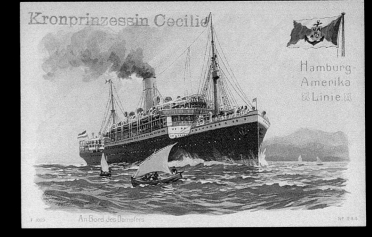

Kronprinzessin Cecilie

Hamburg-
Amerika
Linie

An Bord des Dampfers

INMAN LINE.

CITY OF ROME.

JOHN G. DALE, AGENT, 31 & 33 BROADWAY, NEW YORK.   over.

"Cleveland"

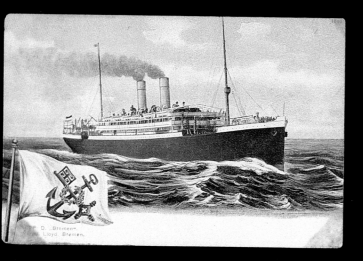

P.D. "Bremen."
Nord Lloyd, Bremen.

HOLLAND-AMERICA LINE.   ROTTERDAM – NEW YORK.

T.S.S. ROTTERDAM.   24170 Tons Register 37190 Tons Displacement.

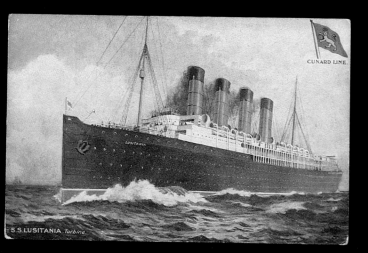

CUNARD LINE.

S.S. LUSITANIA. Turbine.

Gruss von Bord des Dampfers "Prinzess Irene".

RED STAR LINE.

TRIPLE-SCREW "BELGENLAND" 27,200 Tons

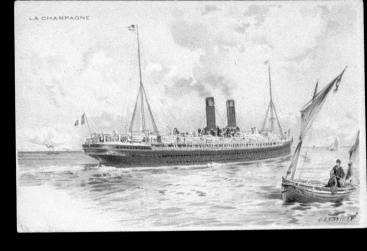

LA CHAMPAGNE

"HANDS ACROSS THE SEA."

R.M.S. CANADA, (DOMINION LINE) 10,000 TONS.

Hands Across the Sea

S.S. CALIFORNIA ANCHOR LINE

R.M.S. CEDRIC (WHITE STAR LINE,) 21,035 TONS.

Nippon Yusen Kaisha S.S. "TAIYO MARU.

SAINT-NAZAIRE. — "L'Espagne" de la Cie Generale Transatlantique. — LL

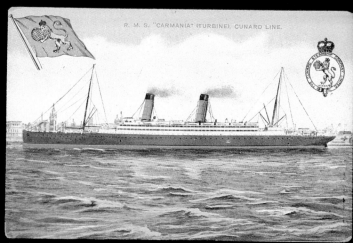

R.M.S. "CARMANIA" (TURBINE), CUNARD LINE.

"We had good times, we had bad times, we had all kinds of things. But by this time we were immune to everything. Most of the people were in so much torture before they got on the boat, not just the examinations but the life we had in general in Europe. And besides, that hope to be in America was so great and so sunny, that it colored all the pain that we had during our trip."

Gertrude Yellin, a Russian Jewish immigrant in 1922

Above: Poster advertising emigration insurance, 1906. Italian emigrants could purchase insurance for 10 lire that would pay up to 1,200 lire in case of death during the 30 days following embarkation. The policy also guaranteed to reimburse the cost of the ticket, up to 200 lire, should the emigrant fail to be admitted into the receiving country.

Right: Immigrants gaze at Statue of Liberty as S.S. Olympic *arrives in New York, ca. 1910. The statue came to symbolize the opportunity and freedom that America offered. It is no wonder that so many immigrants took heart when they first saw Liberty's grand welcoming gesture.*

carried immigrants to the United States. A report drawn up by U.S. immigration inspectors and presented to Congress in 1909 called steerage on most ships "disgusting and demoralizing." Steerage compartments, the inspectors reported, were typically packed with rows of narrow bunks. Mattresses were no more than burlap-covered bags of straw or seaweed, and a life preserver generally served double duty as a pillow. Stewards served meals on deck from twenty-five-gallon tanks. Passengers had to stand in line to get their food, which they ate from their own tin mess kits. The report concluded that steerage was not only inhumanly congested but injurious to health and morals.

Social reformers wanted steerage abolished altogether. Improvements came gradually as competition for the immigrant trade increased and government regulations became more stringent. By the 1910s, many of the newer ships had replaced steerage with third-class accommodations. The enormous dormitories were replaced by four- and six-berth cabins. Stewards served breakfast, lunch, and dinner in dining rooms furnished with long tables set with china and flatware. Despite these improvements on newly built ships, conditions aboard older vessels remained, in the words of another investigator, "dismal, damp, dirty."

Whether on a new or old ship, seasickness was the constant scourge of steerage passengers. On stormy days they were confined to their cramped quarters on the lower decks. Many were hardly able to leave their bunks, and the smell, as one immigrant said, was fierce. Most of these first-time ocean travelers were also deeply afraid of storms. Mary Antin, who came to America in 1894 as a young girl,

"The first time I saw the Statue of Liberty all the people were rushing to the side of the boat. 'Look at her, look at her,' and in all kind of tongues. 'There she is, there she is,' like it was somebody who was greeting them."

Elizabeth Phillips, an Irish immigrant in 1920

"I felt grateful the Statue of Liberty was a woman. I felt she would understand a woman's heart."

Stella Petrakis, a Cretan immigrant in 1916

Immigrants aboard Hamburg-America Line's S.S. Patricia *arriving in New York, 1906. The* Patricia *could carry over 2,100 steerage passengers.*

"My first impression when I got there, I tell you the God's truth, you're in a dream. It's like in heaven. You don't know what it is. You're so happy there in America."

Felice Taldone, an Italian immigrant in 1924

wrote of her crossing: "The perils of the sea were not minimized in the imaginations of us inexperienced voyagers. The captain and his officers ate their dinners, smoked their pipes and slept soundly in their turns, while we frightened emigrants turned our faces to the wall and awaited our watery graves."

Karl Puffe, who emigrated from Austria in 1892, described a memorable storm. "It is magnificent," he wrote in his diary, "to see the waves of the ocean with all its might. So far as your eyes can see [there] is nothing but high waves and a whole ocean in an uproar. In the night a little baby was born. Through all the motion of the ship, it came too soon."

But there were also happy times. Antin recalled "furtive sun-

shine, birds atop the crested waves, band music and dancing and fun." She explored the ship and made friends with the officers and crew. Years later she was able to write in her memoirs, "It was my first experience of the ocean, and I was profoundly moved."

Below: Jewish war orphans arriving from eastern Europe, 1921.

Opposite: Children of many lands arrived at America's gates. Top row: Austrian and Albanian shoes. Bottom row: Greek and Chinese shoes.

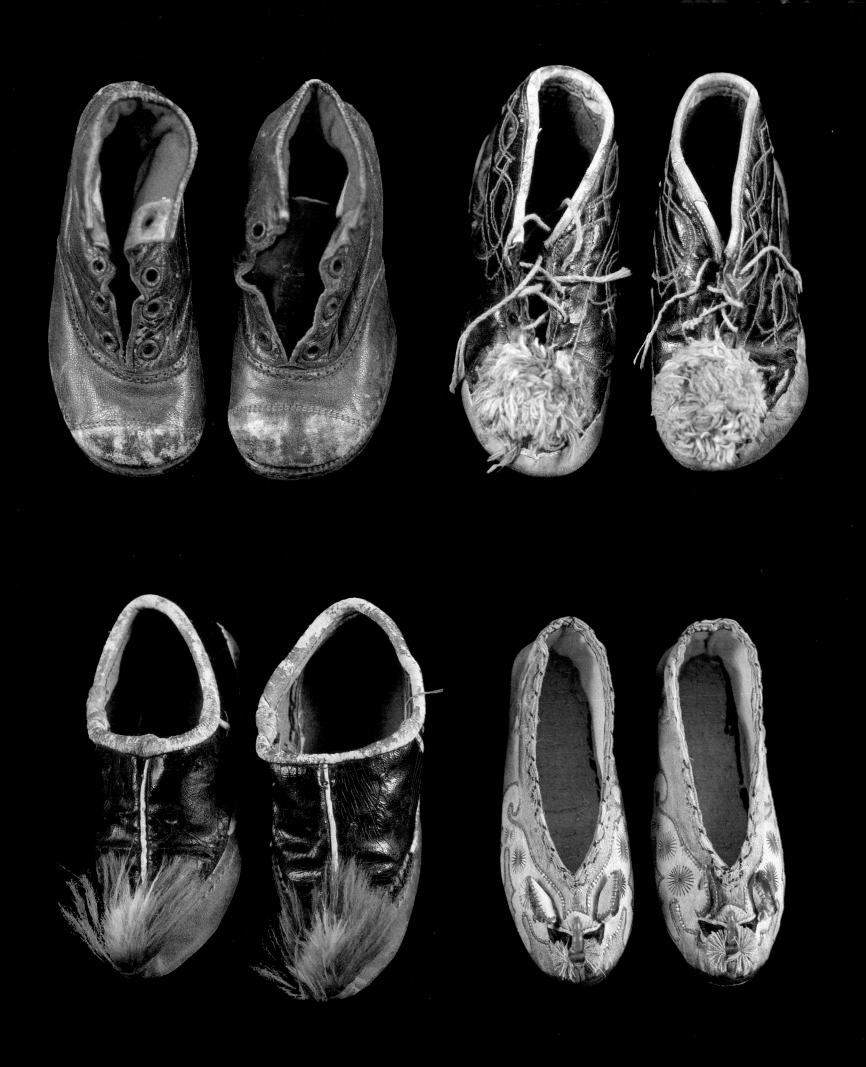

By all accounts, the most exciting part of the journey was its end, the day of arrival, when ships made port and at long last the weary travelers could land. New York City was the principal port of entry for immigrants, their path to America determined by well-established shipping lanes across the Atlantic Ocean. The nation's largest seaport since the 1820s, New York was also a major railroad hub that offered access to nearly every part of the country.

Because of the waves of newcomers entering the city, New York was the first port to open an immigration depot—Castle Garden, a massive stone structure built in 1808 as a fort. It later served as an opera house until 1855, when New York State authorities transformed it into a landing station. Castle Garden's primary purpose was not to inspect, but to protect hapless newcomers from the crooks, prostitutes, and swindlers that prowled the piers looking for easy marks. Within Castle Garden's walls, immigrants could exchange money, purchase food and rail tickets, attend to baggage, and obtain information about boarding houses and employment. By the time it closed in 1890, the old depot, run-down and shabby from hard use, had registered over eight million immigrants.

Castle Garden's successor was Ellis Island, a larger station located in the harbor, a short ferry ride from the city's docks. On Ellis Island, which was operated by the federal Bureau of Immigration, a team of inspectors and doctors examined the new arrivals to weed out the sick, the impoverished, the disabled, and all others who seemed undesirable. All but a few passed the somewhat dehumanizing battery of tests and were soon on their way to their final destinations.

While New York continued to receive about 70% of the immigration flow, other American ports that had steamship and railroad connections were busy as well. As at Ellis Island, federal inspectors greeted the new arrivals. In Boston, the second busiest port during the peak years, the U.S. Immigration Service set up shop in a cavernous wooden shed provided by the steamship companies. Boston was a major gateway for immigrants from Ireland, but by the 1880s it was also receiving many Italians, Greeks, Portuguese, eastern European Jews, Poles, and Armenians.

Throughout the peak years of immigration, Philadelphia received about a million immigrants. Most traveled on ships owned by the American Line Steamship Company, founded with support from the Pennsylvania Railroad. The American Line made weekly crossings between Liverpool and Philadelphia, with a stop at Queenstown, Ireland.

In Baltimore, immigrants were inspected in the Baltimore & Ohio Railroad reception center, an open, shed-like structure located near the piers. Passengers moved directly from the ships, through inspection, and then to the B.&O. station, where they would board trains to westward points—Cincinnati, Chicago, and St. Louis, among others. The B.&O. Railroad coordinated its immigrant business with the German Lloyd Line, which scheduled regular sailings to Baltimore from Bremen, its home port.

After 1910, immigrants arriving in San Francisco, most of whom were Chinese, were processed on Angel Island. Although other nationalities were quickly inspected and sent on their way, the Chinese were usually detained for weeks or months, awaiting permission to land. This discriminatory policy was an outgrowth of the 1882 Chinese Exclusion Act, which barred Chinese from the country unless they were merchants, government officials, students, teachers, visitors, or U.S. citizens. Most Chinese immigrants claimed citizenship by birth or as the children of American-born Chinese. Since they rarely had papers to prove their claims, the Chinese detainees, as well as their relatives, were subjected to rigorous interrogations to determine eligibility for entry.

To avoid these tough interrogations, a small number of Chinese sailed to New Orleans, where the haphazard enforcement of immigration laws made it easier to gain entry to the country. New Orleans did not have the rail connections necessary to attract substantial immigrant traffic but it did receive arrivals from Spain and Latin America. Other ports that received a small but steady stream of newcomers were Key West, Florida; Galveston, Texas; Seattle, Washington; and New Bedford, Massachusetts.

Not all immigrants came across the ocean. Though records on inland points of entry are incomplete, it is estimated that during the years 1880 to 1924, well over two million immigrants crossed the Canadian and Mexican borders into the United States.

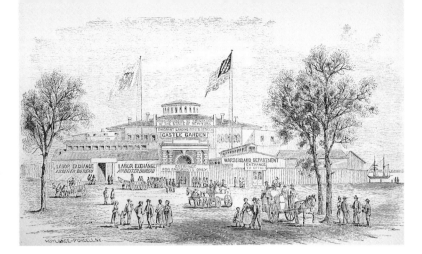

Top: Castle Garden, ca. 1870. Located at the southern tip of Manhattan, America's first immigrant landing station received over eight million immigrants between 1855 and 1890.

Bottom: Immigrants on ship docking at a Boston pier, November 1, 1923. Boston received only 20,000 in 1923, down from a peak of 70,000 immigrants in 1907.

"A thousand sorrows and a hatred ten thousand-
fold burns between my brows.
Hoping to step ashore the American continent is
the most difficult of difficulties.
The barbarians imprison me in this place.
Even a martyr or a hero would change
countenance."

Poem written on barrack wall, Angel Island

Above: Coaching notes and map of Sar Hong village, Sun Woey District, confiscated at Angel Island, ca. 1915. Notes like these were often used by immigrants and their relatives to prepare for the interrogations on Angel Island. Inspectors asked specific questions about family, home life, and village in an attempt to catch "paper sons," immigrants illegally posing as the children of Chinese American "paper fathers." Some of the specific questions (with answers) in these coaching notes are: "How far is your maternal grandparents' village from yours? How large is your village and how many people live there? What direction does your village face? Are there any hills, trees, or bodies of water in the back, front, left, or right of your village? In what alley is the ancestral hall?" If the answers of the immigrant and his father did not match, the immigrant would be deported.

Opposite top: Japanese picture brides detained on Angel Island, 1916. The relatively small detention station could accommodate 200 to 300 men and 30 to 50 women. In addition to the Chinese, who made up the bulk of arrivals, the station also processed other Asians, including over 600 Japanese picture brides a year (until the practice was halted in 1921) and small numbers of Koreans and Hindus.

Opposite bottom: Cape Verdean immigrants on S.S. Savoia, arriving in New Bedford, Massachusetts. Thousands emigrated from the Cape Verde Islands, a Portuguese dependency located 400 miles off the African coast. Most of the islands' population was of mixed African and European ancestry.

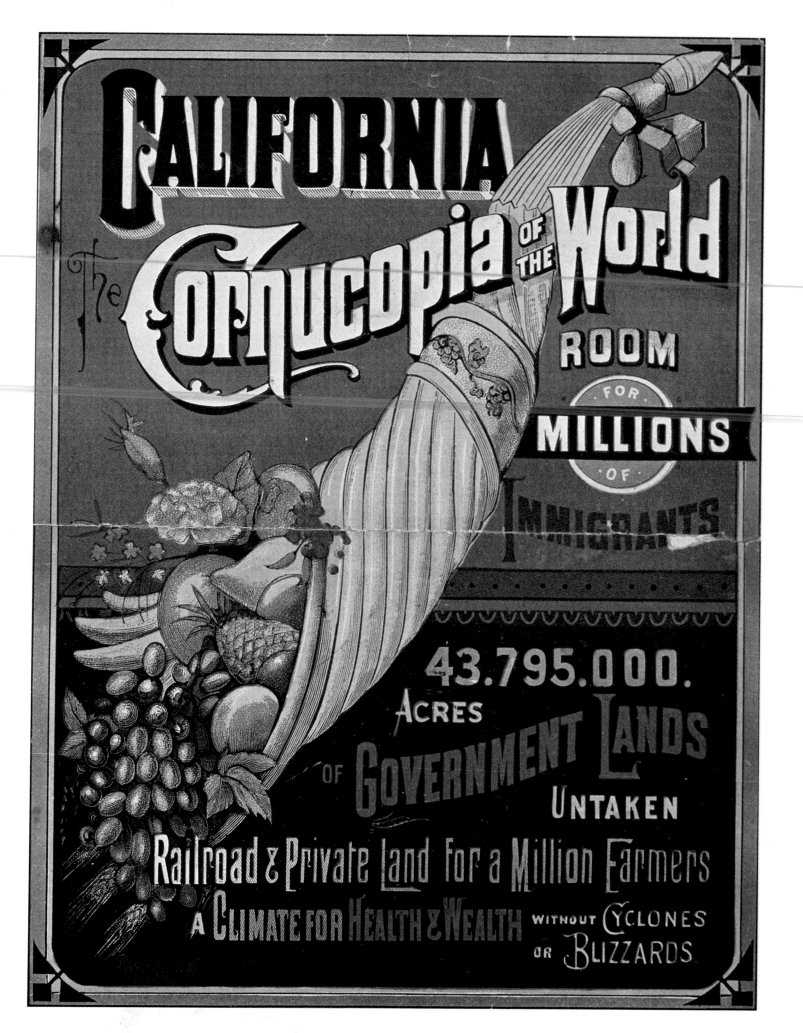

Across the Land

No matter what their port of entry, most immigrants traveled on to other parts of the country. Of the 12 million people who came through Ellis Island, eight million left the New York area for destinations scattered from coast to coast.

By the the late nineteenth century, the majority of immigrants were heading for the industrial northern states, despite vigorous efforts to attract newcomers to less populated regions in the Midwest, West, and South. State governments, local chambers of commerce, immigrant aid societies, and railroad companies were all actively engaged in this endeavor. The railroads were especially aggressive. They were doing more than selling one-way tickets to distant points; they were selling land—great tracts granted to them by the federal government early in the nineteenth century as incentives to extend the railroad into every corner of the nation.

To boost their sales efforts, the railroads printed brochures and broadsides in many languages and distributed them throughout Europe. In railroad stations and seaports, immigrants would see large, colorful posters extolling the virtues of such faraway places as Nebraska, Texas, or California. The Central Pacific Railroad touted California's "climate for health and wealth, without cyclones or blizzards." The St. Paul, Minneapolis and Manitoba Railway called Minnesota "one immense empire of mineral, timbered and agricultural wealth, waiting only to be occupied." Many companies employed overseas agents who were aggressive land salesmen. Prospective buyers could get rebates on their tickets and free room and board while they inspected the land on sale. "Go and see for yourself," a Burlington Lines poster read. "Low round trip rates to all points and return, and the amount paid is refunded to those who buy."

Most of the best farmland was sold by the 1890s, but railroads remained active in the profitable immigrant passenger trade, selling hundreds of thousands of tickets per year. Travel agents in Europe sold package deals that included steamship passage and train travel to American destinations. Railroads also had agents on Ellis Island and at other ports of entry.

While the railroad companies were creative marketers, they did not guarantee customer satisfaction. Marius Larsen, a Danish immigrant in 1912, complained that he was at the mercy of the agents' policy of booking passengers on the first available line: "We left on the New York Central line," he wrote in his diary, "by which we will go on a long detour up into Canada. Immigrants get sent with

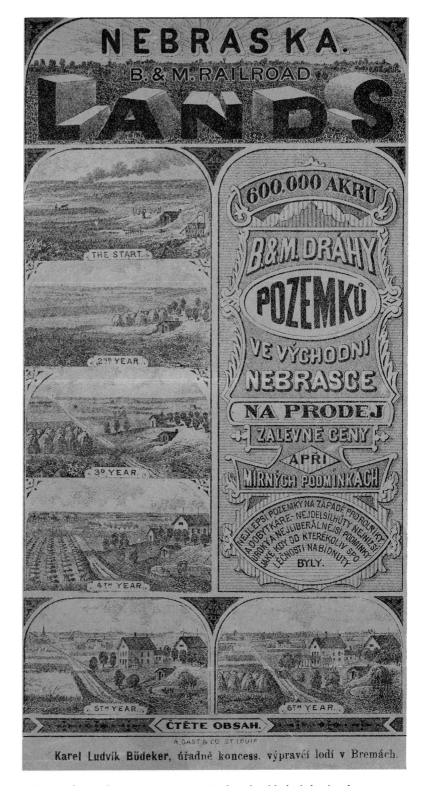

Above: The Burlington & Missouri Railroad published this brochure in 1881 in Czech (shown here) and German. The cover text advertises the sale of 600,000 acres in Nebraska.—"the best land in the West"—at low prices and under "the most liberal credit terms ever offered by any company."

Opposite: Published in 1885 by the California Immigration Commission of the Central Pacific Railroad, this booklet describes California as "not only the land of promise, but the land of real fruition," capable of "supporting easily and prosperously 40,000,000."

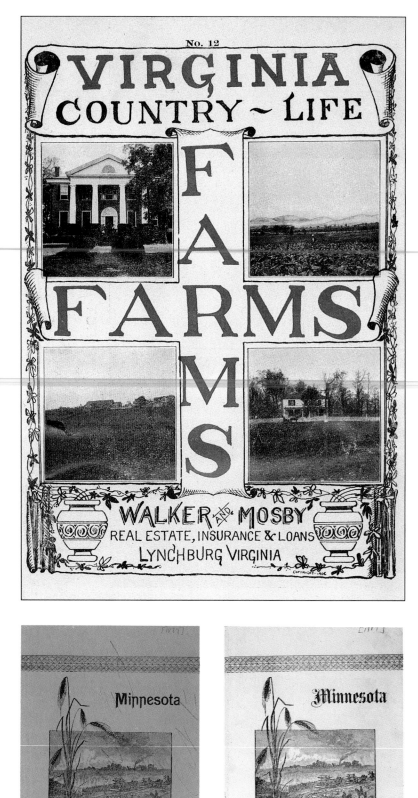

Above and top right: In the early 1900s, the Southern Railway distributed promotional materials in London to attract immigrants to the South. In fact, opportunities in the region were limited because African Americans provided a native labor pool. Only 2% of immigrants in the period 1880–1924 settled in the South.

Bottom: In 1889, the St. Paul, Minneapolis and Manitoba Railway published this promotional booklet in Norwegian (left) and German (right) as well as in English and Swedish.

"Knoxville feels that if the outside world knew of the many real and genuine advantages that are enclosed within the circle of her domain, that people would flock to her from all over the world."

Brochure distributed by the Southern Railway in London, 1906

"TEXAS is an agricultural state of the first rank.... The fertility and cheapness of the TEXAS land surpasses all the other sections of the North American Union.... TEXAS also offers laborers a promising future. The wages are high compared to other countries, since there is not such a large supply of labor in TEXAS as in the eastern states and their large cities."

Broadside distributed in Bremen, Germany, 1906

whichever railroad can accommodate them, regardless of how long the route is, and therefore, if I ever make the trip again, I'll only have a ticket to where we land and purchase the railroad ticket separately. Then I can decide for myself which train I'll take."

The major railroad companies ran special immigrant trains from America's seaports to most inland cities. The trains were notoriously overcrowded and short on comfort. Some of the coaches were no more than converted boxcars outfitted with crude wooden benches. Few services were offered to the immigrant passengers, who often had to depend on box lunches to sustain them for a trip of several days. Transcontinental travelers had sleeping berths but they had to provide their own bedding.

By the turn of the century, fewer immigrants were making the long journey into rural America. Most newcomers had neither the desire nor the capital to buy farmland; they came instead for jobs. They headed for cities and regions where steel plants, textile mills, factories, and mines needed workers. Over 65% of these immigrants went to four industrialized states—New York, Pennsylvania, Illinois, and Massachusetts. After 1900, even Asian immigrants, most of whom entered the country through California, began to travel across the continent to the cities of the Midwest and East.

The influx of newcomers into already crowded and poor urban districts spurred renewed attempts by Jewish organizations to disperse newcomers across the land. The Jewish Colonization Association in St. Petersburg, Russia, which published Yiddish circulars about twenty-one states, tried to make immigrants aware of opportunities beyond New York. The Industrial Removal Office helped urban dwellers relocate to the countryside, and the Galveston Plan attempted to lure travelers away from New York by offering lower transatlantic fares to Galveston, Texas.

These efforts were largely ineffective. The majority of immigrants continued to head for northern industrial cities, following in the footsteps of those who had come before them. They went where they could live with friends or relatives until they got their feet on the ground and found a job.

"Golden Belt Country. Land...in Kansas," announced this Swedish brochure, distributed by the Union Pacific Railway Company in 1887. It also advertised trains to the West Coast.

"We got on the train, the four children and my mother. She couldn't speak a word of English. They asked her where she was going. She said, 'Washington.' And they were heading us for the state of Washington. Finally she took the address and showed it to them and they realized that she meant Washington, D.C. And most of our baggage had gone to the state of Washington in the meantime."

Cosma Tangora Sullivan, an Italian immigrant in 1905

"When we were on trains, all I saw was these little houses in Pennsylvania. And everything looked so smoky, at that time. I was disappointed when I came to America. All the pictures I saw of America was tall buildings. And I thought I was going to live in one of those high-rise apartments."

Mary Kudrna Garba, a Czechoslovakian immigrant in 1923

Right: Immigrant aid societies issued cards like this to help immigrants get proper directions during their overland travels.

Opposite top: Immigrant train, Locust Point, Baltimore, ca. 1900. The immigrant traffic was big business for the railroad companies. In Baltimore, the immigration station was operated by the Baltimore & Ohio Railroad rather than by the government. After inspection, the foreigners traveled to their final destinations by railroad.

Below: Railroad and steamship timetables, 1890–1922. In addition to railroads, steamships were a common form of transportation, especially in New England and the South.

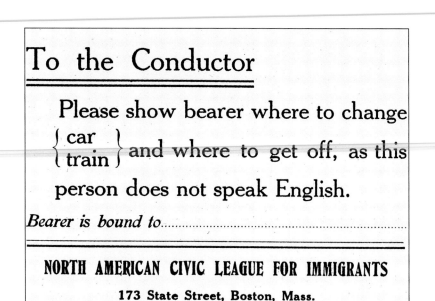

To the Conductor

Please show bearer where to change { car } { train } and where to get off, as this person does not speak English.

Bearer is bound to...

NORTH AMERICAN CIVIC LEAGUE FOR IMMIGRANTS

173 State Street, Boston, Mass.

At Work in America

"Well, I came to America because I heard the streets were paved with gold. When I got here, I found out three things: first, the streets weren't paved with gold; second, they weren't paved at all; and third, I was expected to pave them."

Old Italian story

During the post-Civil War era, America's manufacturing and transportation industries were booming. The late nineteenth century saw the settling of half the American continent, the construction of over 150,000 miles of railroad, and the production of record-breaking amounts of coal and steel. By 1900, the United States was the wealthiest country in the world, far surpassing England, France, and Germany in manufacturing and trade. One of the critical factors in America's growth was the seemingly endless supply of immigrant labor. By 1910, though immigrants were only 14% of the national population, they made up over half of America's industrial workers.

The immigrants helped to fuel a booming economy, but what they got in return often fell short of a decent living wage. Most arrived with little money and took the first jobs they could find, usually the hardest and lowest paid. They typically worked ten to twelve hours a day and six to seven days a week. Annual wages ranged from an average $250 to $300 in the mills to $400 to $450 in the mines. Though the cost of living varied from job to job and place to place, most immigrants were hard-pressed to support their families. In 1907, for example, an average Slavic steelworker's family in Homestead, Pennsylvania, had a weekly income of $13.88. This modest sum covered only the bare essentials: rent for a two-room frame house, $2; food, $5.98; fuel, 38 cents; insurance, 88 cents; and other expenses, such as clothing, medicine, household supplies, and carfare, $3.86. The remainder, 78 cents, went into savings, which was supposed to take care of emergencies. The fragile balance of a family's finances, however, was difficult to maintain, especially when illness struck or when the breadwinner was laid off during a work slowdown or economic depression. For many families, borrowing money became a recurring necessity, and repaying debt, another large bite out of their meager budgets.

As newcomers joined friends and relatives from the old country who were already established, a natural clustering of nationalities occurred. "You came together with your own group," recalled Max Grossman, a Russian Jewish immigrant in 1902. "They found a place for you to live and a place for you to work." Immigrant communities grew up where opportunities matched the newcomers' preferences and skills, with different ethnic groups favoring certain jobs, trades, and regions of the country. Broad patterns of settlement and employment emerged. Many Scandinavians traveled to Minnesota and went into farming, while Slavic groups tended to go to the mines and steel mills in Pennsylvania and slaughterhouses in

Above: Coal miners, ca. 1910. At this time nearly half the coal miners in America were foreign-born, with Poles, Slavs, and Italians the most numerous. Most miners worked ten hours a day, six and a half days a week. The work was grueling, dirty, and highly dangerous. In 1907, over 3,000 miners died in job-related accidents. Living conditions were usually deplorable and dominated by the company, which supplied housing and operated a general store. The old lament "I owe my soul to the company store" described many a miner's situation: surviving on credit and sinking more deeply into debt.

Opposite top: Construction of St. Paul, Minneapolis and Manitoba Railroad, Minnesota, 1897. The Irish and Chinese contributions to building the transcontinental railroad during the 1860s are legendary, but by the turn of the century, rail crews were generally made up of many nationalities.

Opposite bottom: The Farsakians, a family of Armenian immigrants, at their sidewalk fruit stand, Worcester, Massachusetts, 1926. The benefits of working for oneself made the risk and effort of starting and running a business worthwhile. Stores, shops, and peddlers' carts gave ethnic neighborhoods their distinctive character.

> **"That was the standard practice, especially before the First World War. Men would leave for America, spend a few years in the coal mines of Pennsylvania, or the iron mills in Pittsburgh, in Chicago in the slaughterhouses, save enough money to either buy himself a piece of land, put his cottage into shape and live there. They wanted to get back. They would never feel good in America."**
>
> Paul Sturman, a Czechoslovakian immigrant in 1920

> **"The coal mines are one of the worst places to work. You say a prayer while your husband or your son goes to work in the morning. You say another one when he comes home at night."**
>
> Elizabeth Smith Nimmo, an English immigrant in 1920

Chicago. Eastern European Jews were often drawn to New York and the needle trades; French Canadians made up the majority of workers in New England's textile mills. Mexicans, Japanese, Chinese, and Filipinos generally headed for California and other western states, where they worked in farming and manufacturing or opened small shops and restaurants.

The Irish had once dominated the building trades, but by 1897, about 75% of the construction workers in New York City were Italian immigrants, and the same was true of other major cities. "All those bridges, all those roads, all those railroads—they were all built by people who worked hard," said Joseph Baccardo, who arrived from Italy in 1898. "My father had to work his heart out to get anywhere. And yet, no matter how hard he worked, there was never enough money." In 1910, pick-and-shovel laborers earned around $1.75 a day; skilled workers, $2.75. Artisans, those who embellished America's new buildings with mosaics, stone carvings, and other architectural details, were better paid and able to rise to a middle-class living standard. Stonecutters, for example, made around $4.50 a day.

Not all immigrants came to stay. When the American economy was strong, "birds of passage" eager to build up nest eggs came to find jobs in construction, agriculture, and mining. But, once they had saved enough money to buy land or open a business in the old country, they returned home. Many Italian, Greek, Slavic, and British immigrants followed this migration pattern. Canadians and Mexicans made seasonal trips across the border—the Mexicans to harvest and plant crops in the Southwest, the Canadians to work in factories and textile mills in the North.

Dishonest labor brokers actively recruited "birds of passage" and other newcomers who were desperate to find work. The brokers, who came in many ethnic variations, generally victimized their own compatriots, charging them exorbitant fees for sundry expenses—transportation to the work site, food, and housing. The immigrants often wound up with little or nothing to show for their long days of

Top: Pouring copper ingot, Lake Linden, Michigan, 1911.

Bottom: Stone carvers working on sculptures for state capitol, Madison, Wisconsin, ca. 1912.

Opposite top: Finnish lumber crew, Wolf River, Wisconsin, 1904.

Opposite bottom: Salmon-canning factory, Puget Sound, Washington, ca. 1900. Most cannery workers were Chinese, though they were banned from other areas of the salmon fishing industry, dominated by Norwegians and Slovenes.

Overleaf: Coal and ice workers, mostly French Canadians, in Manchester, New Hampshire, ca. 1900. Forty percent of Manchester's population at the turn of the century was French Canadian.

"He who can do a little of everything gets along best. He must not shirk hard work, and he must not shirk being treated like a dog. He must be willing to be anyone's servant, just like any other newcomer here."

Peter Sørensen, a Danish immigrant, letter of April 14, 1885

"My father was a building contractor in Wales. And one of the things that he did, he was an ornamental plasterer. He would go to New York and walk up and down the streets looking for some evidence of some work going on, and try to walk in to get a little job. He'd walk the streets systematically. One street after the other, day after day after day, and come home—nothing, nothing, nothing...."

Donald Roberts, a Welsh immigrant in 1925

Top: Max Stein, a Jewish fruit peddler, Pueblo, Colorado, 1910.

Bottom: Cape Verdean dockworkers who outfitted whaling vessels, New Bedford, Massachusetts, 1904. Immigrants from the Cape Verde Islands established communities in Rhode Island and southeastern Massachusetts.

Top: Mexican laborers picking cotton on a Texas border plantation in 1919. Southwestern agriculture depended on Chicano laborers, 41% of whom worked in agriculture by 1930.

Bottom: Threshing on a Norwegian farm, Grafton, North Dakota, 1911.

Opposite: Sweatshop, New York City, ca. 1900.

back-breaking labor. Ernest Becker, who emigrated from Germany, took a job that paid $16 a week but he had to pay "ten bucks for room and board, five bucks to pay back on the fare. I got one buck," he said. "Indentured labor, that's really what it was." As soon as workers learned a bit of English and enough about American ways to find their own jobs, they avoided the questionable services of the labor broker.

The garment industry, too, was rife with exploitation. The ready-to-wear clothing manufacturers cut labor costs by jobbing out piecework—sleeves, collars, or trouser legs—to sweatshop subcontractors, who hired workers at miserably low wages. In New York City, eastern European Jews made up most of the workers who toiled in dim, hot, cramped sweatshops located all over the Lower East Side. By 1900, many Italians as well were entering the needle trades. The work was seasonal—three months in the summer and three months in the winter. For toiling ten to thirteen hours a day, a worker received minimal pay—about $5 a week, depending on skill and speed.

On the streets below the tenement windows, another form of subsistence commerce was under way. "We had the Jewish peddlers, who took their little pushcarts on Rivington Street or Delancey Street," recalled Pearl Pohrille, who came from Germany in 1921. "If it wasn't too cold or too rainy or too hot, they would have the means to support their families." In 1910, over half the peddlers in the

United States were immigrants. On crowded streets that resembled vast outdoor department stores, scores of these pushcart merchants hawked their wares—clothes, fish, fruit, food, brooms, sewing supplies—almost anything imaginable.

A number of immigrants managed to save or borrow enough capital to open a business—a barbershop, a laundry, a restaurant, or some other small venture. A peddler's pack or pushcart was often the first step to owning a small neighborhood store that stocked ethnic foods and catered to Old World customs. Kosher butchers, for example, were essential for Jewish immigrants who wanted to maintain religious traditions. Those who scrimped and saved to establish their own businesses could sometimes get help from immigrant banks or mutual aid organizations willing to loan money to a compatriot or provide advice and legal services.

Immigrants' livelihoods were precarious, and survival often meant that everyone in the family had to pitch in—not just mother but the children as well. After school and on weekends, youngsters helped with piecework at home or took over household chores so their mothers could go out to work. Children peddled newspapers, sold chewing gum, shined shoes, or ran errands to bring in extra income.

Millions of other children joined the ranks of adult laborers and worked ten to twelve hours a day in textile mills, glass factories, canneries, and coal mines, and on farms. Tessie Argianas, from

"We started work at 7:30 and during the busy season we worked until 9:00 in the evening. They didn't pay overtime and they didn't give you anything for supper money. My own wages when I got to the Triangle Shirtwaist Company [at age eight in 1901] was a dollar and a half a week. And by the time I left in 1909, I had worked my way up to $6!"

Pauline Newman, a Lithuanian Jewish immigrant in 1901

Greece, said she was only 11 years old when her father took her to work at a tailor shop. "She's small," he told the owner, "but she's 16 years old." No one bothered to check her papers and she was hired. Clara Larsen, who emigrated from Russia, went to work when she was 14. "Whenever the inspector used to come in," she said, "the boss would come and grab me by the neck and throw me into the bathroom and lock the door so he would never catch me."

Adelard Janelle, a French Canadian immigrant, started working in a textile mill when he was 12 years old. He worked from six in the morning to six at night. "I started at 55 cents a day. I was the oldest of the children so it was expected that I would enter the mill. It was natural for all French Canadians to work, really." Children were hired as cheap, docile labor to perform unskilled drudgery that was often more hazardous than work done by their elders. The rate of accidents among children was three times that for adults. The National Child Labor Committee, organized in 1904, exposed the cruelties children suffered in the workplace and led the campaign for child labor laws. Reform came slowly, but by 1914, thirty-five states prohibited employment of children under 14 and set an eight-hour workday for children under 16. Most states also required minors to attend school.

While the vast majority of women stayed at home, they earned money by taking in laundry, sewing, or boarders. Others also helped to run a family business. Women who worked outside the home usually entered domestic service but some became farm laborers, factory hands, or textile mill workers. The garment industries employed many women, who stitched and sewed side-by-side with their male co-workers. Employers often preferred hiring women because they were less demanding, worked harder, and cost less than male workers. For most tasks, women earned about half to two-thirds of what their male counterparts earned.

In the late 1800s and early 1900s, social reformers pressed for laws protecting women from exploitation. By 1913, thirty-nine states had enacted legislation limiting the number of hours women could work in a day. Though meant to benefit women, the new regulations often created more hardship, since the shorter day meant less money. Many immigrant women needed the extra hours' pay just to make ends meet.

The needs of immigrant workers often conflicted with those of native-born Americans. At a time when immigration was soaring, foreign-born workers were regarded with a sense of wariness if not downright antipathy. The American trade union movement,

Top: Six-year-old Italian boy carrying home a bundle of work at noon hour, New York City, 1923.

Bottom: Coal-mine breaker boys at lunch, South Pittston, Pennsylvania, January 1911. The Pennsylvania mines employed more than 15,000 boys under age 16. They worked on the surface until age 12 and below ground thereafter, for wages of $1 to $3 a week.

The Mauro family assembling feather-goods, New York City, 1911. The photographer, Lewis W. Hine, noted: "Mrs. Mary Mauro, 309 East 110th Street, 2nd floor. Family work on feathers, make $2.25 a week. In vacation, two or three times as much. Victoria 8, Angelina 10 (a neighbor), Fiorandi 10, Maggie 11. All work except two boys against the wall. Father is street cleaner and has steady job."

Jobbing out piecework to be done at home by entire families was a common practice. The manufacture of clothing, cigars, feather-goods, and artificial flowers all depended heavily on homeworkers, most of whom, by the early 1900s, were Italian women.

primarily concerned with organizing skilled workers, not only disregarded unskilled immigrant labor but supported efforts to curtail immigration. American workers saw the influx of cheap foreign labor as a way for bosses to undermine the union cause, which was then pressing for an eight-hour workday. The immigrants, on the other hand, were desperate to find work. The "birds of passage," who were here only temporarily, and recent arrivals who felt they had no long-term stake in unionization, were not willing to give up their jobs and paychecks to go on strike. Sometimes immigrants recruited by labor brokers acted as strikebreakers, further inflaming bad feelings between native-born and alien.

Certain unions, however, primarily in trades where foreign laborers were most numerous, had to reach out to the immigrants in order to survive. "In unity—there will be power!" became a familiar rallying cry. Organizers had to bring together men and women of many nationalities who spoke different languages and had diverse views and concerns. They had to convince workers to put aside ethnic hostilities and join to create a solid front. As John Mitchell, president of the United Mine Workers, told his members, "The coal you dig isn't Slavish, or Polish, or Irish coal, it's just coal."

New York City's garment workers were also early union activists, waging successful strikes as early as 1909 and 1910. These confrontations and the tragic Triangle Shirtwaist Company fire of 1911, which killed over 140 young workers, strengthened union participation and added a sizable and loyal core to labor's rank and file. By the 1930s, immigrants, because of their sheer numbers, had become a moving force in the American labor movement, providing unions with some of their greatest leaders.

Top: Silk-mill warpers, Paterson, New Jersey, ca. 1920, where Italians and Germans dominated the industry.

Bottom: Immigrant workers painting mowing machines, Cleveland.

Opposite: Scrubwoman, New York City, 1920.

67

Above: Protest against child labor in New York City labor parade, May 1, 1909.

Opposite top: The multiethnic nature of the trade union movement was evident at this 1913 New York City clothing workers' strike, where signs appeared in Italian, Yiddish, Russian, and English.

Opposite bottom left: Identifying victims of the Triangle Shirtwaist Company fire, New York City, March 25, 1911. More than 140 workers, mostly young Jewish and Italian women, died in this terrible fire. Locked doors and inadequate fire escapes prevented workers from fleeing the burning building. Many victims jumped 80 feet from the windows to the pavement below; others burned to death still sitting at their machines. The tragedy helped to galvanize support for the clothing-worker unions.

Opposite bottom right: The Amalgamated Clothing Workers of America call for a strike in English, Yiddish, Italian, and Lithuanian, in Philadelphia, ca. 1919. One of the most powerful labor organizations in the country, this union had a largely Jewish and Italian immigrant leadership and membership.

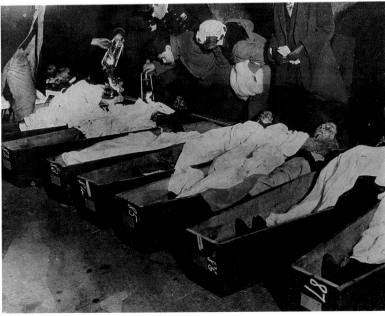

Between Two Worlds

As the influx of newcomers to the United States continued to rise, large ethnic communities grew up in the cities. By 1910, 75% of the residents of New York, Chicago, Detroit, Cleveland, and Boston were immigrants or the children of immigrants. The new arrivals generally went to friends or relatives living in Little Italys, Chinatowns, or Germantowns, or some other ethnic enclave located in one of the city's poorer districts.

It was common for many ethnic colonies to coexist within large immigrant neighborhoods. In New York's Lower East Side, for example, Irish and German immigrants were gradually moving out as Italians and eastern European Jews were moving in. The Italians from Naples clustered near Mulberry Bend, while Genoese settled on Baxter Street and Sicilians on Elizabeth Street. Jews, too, settled in patterns that coincided with old country regions. Galicians, Romanians, Hungarians, and Russians each occupied a different street or block. In these crowded, bustling neighborhoods, the inhabitants sought to preserve their old life styles, so much so that "Rivington Street was only a suburb of Minsk," as Alfred Kazin wrote.

In these oases, immigrants could speak their own languages, buy ethnic foods, exchange news of the homeland, and celebrate traditional holidays and holy days. Those who worked within the neighborhood rarely had to speak English or encounter the demands of American society.

The neighborhoods provided some warmth of familiarity but they also imposed enormous physical hardships on their dwellers. The immigrant districts were squalid, unhealthy, noisy, and crowded. In the words of one observer, "the architecture seemed to sweat humanity at every window and door," a description of the Lower East Side in New York that would be appropriate for many ethnic enclaves. In Manhattan alone, over 1.2 million people lived in buildings designed especially for high-density dwelling—the "dumbbell" tenement, a six- or seven-story structure that occupied a lot that was twenty-five feet wide, and a hundred feet deep. The term dumbbell described the shape of the floorplan: narrower in the middle to allow for a central air shaft between buildings. Each floor of the tenement had two apartments in the front and two in the back.

Mulberry Street, Little Italy, New York City. In 1923, one observer of the city described this area as a "sociable southern Italy, cramped and warped in the unfragrant and ugly tenements of New York."

"Everybody lived in little cliques, the Polish, the Ukrainian, the Russian. So they would help each other out, whatever. Maybe one knew a few words more than the other. They used to live, I don't know how many, maybe ten, twelve people in one room, because one was helping the other to get established here."

Louise Nagy, a Polish immigrant in 1913

"We sort of got ashamed of being Italians, because we were harassed so much after we got here. We didn't realize that things like that were going to happen. It was a shock to us. And that went on for years."

Cosma Tangora Sullivan, an Italian immigrant in 1905

TENEMENT TO LET

The New York Tenement House Law of 1901 mandated a toilet and running water for each unit. But before its enforcement, tenement residents of each floor had to share two water closets located in the hallway. To make matters worse, many families had to take in boarders in order to cover the rent. Not surprisingly, disease, including tuberculosis, cholera, and typhus, was rampant. Jacob A. Riis, a social reformer and photographer, observed that during summer, the death toll was heavy, especially for children: "Little coffins are stacked mountains high," he wrote, "on the decks of the County Commissioners' boat when it makes its semi-weekly trip to the city cemetery."

Despite the severe poverty and hardships, immigrants strove, with gritty determination, to reconstruct their Old World style of life, adapting it, whenever necessary, to suit its new American surroundings. Within the limited perimeters of their separate neighborhoods, they developed self-sufficient cultures of extraordinary intensity and variety. Communication among the inhabitants was maintained by a prolific foreign-language press, which informed, entertained, and educated a broad and varied readership. The foreign-language dailies were as essential to the vitality of the immigrant community as American newspapers were to the native-born. Supported by a loyal readership and advertising from immigrant entrepreneurs, ethnic newspapers and magazines were a marketplace for goods and ideas. Rival papers, espousing divergent political and social ideologies, waged circulation wars. They backed different candidates and causes and attacked each other in scathing editorials. Besides providing a lively forum of opinion, foreign-language papers reported local events and news from the home country. They also offered advice on how to cope with the stresses and strains of living, working, and raising a family in America.

The ethnic press reached its peak of activity during World War I, when news of the homeland was of urgent interest to immigrants. In 1917, over 1,300 foreign-language newspapers were being published. The Italian press claimed a circulation of nearly 700,000, while the Polish, Yiddish, and German presses each claimed one million.

The life of the immigrant community revolved around family

Opposite: Cincinnati's German neighborhood, the "Over the Rhine" district, had all the distinctive features of a German town: beer gardens, restaurants, churches, theatres, and a flourishing German press.

Top: A common sign throughout the period.

Middle: Room in tenement flat, New York City, 1910.

Bottom: Pittsburgh slum, 1908. The outhouse and the yard hydrant were used by sixty tenants.

73

"While I am not a whole American, neither am I what I was when I first landed here; that is, a Bulgarian.... I have outwardly and inwardly deviated so much from a Bulgarian that when recently visiting in that country I felt like a foreigner.... In Bulgaria I am not wholly a Bulgarian; in the United States not wholly an American."

Stoyan Christowe, "Half an American," 1919

"It's very strange coming from another country, to tell you the truth. Very strange...."

Florence Norris, an English immigrant in 1915

"This Christmas approaching, I was here all by myself. In my home, Christmastime, we had so many friends. And we go to church and we go singing carols. It was a great time. And here, on Christmas Eve, I went to bed at 6:29, like a baby, I cry like a baby. I said, 'I can't take it. I got to go back.'"

Joseph Talese, an Italian immigrant in 1920

"Many Swedes are settled here and more come each year, so there will soon be a Little Sweden here, especially around the Swedish church. There is a post office and three stores as well as a Swedish doctor, Carlberg. The name of the place is Nya-Sverige, in English New Sweden."

Letter from Carl and Fred in Texas to their sister in Sweden, January 23, 1896

Opposite: The Hilton family, immigrants from England, on their homestead near Weissert, Custer County, Nebraska, ca. 1889. The British continued to be one of the larger groups of newcomers during the peak immigration years. More than 1.5 million English, 400,000 Scottish, and 50,000 Welsh emigrated to the United States between 1880 and 1924.

Above: Parishioners in front of St. Josaphat Ukrainian Catholic Church after Sunday services, Gorham, North Dakota, ca. 1897. While most Ukrainian immigrants went to northeastern industrial cities, a small number settled in farm communities in North Dakota, Wisconsin, Virginia, Georgia, Texas, and Hawaii. Each community had its own Ukrainian church.

"Everybody had something to give me for help. It wasn't a question of money, it was a question of being a human being to a human being. And in those days people were apparently that way. There were so many nice people that were trying to help us when we came to this country."

Clara Larsen, a Russian Jewish immigrant in 1908

Top: Russian Jewish tea party at Woodbine Agricultural Colony, New Jersey, ca. 1900. Agricultural communities for eastern European Jews provided an alternative to the urban ghettos.

Bottom: The sunflower harvest was traditionally celebrated in Hungary, a large producer of sunflower oil. These Hungarian immigrants continue the tradition at a sunflower party in Cleveland in 1913.

Top: Bahamian immigrants in Coconut Grove, near Miami, late nineteenth century. By 1920, more than 16% of Miami's 30,000 residents were from the Bahamas.

Bottom: Greek miners in Clear Creek, Utah, pose for a photograph to send to relatives in Crete, ca. 1915. The bottles and guns are perhaps signs of affluence.

and religion. These twin institutions sustained deep spiritual values and preserved ethnic identity. Families arrived together or came in "chain" migration, one sending for the other, until parents, aunts, uncles, brothers, sisters, and cousins were reunited in the same American neighborhood or community. "My brother and some sisters brought me here, sent me a ticket," recalled Matthew Murray, who came from Ireland in 1914. He settled in Dorchester, a Boston neighborhood that was almost entirely Irish. "I worked mostly with Irish," he said, "and most of my friends were Irish." Regardless of ethnic background, the network of kin and community played a nurturing and essential role in helping immigrants adjust to the new world.

Building a place of worship was another step in reestablishing continuity with the traditions and customs of the homeland. The church or synagogue was often the center and heart of the immigrant community. Around this ecclesiastical core, a broad spectrum of secular ethnic organizations sprung up, from small local clubs to national associations. Neighborhood social groups sponsored ethnic celebrations, sporting events, card parties, picnics, and dances. Benevolent and mutual aid associations raised funds and dispensed sick and death benefits to their members. Their business meetings, held in lofts, candy stores, or taverns, became friendly exchanges of advice, information, and memories of home. Networking through these ethnic groups made it easier for new arrivals to find housing and employment or to secure a promotion at work. Gradually, as immigrant groups became more established and prosperous, they founded national organizations that promoted their own ethnic culture, funded social programs, and lobbied Congress for legislation beneficial to immigrants.

Top: A children's choir forms the Norwegian flag at the Norwegian Centennial Celebration, a festival in Minnesota in 1925, commemorating the arrival of the first Norwegian immigrants in 1825. President Calvin Coolidge delivered the keynote address, and over 100,000 people participated in the celebration.

Middle: Japanese church picnic, Oakland, California, 1910. The 1910 census counted over 72,000 Japanese Americans, most in California. Like so

many other ethnic groups, they formed their own churches—both Buddhist and Christian.

Bottom: All the members of this group, posing ca. 1917, emigrated from the village of Machgharah, Lebanon, and settled in Methuen, Massachusetts. Many of them belonged to the same extended family.

Above: Parade for Mexican holiday, Cinco de Mayo, in Mogollon, New Mexico, 1914. This holiday commemorates the Mexican victory over the French in the Battle of Puebla in 1862. Ethnic communities thrived on social events. Picnics and dances were favorite activities, but parades seemed to excite the most interest and participation. St. Patrick's Day, Columbus Day, Pulaski Day, and other special holidays were occasions to demonstrate not only ethnic pride but also how much the community had accomplished in its adopted homeland.

Left: San Francisco's Chinatown was home to tens of thousands of Chinese, mostly men who had come to California for temporary work and lived in a "bachelor society." In accordance with Confucian practice, wives remained in China to attend to parents-in-law, raise children, and care for ancestral shrines.

Overleaf: German musicians practicing at a picnic in Madison, Wisconsin, 1897.

"In the Yiddish theatre they always had scenes about Ellis Island, about immigrants coming. For many years they told the story of how the immigrants came here and what they went through and some of them being sent back. And then they had to come again. This was tremendous material for them to play."

Seymour Rexite, a Polish Jewish immigrant in 1920

Boris Thomashefsky, a great star and impresario of the Yiddish theatre for decades, starred in his own production of The Green Millionaire *in 1915. By this time, New York City had almost twenty Yiddish theatres.*

Above: Road companies brought the Yiddish theatre to cities across the country. In 1922, the Academy Theatre in Scranton, Pennsylvania, presented The Lunatic.

Opposite: Irish and German subjects were featured in these shows. Ethnic themes were popular, not only in foreign-language theatres but in English-language productions that toured the country.

The neighborhood ethnic theatre presented evenings of entertainment, melodrama, low comedy, and historical pageantry. In these productions—in Yiddish, German, Slovak, Italian, Danish, Chinese—the audience found escape from the everyday. Most immigrants were captivated by the theatre, which was dedicated to providing "cheap wholesome entertainment for the masses." On stage the players spoke a familiar language, told favorite jokes and stories, pranced through routines of pratfalls and slapstick, grappled with social dilemmas, and portrayed the disappointments, successes, and ironies of adjusting to life in America. The productions presented the ridiculous and the sublime, sometimes within one evening, and provided an emotional outlet for lively, responsive audiences. During the early decades of the twentieth century, ethnic productions played in school basements and small-town theatres as well as in great halls, such as San Francisco's Italian Washington Theatre and New York City's Yiddish Grand Theatre.

Overleaf: Ethnic songs published as sheet music were another immensely popular form of entertainment. They addressed the incongruities that emerged when the Old World confronted the New. Songwriters, sometimes immigrants themselves but more often the children of immigrants, freely lampooned the foibles of ethnic Americans, using ludicrous stereotypes that today would be considered insensitive and demeaning.

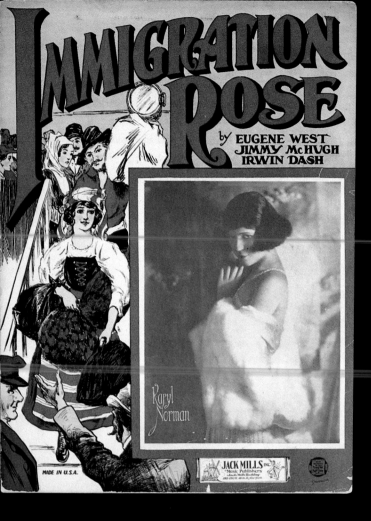

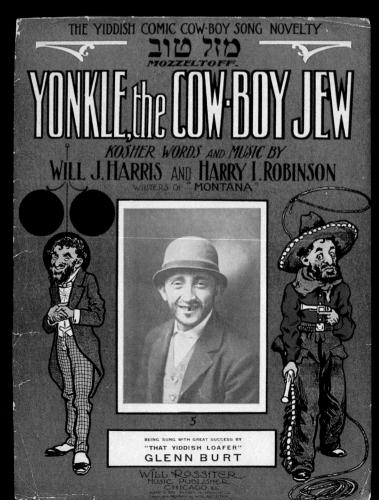

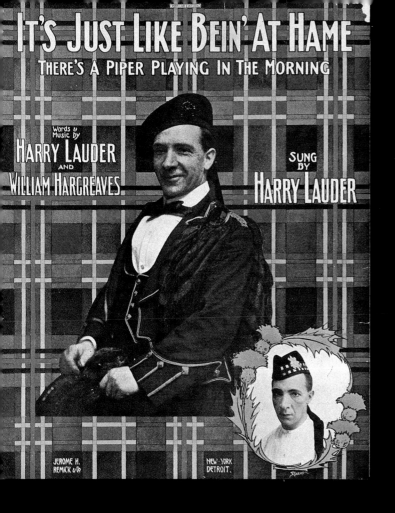

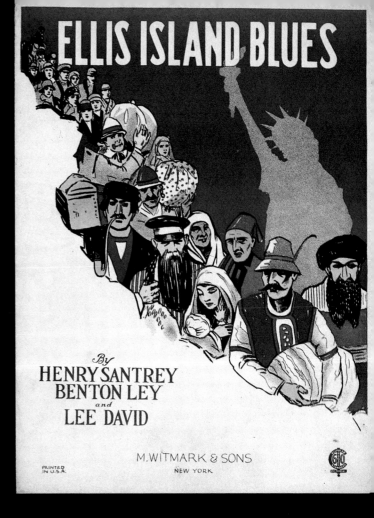

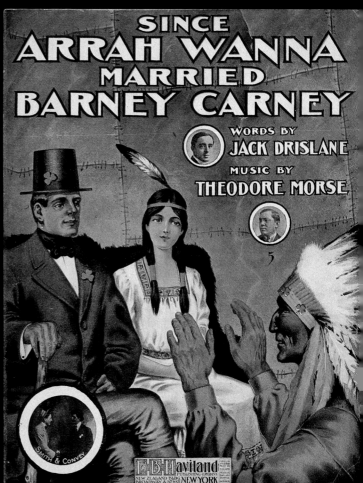

The immigrant community was a market for all kinds of products and services, and the ethnic press provided a way to reach that market. A dentist and doctor advertise in Yiddish in a New York magazine. The Western Union Macaroni Co. seeks Italian customers in Denver, Colorado. The Milwaukee-based F. Mayer Boot & Shoe Co. tries to spark some business among Czechs. A Brooklyn fish market advertises to Finns, and an Iowa farm equipment company sells its wares (including the disk harrower shown opposite) to Czech immigrants.

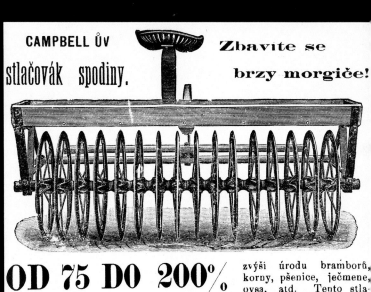

"I had beautiful, rosy cheeks when we came to this country. And my mother used to say, 'What happened to your beautiful rosy cheeks? This American air doesn't seem to be as good as the Italian air.' And she used to think, well, that was it, the change."

Josephine Reale, an Italian immigrant in 1920

"We wanted to be Americans so quickly that we were embarrassed if our parents couldn't speak English. My father was reading a Polish paper. And somebody was supposed to come to the house. I remember sticking it under something. We were that ashamed of being foreign."

Louise Nagy, a Polish immigrant in 1913

Immigrant children walked a fine line between two opposing cultures. On one side were their parents and centuries of Old World tradition; on the other, new friends from many ethnic backgrounds and public school teachers who frowned on foreign ways. The children found themselves thrown into radically new environments that demanded extreme adjustments. "It was sink or swim," said Anne Littman, who came from the Ukraine when she was just eight years old. "Our parents couldn't help us."

The public schools were prime agents for Americanizing the young newcomers. Teachers urged students to turn their backs on their immigrant past and get in step with America's future. In 1896, New York City's Commissioner of Common Schools issued a statement that expressed the views of many American educators. It was the paramount duty of the public schools, he said, to obliterate "all the distinguishing foreign characteristics and traits...as obstructive, and warring, and irritating elements." The shock of entering a world where your background and culture were not only not esteemed but reviled scarred the feelings of many youngsters. The teachers' disapproval made them even more intent on shedding their old habits and customs. The children's efforts, however, drove an emotional wedge between them and their parents.

Learning English as soon as possible seemed to be the only way to navigate the affairs of daily life and survive in America. Since most children were able to pick up the new language with comparative ease, they often served as their parents' translators and envoys. Jacob A. Riis called them "go-betweens," shuttling back and forth like emissaries, carrying messages and money to doctors, landlords, or shopkeepers for their non-English-speaking parents. "I was the one who always went to the gas company to complain about the bill," said Lou Winnick, a Romanian Jewish immigrant who came here as a child in 1922. "And I was the one who dealt with the landlords, the real estate agents. I could read the contract or the lease and speak English. I became in a sense a sort of junior father of the family."

Top: Greek newsboys, New York City.

Bottom: Children standing in front of kosher grocery store at 6th Avenue North and Lyndale, Minneapolis, 1908.

Opposite: "Outdoor play on school roof," North Bennet Street Industrial School, North End, Boston.

New Americans

Each immigrant had to learn how to balance old ways with new. But making adjustments and concessions to their adopted country was a long and painful process. It meant giving up pieces of a cherished past and exchanging them for new customs that lacked the resonance of traditions followed since childhood and blessed by generations of observance.

Immigrants living in American urban ghettos could no longer depend on the kind of social and spiritual framework that had once given their lives meaning in European towns and villages. They were less constrained by rigid class structures or by the authority of the local rabbi, prelate, or nobleman. For some, this new freedom was exhilarating, but others found it troubling, creating a burden of doubt and uncertainty. How much of the old should they preserve? How much of the new should they embrace? For deeply religious immigrants, this meant more than simply adjusting to a new environment, it meant making countless moral decisions, redefining concepts of vice and virtue and good and evil.

The observation of the Sabbath was often the first sacred duty to be sacrificed to necessity. "If you can't come in on Sunday, don't come in on Monday" seemed to be a ubiquitous directive in factories and other industrial sites. Some Jewish immigrants would only work for Jewish-owned shops that allowed them to keep their Saturday Sabbath. Others, however, found that they had to compromise. Morris Moel, who emigrated from the Ukraine in 1922, recalled his mother's anguish when his father, instead of going to synagogue on Saturday, went to work. "My mother cried like a baby," he said. "But then, she realized that you had to make a living. And that's the way it was."

While immigrants wrestled with these moral dilemmas, native-born Americans grew impatient and then alarmed at the large numbers of unassimilated foreigners clustering in impoverished, disease-ridden ghettos. By the 1910s, this alarm led to the creation of many programs to educate immigrants and hasten assimilation. "Greenhorns," as the immigrants were sometimes called, received ample advice from all sides. Employers, teachers, bureaucrats, and social workers urged them to submerge themselves in America's melting pot, learn English, become citizens, and vote. In heavily populated immigrant neighborhoods, local schools and neighborhood settlement houses often set up evening classes for immigrants. Henry Ford initiated an aggressive Americanization program at his Detroit automobile plant, where citizenship and English classes

"It was kind of bad for awhile till we got to know people and speak the language and quit being called greenhorns. People say, you ought to preserve your own heritage or something, but all we could think of was, we didn't want to be different, we wanted to be like the rest of the Americans."

Walter Wallace, a Lithuanian immigrant in 1923

Opposite top: The Syrian-American Commercial Press published the maxims and sayings of Benjamin Franklin in 1917, to raise money for the Lebanese Refugee and Victims Aid Committee Project.

Opposite bottom: A 1917 poster in six languages (English, Slovene, Italian, Polish, Hungarian, and Yiddish) encourages immigrants to learn English and become citizens.

Top: English class at Chicago plant of Barrett Company, 1919. Many companies set up ambitious programs to Americanize their immigrant workers. They offered classes in English and citizenship, had doctors and dentists demonstrate American health care practices, or sent company nurses into homes to teach hygiene and child care.

Bottom: Immigrant women learn about the U.S. flag in citizenship class, New York City.

"There is no room in this country for hyphenated Americanism.... Our allegiance must be purely to the United States. We must unsparingly condemn any man who holds any other allegiance. But if he is heartily and singly loyal to this Republic, then no matter where he was born, he is just as good an American as anyone else."

Theodore Roosevelt, 1915

Top: Chinese Americans portraying China, the Statue of Liberty, and Uncle Sam at New York City bond rally, ca. 1917.

Bottom: World War I poster urging America's most recent arrivals to buy War Savings Stamps.

were mandatory for foreign employees. The first sentence they learned was "I am a good American."

In 1916, one educator wrote that it was not only desirable but necessary to offer instruction to immigrant adults, citing two reasons: "For our own protection and for the immigrant's benefit. Today the majority of the immigrants," he continued, "come to better their economic condition. Therefore it is our first business to teach him English—the colloquial English that will enable him to get on in life; to get a job, to keep it and then to get a better one; to find his way about the streets and to familiarize himself with American life."

While much of the help available to new arrivals was offered with the best of intentions, its underlying message became gradually more overbearing: that immigrants should renounce their heritage and become Americans. The entrance of the United States into World War I in 1917 gave fresh impetus to social reformers' efforts to Americanize the immigrant. The tolerant sentiment "Many Peoples, But One Nation" gave way to the insistent slogan "100% American." Immigrants were not simply encouraged to speak, dress, and act American; they were now called upon to declare their loyalty, help the war effort, buy a war bond, join the army, even die for America. Immigrants who refused to be goaded into patriotic conformity, or whose surnames were German, were harassed by an assortment of jingoists who believed that any hint of divided loyalty invited America's defeat in Europe.

Immigrants reacted to this cultural barrage in a variety of ways. Assimilation was a gradual process, but newcomers generally took advantage of the educational and social programs offered for their benefit. The settlement house movement, started in the United States by Jane Addams, who opened Hull House in Chicago in 1889, was a vital source of help. Addams's successful example was followed by social reformers in most major cities, especially Boston, New York, and Philadelphia. Each settlement offered as much as possible to as many as possible, shaping its programs and services to the particular needs of the neighborhood. Immigrants came to the settlement for medical services, emergency relief, counseling or vocational training, help in getting a job or lessons in cooking, hygiene, or home economics. Children came after school to take music lessons, rehearse for a play or concert, use the library, or get help with homework. While the settlement house program varied from place to place, it always included English and citizenship courses. These lessons were

Above and opposite: World War I posters asking immigrants to contribute money and service. Americans of all ethnic groups—from the French DuBois to the Mexican Gonzales—were celebrated in a Victory Liberty Loan appeal. Another poster invokes the names of Kosciuszko and Pulaski, Polish patriots who fought in the American Revolution: "They fought for freedom in America. Can you help Americans fight for freedom in Poland? EAT LESS." A third poster reads "Stand by the Boys" in Italian, Croatian, Slovene, Polish, Hungarian, and German.

"My mother began to go to night school, and she immediately began to study for citizenship. She and I studied together about the Constitution, about the presidents, about the portions of the government, the executive, the judicial, and the congressional. She knew all these things and she did pass the examination and it was one of the happiest days of her life when she became a citizen."

Morris Moel, a Ukrainian Jewish immigrant in 1922

Top: Immigrant being sworn in as citizen.

Bottom: Naturalization certificate of Sadie Hazar, who emigrated from Lebanon in 1921 and became a citizen in 1943. Many immigrants waited decades before applying for their citizenship papers.

Opposite: In the early 1920s, the Metropolitan Life Insurance Company published citizenship booklets for immigrant policyholders.

supposed to give immigrants the means and knowledge, and also the will, to become loyal Americans.

Throughout the nineteenth century, becoming a citizen of the United States was a simple matter of taking an oath before a judge. Political machines often took advantage of this easy process by corralling newly arrived immigrants at election time, quickly getting them naturalized, and then marching them off to the polls to cast their votes for certain candidates. By 1906, the federal government had taken steps to stop these abuses by standardizing the country's naturalization process, which had previously been regulated by each state. Federal law required candidates for citizenship to prove that they had been in the country for at least five years. They also had to appear before a federal judge, prove that they could speak English, and answer questions about American history and civics. Not everyone could apply for naturalization, however. The government denied this privilege to certain immigrant groups—the Chinese, for example, in 1882; and after 1911, the Japanese and most other Asians. These bans, grounded in entrenched racist attitudes, were not completely revoked until 1952.

Eligible newcomers sometimes made great sacrifices to qualify for naturalization once their five-year residency was fulfilled. Many, however, found it difficult if not impossible to attend night school, study, and memorize all the facts and dates that might be asked on a citizenship test. Immigrants were either too busy in the evening taking care of their children or doing housework or too exhausted after working a ten-hour day. Those who persevered sometimes found help along the way. Moses Kirshblum, who came to America in 1923 from Bialystok, Poland, applied for citizenship even though he had not been able to learn English. His son described the judge's questioning:

"Are you a bigamist?" My father had never heard the word, and he said "Yes" with great pride. "Do you have any prison record?" and again he said "Yes." He figured he can't go wrong by saying "Yes." Then the judge began to ask him about certain American holidays: He said: "Do you remember what the Fourth of July is?" And he said "Labor Day." But toward the end he turned pleadingly to the judge and said, "Mr. Judge, please do me a taver [a version of the Hebrew word tovah, meaning a favor]. Do me a taver. I want to be an American citizen." And the judge, because he was

> "We allow the foreigner to join our self-governing electorate almost before he has had time to step off the Ellis Island ferryboat. No wonder he votes not as an American but as the foreigner that he still is! And the American politician, knowing that full well, panders to his foreign feeling in order to get his foreign vote."

Henry H. Curran, commissioner of immigration at Ellis Island, 1924

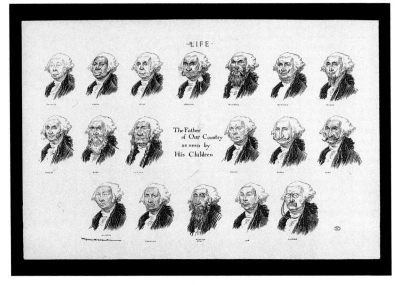

Top: A disgruntled Uncle Sam watches a long line of immigrant voters cast their ballots. This 1899 Puck *cartoon pokes fun at the immigrants' purported divided loyalties.*

Bottom: Many ethnic groups claim George Washington as their own in this 1907 Life *cartoon.*

deeply moved by this old man pleading for American citizenship, said tearfully, "A citizen you shall be," and granted him papers.

Naturalized immigrants and their children gradually formed a sizable bloc of voters. Ethnic support was important in big-city politics, where machines such as Tammany Hall in New York retained their power by dispensing jobs and emergency help to each successive wave of new arrivals. Republicans and Democrats as well as Socialists actively courted the immigrant vote. Socialists appealed strongly to the working classes, especially among Finnish and Jewish immigrants, many of whom had brought socialist ideas with them from Europe. Republicans found support in the German community, while Democrats could generally count on a large Irish vote. Standard campaign strategy included the wide distribution of flyers and broadsides in a variety of translations. Most politicians on the stump were able to say a few words in several languages and had a store of favorite expressions and jokes appropriate for nearly every ethnic occasion.

Eventually, immigrants themselves entered the political arena. One successful candidate was Anton J. Cermak, who had emigrated from Prague with his parents in 1873, when he was a baby. In 1930, when Cermak ran for mayor of Chicago, his opponent openly ridiculed the idea of a foreigner being elected. "Tony, Tony, where's your pushcart at?" taunted Cermak's adversary. "Can you imagine a World's Fair mayor with a name like that." Cermak's answer became a classic immigrant retort and helped to win his campaign. "It's true," he said, "I didn't come over with the *Mayflower*, but I came as soon as I could."

Opposite: District Attorney William Travers Jerome, running on the Republican ticket, distributed sample ballots in Hungarian (top), Italian (bottom), Yiddish, and English during the 1905 election in New York City.

Top ballot (Hungarian)

MIKÉPEN SZAVAZZON
JEROME Részére es a
Republikanus Partra.

MIKÉPEN SZAVAZZ ON
JEROME Részére es a
Republikanus Partra.

Jegyezze a Szavazó ivet az alanti mód szerint.
AZ EGYIK KERESZTET **X** UGY HELYEZZE EL A SZAVAZÓ ROVATBA, HOGY AZ A JEROME NEV BAL OLDALÁRA, A MASIK PEDIG A **SAS** CZIMER ALANTI KARIKÁJÁBA ESSEN:
NE TEGYEN MÁS MEGJEGYZÉSEKET AZ IVEN KI NE KARCOLJON VALAMELY NEVET.

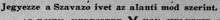

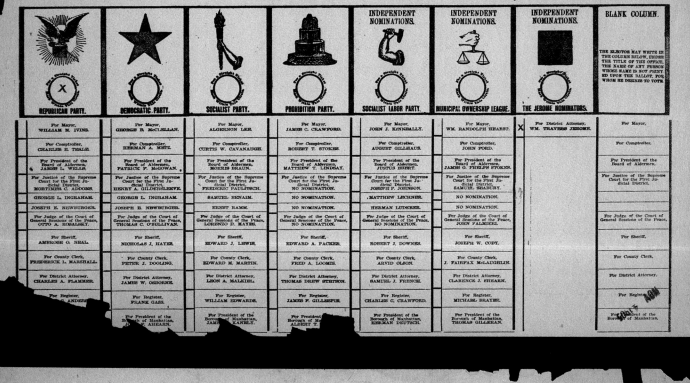

Office	REPUBLICAN PARTY (X)	DEMOCRATIC PARTY	SOCIALIST PARTY	PROHIBITION PARTY	SOCIALIST LABOR PARTY	MUNICIPAL OWNERSHIP LEAGUE	THE JEROME NOMINATORS	BLANK COLUMN
For Mayor	WILLIAM M. IVINS	GEORGE B. McCLELLAN	ALGERNON LEE	JAMES C. CRAWFORD	JOHN J. KINNEALLY	WM. RANDOLPH HEARST		For Mayor,
For Comptroller	CHARLES E. THALL	HERMAN A. METZ	CURTIS W. CAVANAUGH	ROBERT T. STOKER	AUGUST GILLHAUS	JOHN FORD		For Comptroller,
For President of the Board of Aldermen	JAMES I. WELLS	PATRICK F. McGOWAN	MORRIS BRAUN	MATTHEW T. LINDSAY	JUSTUS EBERT	JAMES G. PHELPS STOKES		For President of the Board of Aldermen,
For Justice of the Supreme Court for the First Judicial District	MORTIMER C. ADDOMS	HENRY A. GILDERSLEEVE	FREDERIC PAULITSCH	NO NOMINATION.	JOSEPH P. JOHNSON	SAMUEL SEABURY		For Justice of the Supreme Court for the First Judicial District,
	GEORGE L. INGRAHAM	GEORGE L. INGRAHAM	SAMUEL BENAIM	NO NOMINATION.	MATTHEW LECHNER	NO NOMINATION.		
	JOSEPH E. NEWBURGER	JOSEPH E. NEWBURGER	ERNST RAMM	NO NOMINATION.	HERMAN LUDERER	NO NOMINATION.		
For Judge of the Court of General Sessions of the Peace	OTTO A. ROSALSKY	THOMAS C. O'SULLIVAN	LORENZO D. MAYES	NO NOMINATION.	NO NOMINATION.	JOHN PALMIERI		For Judge of the Court of General Sessions of the Peace,
For Sheriff	AMBROSE O. NEAL	NICHOLAS J. HAYES	EDWARD J. LEWIS	EDWARD A. PACKER	ROBERT J. DOWNES	JOSEPH W. CODY		For Sheriff,
For County Clerk	FREDERICK L. MARSHALL	PETER J. DOOLING	EDWARD M. MARTIN	FRED A. LOOMIS	ARVID OLSON	J. FAIRFAX McLAUGHLIN		For County Clerk,
For District Attorney	CHARLES A. FLAMMER	JAMES W. OSBORNE	LEON A. MALKIEL	THOMAS DREW STETSON	SAMUEL J. FRENCH	CLARENCE J. SHEARN	WM. TRAVERS JEROME (X)	For District Attorney,
For Register	... ANDERSON	FRANK GASS	WILLIAM EDWARDS	JAMES F. GILLESPIE	CHARLES C. CRAWFORD	MICHAEL BRAYER		For Register,
For President of the Borough of Manhattan	... DUFFY	JOHN F. AHEARN	JAMES C. KANERLY	ALBERT T. ...	HERMAN DEUTSCH	THOMAS GILLERAN		For President of the Borough of Manhattan,

BLANK COLUMN. THE ELECTOR MAY WRITE IN THE COLUMN BELOW, UNDER THE TITLE OF THE OFFICE, THE NAME OF ANY PERSON WHOSE NAME IS NOT PRINTED UPON THE BALLOT, FOR WHOM HE DESIRES TO VOTE.

Bottom ballot (Italian)

MODO DI VOTARE PER
JEROME ED IL PARTITO
REPUBLICANANO.

MODO DI VOTARE PER
JEROME ED IL PARTITO
REPUBLICANANO.

Si marco il foglio voto come si Vede piu sotto.
Un segno **X** nello spazio alla sinistra del nome di Jerome ed un segno **X** nel sircolo che sta sotto l'emblema Republicano.
Non fate altri segni sul foglio voto.
Non cancellate alcun nome.

Office	REPUBLICAN PARTY (X)	DEMOCRATIC PARTY	SOCIALIST PARTY	PROHIBITION PARTY	SOCIALIST LABOR PARTY	MUNICIPAL OWNERSHIP LEAGUE	THE JEROME NOMINATORS	BLANK COLUMN
For Mayor	WILLIAM M. IVINS	GEORGE B. McCLELLAN	ALGERNON LEE	JAMES C. CRAWFORD	JOHN J. KINNEALLY	WM. RANDOLPH HEARST		For Mayor,
For Comptroller	CHARLES E. THALL	HERMAN A. METZ	CURTIS W. CAVANAUGH	ROBERT T. STOKES	AUGUST GILLHAUS	JOHN FORD		For Comptroller,
For President of the Board of Aldermen	JAMES I. WELLS	PATRICK F. McGOWAN	MORRIS BRAUN	MATTHEW T. LINDSAY	JUSTUS EBERT	JAMES G. PHELPS STOKES		For President of the Board of Aldermen,
For Justice of the Supreme Court for the First Judicial District	MORTIMER C. ADDOMS	HENRY A. GILDERSLEEVE	FREDERIC PAULITSCH	NO NOMINATION.	JOSEPH P. JOHNSON	SAMUEL SEABURY		For Justice of the Supreme Court for the First Judicial District,
	GEORGE L. INGRAHAM	GEORGE L. INGRAHAM	SAMUEL BENAIM	NO NOMINATION.	MATTHEW LECHNER	NO NOMINATION.		
	JOSEPH E. NEWBURGER	JOSEPH E. NEWBURGER	ERNST RAMM	NO NOMINATION.	HERMAN LUDERER	NO NOMINATION.		
For Judge of the Court of General Sessions of the Peace	OTTO A. ROSALSKY	THOMAS C. O'SULLIVAN	LORENZO D. MAYES	NO NOMINATION.	NO NOMINATION.	JOHN PALMIERI		For Judge of the Court of General Sessions of the Peace,
For Sheriff	AMBROSE O. NEAL	NICHOLAS J. HAYES	EDWARD J. LEWIS	EDWARD A. PACKER	ROBERT J. DOWNES	JOSEPH W. CODY		For Sheriff,
For County Clerk	FREDERICK L. MARSHALL	PETER J. DOOLING	EDWARD M. MARTIN	FRED A. LOOMIS	ARVID OLSON	J. FAIRFAX McLAUGHLIN		For County Clerk,
For District Attorney	CHARLES A. FLAMMER	JAMES W. OSBORNE	LEON A. MALKIEL	THOMAS DREW STETSON	SAMUEL J. FRENCH	CLARENCE J. SHEARN	WM. TRAVERS JEROME (X)	For District Attorney,
For Register	HENRY A. C. ANDERSON	FRANK GASS	WILLIAM EDWARDS	JAMES F. GILLESPIE	CHARLES C. CRAWFORD	MICHAEL BRAYER		For Register,
For President of the Borough of Manhattan	...	JOHN F. AHEARN	JAMES C. KANERLY	ALBERT T. HULL	... DEUTSCH	THOMAS GILL...		For President of the Borough of Manhattan,

BLANK COLUMN. THE ELECTOR MAY WRITE IN THE COLUMN BELOW, UNDER THE TITLE OF THE OFFICE, THE NAME OF ANY PERSON WHOSE NAME IS NOT PRINTED UPON THE BALLOT, FOR WHOM HE DESIRES TO VOTE.

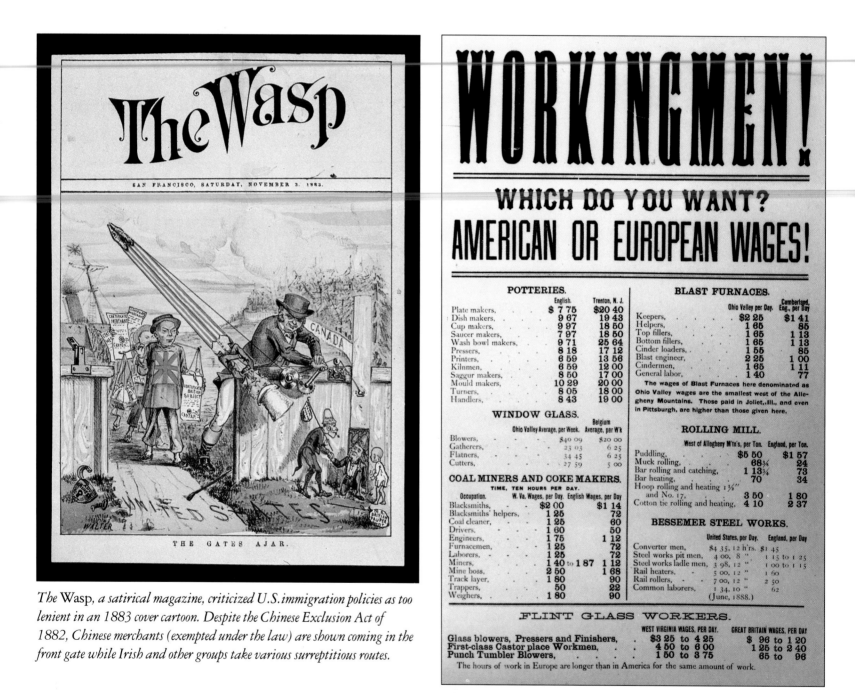

The Wasp, *a satirical magazine, criticized U.S. immigration policies as too lenient in an 1883 cover cartoon. Despite the Chinese Exclusion Act of 1882, Chinese merchants (exempted under the law) are shown coming in the front gate while Irish and other groups take various surreptitious routes.*

This late-nineteenth-century broadside expresses fears that immigrant labor would undermine American wages. Organized labor officially opposed unrestricted immigration, but many union members, immigrants themselves, privately supported an open-door policy that would allow relatives and friends to join them.

The Closing Door

"The present predominating immigration from southern and eastern Europe is inferior on the whole to the old north European immigration. It contains many undesirable and unintelligent people."

William Williams, commissioner of immigration at Ellis Island, 1903

America's immigration policies provoked a national debate during the late nineteenth and early twentieth centuries. Though unrestricted immigration had helped build and strengthen the United States, many believed that the country could not continue to absorb the steadily increasing numbers of new arrivals. The restrictionist movement's noisiest champions were the nativists, whose anti-Catholic, anti-Semitic, and anti-Asian rhetoric preyed on the country's fear of strangers. There was, to be sure, widespread apprehension about the soaring number of arrivals from southern and eastern Europe, but many Americans who favored restriction were reacting to practical social concerns, especially the impoverished conditions of immigrant slums, viewed as impenetrable pockets of violence, crime, and disease. With record-breaking numbers of immigrants arriving each year, the extreme poverty and its tragic consequences seemed to worsen. Social welfare agencies complained that they could not care for the large numbers of impoverished, mentally ill, or sickly immigrants who needed help.

Public pressure and congressional investigations gradually moved the federal government to take cautious measures to inspect and sift new arrivals, turning away certain categories of undesirables. The first federal immigration bill, passed in 1875, barred convicts, prostitutes, and Chinese contract laborers. In 1882, two more bills were passed: a law barring lunatics, idiots, and paupers, and the Chinese Exclusion Act, which barred all Chinese laborers. The exclusion laws, renewed periodically, and the 1907 Gentlemen's Agreement, which curtailed Japanese immigration, enacted racist policies that had been vigorously and viciously promoted by nativist groups.

In 1885, Congress passed the Alien Contract Labor Law, which outlawed the importation of foreign workers. America's labor leaders had lobbied aggressively for this legislation, intended to protect American jobs from being usurped by cheap labor from abroad. Even after this law was passed, American unions remained staunch restrictionists, maintaining that immigrants undermined efforts to gain higher wages. In 1895, a congressional investigation reported that over a period of ten years, 10,000 immigrants had taken jobs in Pennsylvania alone, "gradually supplanting the practical [American] miners, who have found it impossible to live at the low rate of wages established by the immigrants."

The Immigration Act of 1891 marked an important change in American policy. With this law, the federal government assumed

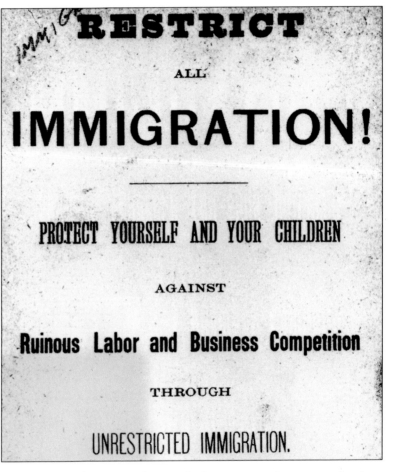

This 1885 brochure, an early example of restrictionist literature, takes the most extreme position in calling for the complete curtailment of immigration. It directs its message to Americans afraid of losing their livelihoods to foreigners.

THE FOOL PIED PIPER.

THE MODERN MOSES.

"The new immigration...contained a large and increasing number of the weak, the broken and the mentally crippled of all races drawn from the lowest stratum of the Mediterranean basin and the Balkans, together with hordes of the wretched, submerged populations of the Polish Ghettos. The whole tone of American life...has been lowered and vulgarized by them."

Madison Grant, *The Passing of the Great Race*, 1918

"Those who are loudest in their cry of 'America for Americans' do not have to look very far back to find an ancestor who was an immigrant."

New Immigrants' Protective League, 1906

PUCK.

LOOKING BACKWARD.
THEY WOULD CLOSE TO THE NEW-COMER THE BRIDGE THAT CARRIED THEM AND THEIR FATHERS OVER.

Opposite top: In this 1909 cartoon, European leaders cheer as Uncle Sam leads an assorted group of cutthroats and members of the "Black Hand" (a criminal society also known as the Mafia) out of Europe.

Opposite bottom: When Puck *published this cartoon in 1881, the editor of the* Jewish Messenger *criticized its use of German and Austrian anti-Semitic caricatures to render eastern European Jewish immigrants.*

Above: In 1893, Joseph Keppler, the founder of Puck *and one of the nation's leading cartoonists, poked fun at successful immigrants who, forgetting their own backgrounds, would now keep out their compatriots.*

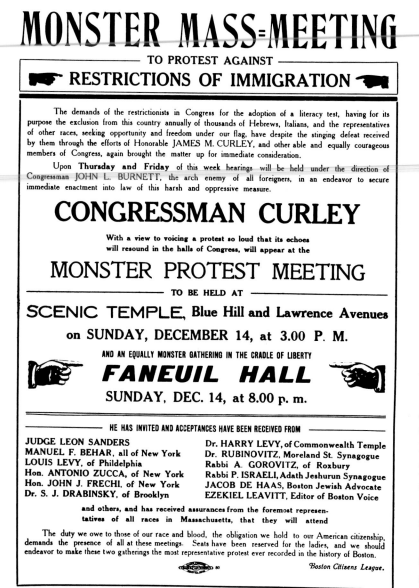

Above: Congressman James Michael Curley was the featured speaker at this 1913 Boston rally protesting the literacy test. Curley, America's most prominent and beloved Irish politician, was the son of immigrants from County Galway. He served three terms as congressman, four as mayor of Boston, and one as governor of Massachusetts.

Opposite: The front page of this 1898 Judge *shows the positive side of immigration and the nation's ability to assimilate immigrant groups.*

control of inspecting immigrants, previously a state responsibility, and authorized a Bureau of Immigration. The new federal bureau devised an inspection system and assigned officers to guard America's gates, including Ellis Island, which would open the following year. The new law also itemized a long list of excluded classes: "All idiots, insane persons, paupers or persons likely to become a public charge, persons suffering from a loathsome or a dangerous contagious disease, persons who have been convicted of a felony or other infamous crime or misdemeanor involving moral turpitude, polygamists and ... contract laborers." In 1903, epileptics and anarchists were added to the list; and in 1907, tuberculars, persons with physical defects that could impair their ability to earn a living, and children under 16 unaccompanied by their parents.

Though most Americans agreed that undesirable characters ought to be kept out, a diversity of opinion existed as to *who* was indeed undesirable. There was still considerable sentiment for maintaining an open door for those who were able and healthy. Industrialists from northeastern states wanted to maintain a free influx of cheap labor. Congress, too, was mindful of a growing bloc of naturalized citizens and their children, who consistently voted for those candidates who favored liberal immigration policy. As immigrants and their descendants began running for and winning elective office, their sentiments found substantial support. In a 1908 speech, Representative Bourke Cockran of New York stated the liberal position that unrestricted immigration benefits everyone: "I welcome this tide of immigration, because I believe there is nothing that can enter our ports so valuable to us as a pair of human hands eager and anxious to engage in labor upon our soil, to increase the volume of commodities available for you and me, to widen the field of production in which highly paid American laborers can find employment."

Pro-immigration forces, however, gradually lost ground to well-established nativist groups, such as the Immigration Restriction League, founded in 1894 by a group of wealthy Bostonians. Influenced by pseudo-Darwinian concepts of heredity and natural selection, the nativists maintained that the so-called inferior races from southern and eastern Europe would surely corrupt America's superior Anglo-Saxon stock. These aliens, said Senator Henry Cabot Lodge, threatened the "very fabric of our race."

The nativists, appalled by the hundreds of thousands of immigrants that trooped through Ellis Island each year, pinned their

VOL. 35 NO. 893   NOVEMBER 26 1898   PRICE 10 CENTS

Judge

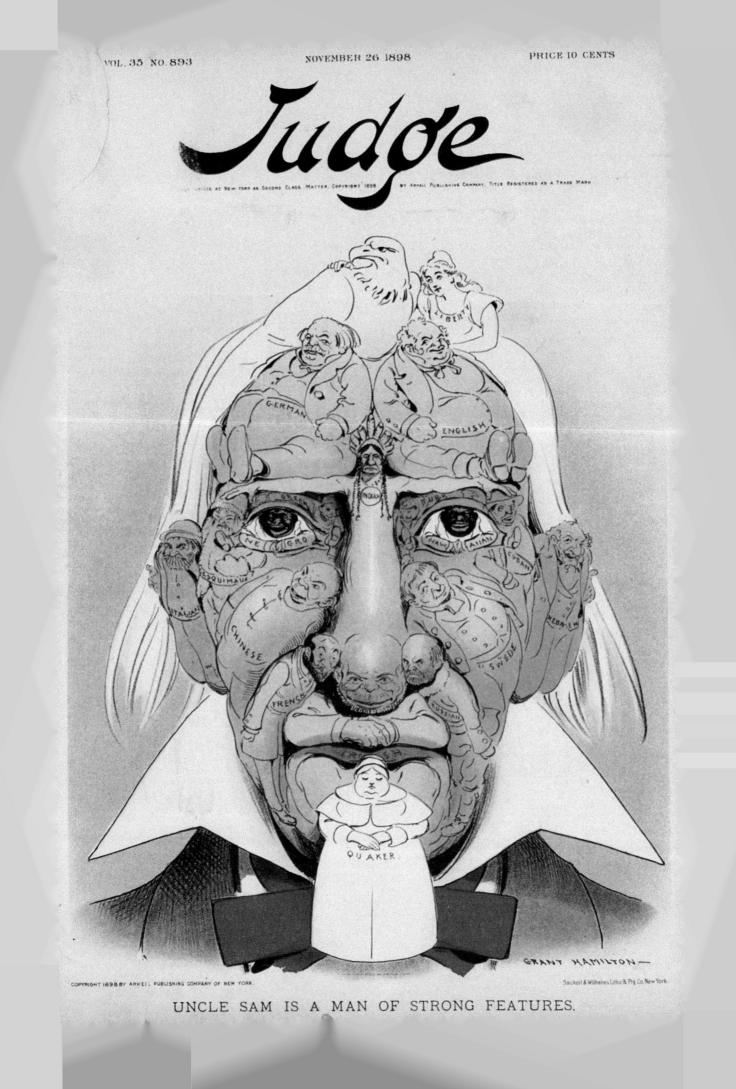

UNCLE SAM IS A MAN OF STRONG FEATURES.

> "The melting pot is destructive to our race.... The danger the 'melting pot' brings to the nation is the breeding out of the higher divisions of the white race and the breeding in of the lower divisions."

Dr. George B. Cutten, president, Colgate University, 1923

Above: Songsters as well as cartoonists expressed the country's anti-immigration sentiments. This 1923 doggerel laments the lack of patriotism in recent arrivals and strongly urges: "O, what will become of our country in a few more years to be, if foreign immigration isn't barred from the U.S.A. Our flag they do not honor, our rights they will betray. O! close the gates of our nation, yes before that awful day. O! close the gates of our nation, lock them firm and strong, before this mob from Europe shall drag our Colors down. There are places here already, our flag is forbidden to wave. O! close the gates of our nation, our liberty to save."

Top right: A woman in Hollywood proudly points to anti-Japanese signs on her house, ca. 1922. Such sentiment peaked on the West Coast between 1914 and 1924. A "Swat the Jap" campaign swept Los Angeles in 1922.

hopes on legislation enacting a literacy test that would require adult immigrants to read a short passage in their native language. Though Congress had passed a literacy-test bill in 1896, 1904, and 1916, it was defeated each time by a presidential veto. In 1917, however, in the midst of World War I, restrictionists managed to push the Immigration Act of 1917 through Congress over the veto of President Woodrow Wilson. The new law barred thirty-three categories of undesirables, including illiterates.

When the literacy test failed to be effective, restrictionists set to work to devise a radically different mechanism for curtailing immigration. The results of their labors were the quota acts, two major laws that marked a departure from previous immigration policies. The First Quota Act of 1921 sharply reduced immigration to 350,000 admissions per year. Immigration from southern and eastern Europe was especially hard hit, as the law intended. The annual quota for these regions would be 155,000 admissions, far below the previous annual average of 783,000.

In 1924, a second quota law imposed more severe restrictions. It set an annual ceiling of 150,000 admissions, further reducing the number of southern and eastern European immigrants to below 25,000. The new act introduced a "national origins" system of allocating quotas to maintain the nation's ethnic composition as it was in 1920. The *New York Times* announced the bill's passage with the headline, "America of the Melting Pot Comes to End." The law's chief aim, explained the subhead, was to "preserve racial type as it exists here today." In addition, the new law denied entry to "aliens ineligible to citizenship," reaffirming Chinese exclusion and effectively barring Japanese without mentioning them by name.

The restrictionists had won their long battle to close America's gates, but it was in many ways an empty victory. The millions of men, women, and children who came to America during its peak years of immigration had a profound impact on the country. They brought with them traditions, customs, and values that would gradually enter the texture of our national life, forever changing the temperament and culture of the United States.

"The welfare of the United States demands that the door should be closed to immigrants for a time. We are being made a dumping-ground for the human wreckage of the war. And worst of all, they are coming in such numbers at a time when we are unable adequately to take care of them."

Rep. Albert Johnson of Washington, sponsor of Immigration Quota Act, 1920.

Above: This 1921 cartoon from the Providence Evening Bulletin *depicts the effects of the First Quota Act, passed that year.*

Left: Ku Klux Klan pamphlet, mid-1920s. The Ku Klux Klan arose after the Civil War as an effort to suppress the newly won freedoms of southern African Americans. It fell into disarray but was revived in 1915, with anti-immigrant feeling providing a new source of support. At the Klan's popularity peak in the 1920s, it campaigned just as vigorously against immigration as against the rights of African Americans. The Klan declared: "Jews dominate the economic life of the nation, while the Catholics are determined to dominate the political and religious life....The vast alien immigration is, at the root, an attack upon Protestant religion with its freedom of conscience, and is therefore a menace to American liberties."

Overleaf: Immigrant-laden barges waiting in front of Ellis Island's main building, 1907.

"My mother had to try and keep track of us. She finally took us and tied us all together so that we would stay together. And that's the way we came off the boat."

Gertrude Schneider Smith, a Swiss immigrant in 1921

"Ellis Island—You got thousands of people marching in, a little bit excited, a little bit scared. Just imagine you're 14½ years old and you're in a strange country and you don't know what's going to happen."

Albert Mardirossian, an Armenian immigrant in 1921

Above: A mother, flanked by her neatly dressed children, gives the camera a determined look as she arrives at Ellis Island. Immigrants often dressed in their best clothes, not just to impress the inspectors but also to greet friends and relatives waiting to meet them.

Opposite top: Antoinette Cammarata Forgione brought this trunk through Ellis Island from Sicily in 1919.

Opposite bottom left: Ships issued landing cards to steerage passengers. This one belonged to Miriam Lowenfish, a Polish Jew who arrived in 1923. The number printed on each card corresponded to the page in the ship's manifest where the passenger's name and other information were recorded.

Opposite bottom right: In 1916, Theodore Anderson, a young Finnish immigrant, made this small wooden suitcase for his journey to America.

108

As immigrant ships steamed into New York's harbor, past the welcoming Statue of Liberty, the excitement of arrival invariably faded when the red brick reality of Ellis Island slipped into view. For many immigrants, Ellis Island was the last hurdle in a long journey that had already surmounted many obstacles.

The federal immigration depot, which opened for business on January 1, 1892, was designed to inspect thousands of immigrants each day, though often the number exceeded 5,000. On April 17, 1907, the island's busiest day, 11,747 immigrants were processed; 1907 was also the island's busiest year, with over one million arrivals.

The inspection routine was supposed to operate much like an efficient assembly line, with a team of federal officers systematically checking each immigrant to make sure that he or she was "without a doubt entitled to land," according to the U.S. immigration laws. Each doctor and inspector had certain tasks, certain papers to stamp or questions to ask. When all was moving smoothly, the process of inspection took three to five hours. Though all but 2% of immigrants were ultimately admitted, about 20% were detained overnight, sometimes for many nights, pending investigation.

Ellis Island was intended only for working-class travelers—those who came in steerage. First- and second-class passengers enjoyed the

"Getting off on Ellis Island, my mother was dressed up. She had been making this suit for a year to land in. And I was dressed up with handmade lace and all. It was jampacked with mostly Europeans. And most of these people were dirty, actually dirty. I was terrified."

Ayleen Watts James, a Panamanian immigrant in 1923

"We were put on a barge, jammed in so tight that I couldn't turn 'round, there were so many of us, you see, and the stench was terrible."

Eleanor Kenderdine Lenhart, an English immigrant in 1921

privilege of being inspected on board ship and, if all was well, of disembarking at the pier. This was generally a cursory examination, and some immigrants, unsure of passing the more rigorous inspection on Ellis Island, managed to pay the extra cost (about $20 more in 1905) to travel second class.

Once the ship docked at one of the Hudson River piers, its officers ordered steerage passengers to gather up their belongings and assemble for a last roll call. Each passenger wore pinned to his or her clothes a boldly numbered card that corresponded to the ship's manifest, or passenger list. The immigrants, sorted by their numbers, were led out of the ships and onto ferries that would take them down the Hudson River to Ellis Island.

The ferries, chartered by the steamship companies, were usually overcrowded and ill equipped, bitter cold in the winter and unbearably hot in the summer. Yet men, women, and children were confined to these tiny, barely seaworthy vessels without food or water for hours at a time. During the busy season (spring to fall) it was not unusual to see several crowded ferries lined up in front of Ellis Island's main building.

Stephen Graham, a British writer who traveled with immigrants in 1913, called the ferry he was on "a floating waiting room. A hot sun beat upon its wooden roof; the windows in the sides were fixed; we could not move an inch from the places we were awkwardly standing...babies kept crying sadly, and irritated emigrants swore at the sound of them."

Finally, officers shouting in several languages ordered the passengers to disembark, form a line, and hurry into the formidable main building, constructed in 1900 to replace an earlier wooden structure that had burned down in 1897. The immigrants, often burdened with an assortment of bundles, baggage, and children, hastily complied with the brusque commands.

What were the immigrants' thoughts as they scurried past the shouting officers? According to Stephen Graham, "All were thinking—'Shall I get through?' 'Have I enough money?' 'Shall I pass the doctor?'" Many were also rehearsing their answers for the inspectors. They knew from friends and relatives who had gone before them what they would be asked and how they should answer.

Above: Two Scandinavian girls, with manifest tags and worried expressions, hold each other's hands as they disembark.

Opposite top: Waiting to disembark at Ellis Island.

Opposite bottom: Immigrants on ferry to Ellis Island, ca. 1908. Immigration hit an all-time high in 1907, when over one million arrivals landed at Ellis Island. On some days, there were so many immigrants waiting for inspection that steerage passengers had to stay on board ships for two or three days before they could be brought to Ellis Island. They had to spend hours more waiting on ferries for their turn to disembark and go through inspection.

The Inspection Maze

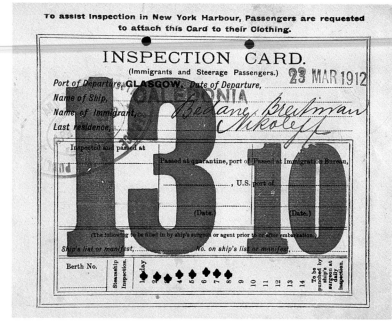

Once inside the main building, the immigrants could check parcels and belongings in the Baggage Room, which occupied nearly the entire ground floor. But many, fearing that they would never see their belongings again, insisted on carrying them throughout the inspection routine.

The examination process began almost immediately. As soon as immigrants started up the stairs, a U.S. Public Health Service doctor stationed at the top of the stairwell watched them for signs of lameness or exertion that might indicate heart disease or some other frailty. Immigrants presented their medical inspection cards to the doctor, who checked and stamped them. Once inside the Registry Room, the newcomers encountered another doctor, who quickly scrutinized each individual from head to toe for signs of disease or deformity. He lifted hats or pushed back shawls to check for favus, a disease of the scalp, scrawling a chalk mark on the lapels or shoulders of those who aroused his suspicions. A third doctor examined immigrants for trachoma, an eye disease, by turning back their eyelids. Trachoma and favus, considered highly contagious and difficult to cure, were common in southeastern Europe but relatively unknown in the United States. Trachoma, if left untreated, could sometimes cause blindness. Doctors checked for this disease by pulling the eyelids up and over a buttonhook, a hairpin, or their fingers, a severely painful procedure.

A doctor who found indications of disease would mark the immigrant with a piece of chalk: L for lameness, C for conjunctivitis, Ct for trachoma, E for eyes, H for heart, K for hernia, Pg for pregnancy, and so forth. The marked immigrant would be taken out of the inspection line and sent to another room for further examination. This generally caused scenes of great anxiety. If a parent or child were separated from a family group, the others were pushed forward without a calming explanation. The inspectors' prime concern was to keep the line moving.

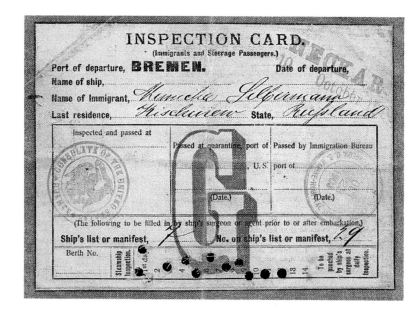

Right: Medical inspection cards. During the transatlantic journey, passengers received inspection cards that recorded how often they had been examined by the ship's physician. Each immigrant had to present the card to an Ellis Island doctor, who stamped it "passed" if the card carrier seemed healthy.

Opposite: A startled immigrant clutching his inspection card as an Ellis Island doctor performs a routine eye examination, ca. 1905.

Above: Doctor using a buttonhook to check eyes for trachoma, ca. 1914. New arrivals feared this painful examination, whose notoriety had traveled back to the homeland. The line doctor had to turn up both eyelids of every immigrant. Grover A. Kempf, a U.S. Public Health Service doctor on Ellis Island from 1912 to 1916, said that the preferred instrument for examining eyes was "the good old buttoner, a little loop to button shoes, the most efficient way of turning the eyes ever devised."

Top right: Buttonhook typical of the kind used by Ellis Island doctors.

Bottom right: During the line inspection, doctors chalk-marked anyone who appeared to be ill. This woman bears the "E" that indicates eye disease, perhaps trachoma.

"My sister developed warts on the back of her hand so they put a chalk 'X' on the back of her coat. The Xs were put aside to see whether they had to be reexamined or deported. If they deported my sister we couldn't let her go. Where would she go if they deported her? Some kind man, I don't know who he was, told my sister to turn her coat around. She had a nice plush coat with a silk lining, and they turned her coat around."

Victoria Sarfatti Fernández, a Macedonian immigrant in 1916

"People who had come to this country in the earlier years had told me, you'll be sorry when you get to Ellis Island. But I wasn't really sorry, I was just maybe upset a little bit. What upset me the most was having to go through so many people's hands and take such a long time."

Mary Dunn, a Scottish immigrant in 1923

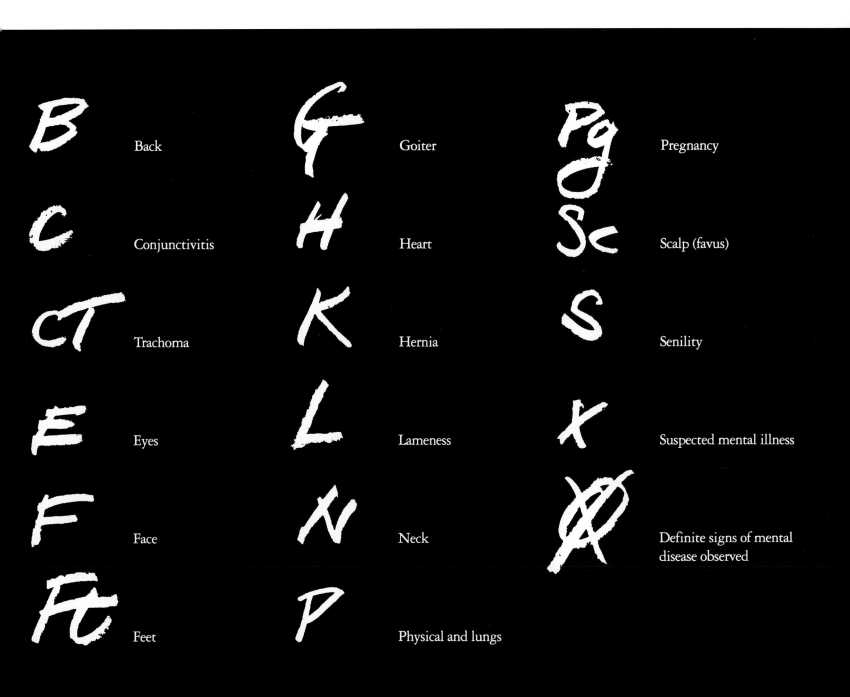

B	Back	G	Goiter
C	Conjunctivitis	H	Heart
CT	Trachoma	K	Hernia
E	Eyes	L	Lameness
F	Face	N	Neck
Ft	Feet	P	Physical and lungs

Pg	Pregnancy
Sc	Scalp (favus)
S	Senility
X	Suspected mental illness
Ⓧ	Definite signs of mental disease observed

Chalk marks used by Ellis Island doctors.

"To me, it was like the House of Babel. Because there were so many languages and so many people and everybody huddled together. And it was so full of fear."

Barbara Barondess, a Russian Jewish immigrant in 1921

Above: Registry Room in the main building of Ellis Island, ca. 1905. After the medical inspection, immigrants, grouped according to the numbers on their manifest tags, waited to present their papers to and be questioned by an inspector.

Top: U.S. Immigration Service inspector's cap.

The initial medical examination took perhaps two or three minutes and was meant only to detect those who should be held for more careful examination. Within the medical profession, Ellis Island was known as the best school for physical diagnosis in the world, and the doctors stationed there were very proud of their diagnostic skills. They estimated that on busy days a doctor had only six seconds to spot more than sixty possible ailments—from anemia to varicose veins—during the brief line inspection. The immigrants who came to Ellis Island, however, were remarkably healthy. As one doctor observed, most were sturdy young peasants accustomed to hard work outdoors.

Once they passed the medical examination, immigrants sat down on wooden benches in the center of the Registry Room, where they awaited their final interrogation. Stephen Graham described the inspection experience as "the nearest earthly likeness to the final 'Day of Judgment,' when we have to prove our fitness to enter heaven." The inspector, much like St. Peter, sat behind his tall desk with a large ledger opened before him. The book contained the ship's manifests, on which each immigrant's name appeared together with his or her age, birthplace, occupation, and other personal data. Ellis Island inspectors used the manifests as a basis for cross-examining each new arrival.

The manifests were a major organizing agent in the processing routine. Immigrants were grouped for inspection according to the numbers on their landing tags (worn prominently on their chests), each number corresponding to a manifest page that listed thirty names. In this way, inspectors could examine thirty immigrants, one at a time, without searching and turning pages.

The examination was further expedited by interpreters stationed near the inspectors' desks, ready to translate questions and answers. Collectively fluent in all major languages and any number of obscure dialects, they were rarely stumped. For a time, their ranks included Fiorello La Guardia, later mayor of New York City (1934–46). Certified to speak Italian, German, and Croatian, La Guardia served as an interpreter on Ellis Island from 1907 to 1910, while he attended law school at night.

Immigrants often had to wait hours for their interrogation, but once they stepped to the inspector's desk the questions came in rapid-fire succession: Name? Where were you born? Married or single? Where are you going? How much money do you have? Have you ever been in jail? What's your trade? Do you have a job?

Top: The last remaining Registry Room inspector's desk, ca. 1905.

Bottom: Answering the inspector's questions, ca. 1910. The first query was usually "What's your name?" Andrjuljawierjus, Grzyszczyszn, Koutsoghianopoulos, and Zemiszkicivicz are a few of the names encountered by Ellis Island inspectors. Scores of immigrants contend that in the inspection process their names were changed or simplified. The legendary name changes, however, have never been documented on paper. Ellis Island inspectors actually had no occasion to write out the immigrants' names. Their job was simply to verify information already written in the ships' manifests.

The question about having a job caused difficulties. The Alien Contract Labor Law of 1885, which had been sponsored by American trade unions, excluded all immigrants who came under contract for work. The law was supposed to protect the American workingman's wages from being undermined by cheap labor imported from abroad. Inspectors, however, often applied the law even to those who said they had been promised jobs by relatives or friends who had immigrated before them. To avoid exclusion, newcomers had to convince the inspectors that they were able to work and support themselves, but they could not mention that they had a job waiting for them.

"How much money do you have?" Immigrants had to show some money to prove they were not paupers. How much was enough was left to the inspector's discretion until 1909, when Ellis Island's commissioner of immigration, William Williams, ordered that all immigrants must have railroad tickets to their destinations and at least $25, at that time roughly the equivalent of an inspector's weekly salary.

Williams imposed his directive without advance warning and applied it immediately, even to those who had sailed to New York before the rule was made public. Protest was immediate. As headlines announced that hundreds were being denied admission at Ellis Island, editorials railed against Williams and his arbitrary order. "Had we known about the rule," said one immigrant, "we should have managed in some way or another to scrape together the required $25." Within a few months, public pressure forced Williams to withdraw his order. He had made his point, however, and for many years to come, inspectors on Ellis Island would ask prospective immigrants to show their $25.

The issue in question was simply whether an immigrant was "liable to become a public charge." This clause, which has been the cornerstone of federal immigration policy since 1882, refers to those newcomers who lack resources and appear likely to wind up on the public dole. Pressured by American social welfare agencies, Ellis Island officials tried to divine the economic prospects of each new arrival, sifting out the most vulnerable: single women, children traveling alone, the sick, and the disabled.

Over the years, to meet the requirements of new laws, Ellis Island's inspectors asked more questions, and doctors checked for more diseases and disabilities. After 1903, inspectors routinely queried newcomers, "Are you an anarchist?" After 1907, they had to verify the ages of children unaccompanied by parents; those under age 16 were not allowed to land. Doctors had to check for tuberculars and epileptics, and judge whether immigrants appeared able to earn a living. The greatest changes came after the Immigration Act of 1917, which itemized thirty-three categories warranting exclusion. The new law required a complete physical of every immigrant, not just those who had been pulled out of the line inspection. Also, all immigrants 16 years and older had to pass a literacy test in their native language. The added examinations demanded more time and reduced the inspection capacity to barely 2,000 immigrants a day.

"Twenty-five dollars? I didn't have it. I told him I had it but I didn't have it. I spent it already. I didn't have a red cent in my pocket when I landed on that boat. They didn't check. He just said something like, 'Have you got $25?' So I just said yes, and that's it. I had nothing. That's something I put over on them."

Charles T. Anderson, a Swedish immigrant in 1925

Top: Registry Room, ca. 1912. The large open volumes on the inspectors' desks are the ship's manifests.

Bottom: "Pay as you enter, Christopher," demand President Taft and Commissioner of Immigration Williams, July 1909. This cartoon lampoons Williams's order that all immigrants must have at least $25 to qualify for admission.

Opposite: Page from passenger manifest of R.M.S. Teutonic, 1897.

"The doctors and everybody that were supposed to interrogate us were dressed in uniforms. That had a terrible effect on me. We were scared of uniforms. It took us back to the Russian uniforms that we were running away from."

Katherine Beychok, a Russian Jewish immigrant in 1910

"He asked me a lot of silly questions. You know what I mean? About America, if I knew all about America. Well, I didn't know anything about America."

Florence Norris, an English immigrant in 1915

CUSTOMS LIST OF PASSENGERS.

District of the City of New York, Port of New York.

"The Passenger Act, Department Decision 217. Regulations, Bureau of Statistics.

I, John G. Cameron Master of the s.s. "Teutonic" do solemnly, sincerely and truly swear that the following List or Manifest subscribed by me, and now delivered by me to the Collector of Customs of the District of the City of New York, is a full and perfect list of all the passengers taken on board said vessel at Liverpool & Queenstown from which port or ports the said vessel has now arrived; and that on said list is truly designated the age, sex, calling or occupation, the port of embarkation, the number of pieces of baggage, of all the passengers, the date and cause of death of any such passengers who may have died on the voyage, and also a statement, so far as it can be ascertained, with reference to the intention of each immigrant passenger as to a protracted sojourn in this country, and also, in regard to Cabin passengers, the country of which they are citizens, and of passengers other than cabin passengers, their native country, their intended destination or location in the United States, and whether they are citizens of the United States or not, and the location of the compartment or space occupied by each, as required by the Passenger Act of 1882 and the Regulations of the Secretary of the Treasury. So help me God.

Sworn to before me this 15 day of April 1897.

Deputy Collector.

† To be used for all passengers.
†† To be used for cabin passengers only.
✱ To be used for passengers other than cabin passengers.

Master.

No.	NAME IN FULL.	Age. Years.	Age. Months.	Sex.	Calling or Occupation.	Country of which they are Citizens. Last Residence	Native Country.	Intended Destination or Location. State or Territory.	State of passengers other than Cabin, whether Citizens of the United States.	Transient, In Transit or intending protracted sojourn.	Location of Compartment or Space occupied forward, amidships or aft.	Number of pieces of Baggage.	Port of Embarkation.	Date and Cause of Death.
1	John McKenna	19		m	Labr	Corleagh	Ireland	New York	No	Permanent	No 2 Upper deck	1	Liverpool	
2	James Connell	25		"	"	Lpool	"	"	"	"	"	1	"	
3	Rose Leddy	20		F	Servant	Dromconda	"	"	"	"	No 5	1	"	10 - 12
4	Kate "	19		"	"	Gartin	"	"	"	"	"	1	"	
5	Patrick Donohue	22		m	Servt Farmer	Killeshandra	"	"	"	"	No 2	1	"	
6	Bessie Wilson	19		F	Servt	Ballyardle	"	Pittsburgh	"	"	No 4 Main	1	"	
7	Joseph Shanahan	16		m	Labr	Limerick	"	New York	"	"		5	"	
8	Samuel Rooney	51		"	"									
9	Jane	48		F	Wife									
10	Ellen	15		"	Spinster									
1	Thomas	12		m	Labr									
2	Dinah	11		F	Child									
3	Michael Whalen	52		m	Miner	Cleator Moor	"	Butte City Mon		"	No 2 Upper	1	"	
4	Sarah Jane Rankin	19		F	Milliner	Cookstown	"	New York		"	No 5	1	"	
5	George Todd	26		m	Cotton Bleacher	Leeds	U. S. A.	Kearney N.J.	Yes	"	No 2	2	"	1 - 0
6	Mary Scott	53		F	Seamstress	Liverpool	England	Wassaic N.Y.	No	"	No 5	2	"	2 - 2
7	Geo. R. Green	40		m	Farmer	Gosbeilin	"	Ithaca		"	No 4 Main	3	"	
8	Mary "	38		F	Wife	"		"						
9	Thomas "	17		m	Labr	"		"						
20	James Shannon	21		"	"	Glassdrummond	Ireland	New York		"	No 2 Upper	1	"	
1	Ellen Maguire	16		F	Servt	Swanlinbar	"	Trenton		"	No 5	1	"	
2	Bridget Rooney	18		"	"	"		Newark				1		
3	Mary Maguire	19		"	"	"		Trenton N.J.				1		
4	Sarah McGann	44		"	Wife	Rathfriland		New York				2		
5	John "	21		m	Farmer	"		"			No 2	1		
6	Michael McDonough	59		"	Ironworker	Bilston		Edwardsville Pa			No 4 Main	3		
7	Winifred "	50		F	Wife	"		"				1		13 - 14 - 27

Class No. 2   Serial Number 2638   Finnish (Gothic)

Sanoi siis Herra Salomolle: että se on tapahtunut sinulta, ja et sinä pitänyt minun liittoani ja minun säätyjäni, kuin minä sinulle säätin; niin minä totisesti reväisen valtakunnan sinulta, ja annan sen sinun palvelialles.

Wherefore the Lord said unto Solomon, Forasmuch as this is done to thee, and thou hast not kept my covenant and my statutes, which I have commanded thee, I will surely rend the kingdom from thee and will give it to thy servant.

(I. Kings 11:11)

Class No. 5   Serial Number 1649   Syriac

[Syriac text]

I will meditate in thy precepts, and have respect unto thy ways.

I will delight myself in thy statutes: I will not forget thy word.

Deal bountifully with thy servant, that I may live, and keep thy word.

Open thou mine eyes, that I may behold wondrous things out of thy law.

I am a stranger in the earth: hide not thy commandments from me.

(Ps. 119:15-19)

Class No. 5   Serial Number 1805   Arabic

[Arabic text]

While he was yet speaking, there came also another, and said, Thy sons and thy daughters were eating and drinking wine in their eldest brother's house. And, behold, there came a great wind from the wilderness, and smote the four corners of the house, and it fell upon the young men, and they are dead; and I only am escaped alone to tell thee.

(Job 1:18,19)

Class No. 1   Serial Number 2638   Dutch

Die waarheid voortbrengt, maakt gerechtigheid bekend, maar een getuige der valschheden bedrog.

Daar is een die woorden als steken van een zwaard onbedachtelijk uitspreekt; maar de tong der wijzen is medicijn.

He that speaketh truth sheweth forth righteousness: but a false witness deceit.

There is that speaketh like the piercings of a sword: but the tongue of the wise is health.

(Prov. 12:17,18)

Class No. 3   Serial Number 5649   Croatian

A jedan dan kad sinovi njegovi i kćeri njegove jedjahu i pijahu vino u kući brata svojega najstarijega.

Dodje glasnik Jobu i reče: volovi orahu i magarice pasijahu pokraj njih.

And there was a day when his sons and daughters were eating and drinking wine in their eldest brother's house.

And there came a messenger unto Job and said, The oxen were ploughing and the asses feeding beside them.

(Job 1:13,14)

Class No. 5   Serial Number 4654   Yiddish

[Yiddish text]

This our bread we took hot for our provision out of our houses on the day we came forth to go unto you; but now, behold, it is dry, and it is mouldy.

(Josh. 9:12)

Class No. 4   Serial Number 3638   Italian

Per la bocca de' piccoli fanciulli, e di quelli che poppano, tu hai fondata la tua gloria, per cagione de' tuoi nemici, per far restare il nemico e il vendicatore.

Out of the mouths of babes and sucklings hast thou ordained strength because of thine enemies, that thou mightest still the enemy and the avenger.

(Ps. 8:2)

Class No. 3   Serial Number 5688   Polish

Bądźcie posłuszni przewodnikom swoim, i ulegajcie im; albowiem oni czuwają nad duszami waszemi, jako mający zdać sprawę, aby to z radością czynili, a nie wzdychając; bo dla was to niepożyteczne.

Obey them that have the rule over you, and submit yourselves: for they watch for your souls, as they that must give account, that they may do it with joy, and not with grief: for that is unprofitable for you.

(Hebrews 13:17)

Class No. 3   Serial Number 2725   Russian

Храни меня, какъ зѣницу ока; тѣнью крылъ Твоихъ укрой меня. Отъ нечестивыхъ, которые нападаютъ на меня, отъ смертельныхъ враговъ, которые окружаютъ меня.

Они заградили сердце свое; устами своими говорятъ гордо.

Keep me as the apple of the eye; hide me under the shadow of thy wings.

From the wicked that oppress me, from my deadly enemies, who compass me about.

They are inclosed in their own fat: with their mouth they speak proudly.

(Ps. 17:8,9,10)

Class No. 5   Serial Number 1638   Armenian (Modern)

[Armenian text]

Let my sentence come forth from thy presence; let thine eyes behold the things that are equal.

Thou hast proved mine heart; thou hast visited me in the night; thou hast tried me, and shall find nothing: I am purposed that my mouth shall not transgress.

(Ps. 17:2,3)

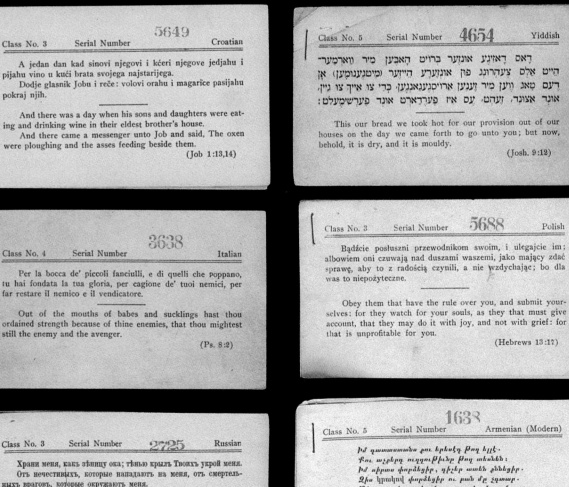
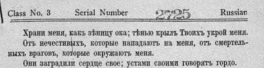

"Every so often somebody called out names of immigrants who were called in to be questioned. I was very nervous because it was so noisy. I couldn't hear the names and I was afraid that I would miss my name and remain there forever."

William Chase, a Russian immigrant in 1914

"I remember my grandfather always telling me how he knew he could be rich in America because he saw riches in the architecture of Ellis Island. He felt that if they let the poor in such a gorgeous hall then life in this country was just."

Rosanne Welch, granddaughter of Giuseppe Italiano, an Italian immigrant in 1904

Opposite: Literacy test cards, 1919. Anti-immigration forces had been trying to impose a literacy test since the 1880s as a means of restricting immigration. They finally succeeded with the Immigration Act of 1917, passed over President Woodrow Wilson's veto. This law required all immigrants 16 years and older to read a forty-word passage in their native language.

Above: Registry Room, ca. 1912. In this view, wooden benches have replaced the iron-pipe railings that once guided the inspection lines. Also, the open staircase has been removed from the center of the room to create more floor space. A new flight of stairs was installed at the east end of the hall.

For most immigrants, about 80%, the Ellis Island odyssey through medical and legal examinations lasted three to five hours. Once the inspector had waved them forward and beckoned the next in line, they had permission to land. No one congratulated them. They were simply hurried down a flight of stairs that led to the New York ferry pier or to the railroad ticket office.

Relatives and friends were often waiting for them near an exit that came to be called the "Kissing Post" because of all the joyful reunions that took place there. In 1910, an Ellis Island matron, Maud Mosher, described the scene: "The Italian kisses his little children, but scarcely speaks to his wife.... The Hungarian and Slavish [sic] people put their arms around one another and weep. The Jew of all countries kisses his wife and children as though he had all the kisses in the world and intended to use them all up quick."

As the world's largest and busiest landing depot, Ellis Island offered an array of travel-related services. Before leaving the island, immigrants could buy railroad tickets to their final destinations, get something to eat, send telegrams to loved ones, and exchange their foreign currency for U.S. dollars. All of these options were offered by private concessions that operated under contract to the U.S. Immigration Service. Unfortunately, in the early years the government failed to closely regulate the concessions, an oversight that gave dishonest owners and employees ample opportunity to fleece unsuspecting newcomers.

One notorious transgressor was the transportation pool, made up

Above: The railroad ticket office, ca. 1910. Twelve major lines shared the business on Ellis Island. They included the Erie, Delaware, Lackawanna and Western, New York Central, Southern Pacific, and Baltimore and Ohio. Only one-third of the immigrants who arrived at Ellis Island planned to stay in the New York area. The great majority were bound for other regions, mostly in the Northeast or Midwest. Fewer numbers made the transcontinental trip to the western states or to the South, where job opportunities for immigrants were scarce.

Left: Immigrant's telegram sent from Ellis Island to relatives in New Jersey. Freide Goldfusz arrived in 1912 to join her husband, Morris, who had come in 1910. Women traveling alone could not leave the island until immigration officers were sure they would be in safe hands.

Opposite: Woman and young girl waiting to board a ferry to the Baltimore and Ohio Railroad. The tags let conductors know what connections travelers had to make to complete their journey.

"I saw this man coming forward and he was beautiful. I didn't know he was my father. Later on I realized why he looked so familiar to me. He looked exactly like I did. But that's when I met him for the first time. And I fell in love with him and he with me."

Katherine Beychok, a Russian Jewish immigrant in 1910

"When we were getting off of Ellis Island, we had all sorts of tags on us. Now that I think of it, we must have looked like marked-down merchandise in Gimbel's basement store or something."

Anna Vida, a Hungarian immigrant in 1921

"Instructions received as to the desired disposition of new arrivals are complied with so far as practicable.... An alien destined to 'Farroceve,' was sent to the correct address, namely Far Rockaway, and one who showed an address 'mai Denlen Street' found his friends on Maiden Lane. 'Docsven' was found to mean Dutchess Avenue. 'Sciozzali' proved to be Schutts Alley and 'Psywij,' Pacific Street."

Comedies and Tragedies at Ellis Island, ca. 1913

of twelve major railroads. Ticket agents often conspired to split the profitable immigrant trade equally among the various lines, sometimes booking passengers on roundabout routes just to give less traveled lines their share of the business. Because of this common practice, many immigrants found themselves traveling to Chicago via Norfolk, Virginia.

The money exchange was another troubled enterprise. Not only did it pay slightly less than the market rate for foreign currency, but its employees often shortchanged customers, refused to give receipts, and, in at least one instance, paid out shiny pennies instead of dollars. Food-stand clerks would threaten immigrants with deportation if they refused to buy a box lunch. One clerk was dismissed for charging $5 for a dollar bag of food. The baggage concession also had problems. It was often accused of extortion, gross overcharging, mismanagement, and occasionally theft.

Most of these abuses were cleaned up when Theodore Roosevelt became president. In 1902, T.R. appointed a new commissioner of immigration, William Williams, whose reforms on the island won immediate praise. New York's *Evening Post* chimed: "A new era begins today at Ellis Island. Cigars no longer net 700 percent profit as in the palmy days before William Williams became commissioner, and milk at two cents a glass takes the place of lacterized water at five cents. The feeding, money exchange, and baggage transfer privileges pass out of the control of a political faction and the Augean stables of the Immigration Bureau are being laboriously swept clean."

The new commissioner's reforms, however, applied not only to the treatment of immigrants but also to the execution of the law. Williams charged that lax application of the law had allowed into the United States many immigrants who were physically incapable of earning a living. Under Williams, the inspection of arrivals was carried out much more rigorously, with the result that many more immigrants were excluded (denied permission to land) and deported (sent back to their port of embarkation). His record for exclusions ranged between 1% and 3.5% of monthly arrivals. "During other administrations," he boasted, "the range was very much lower."

Top: Sign used on Ellis Island, ca. 1901.

Bottom: Immigrants lining up to exchange their money for U.S. dollars. Once they had some American money, immigrants could stop at the food stand, prominently marked in five languages, "Provisions cheaper here than on the railroad." They could purchase a box lunch containing sandwiches, fruit, and pie for 50 cents to a dollar. In the Baggage Room they could arrange to have trunks shipped to their new homes; at the telegraph office they could send messages to stateside friends and relatives.

Opposite: Foreign money typical of Ellis Island's busy era, 1892 to 1924. The money exchange could deal in nearly any currency. The rate of exchange, however, was generally less than that of commercial banks.

"So, we all went down and got on the ferryboat. And the ferryboat ran to the Battery. And then, we just walked off, just like letting the birds out of the cage."

Donald Roberts, a Welsh immigrant in 1925

Top: People waiting outside the Ellis Island Ferry Station at the Battery in lower Manhattan.

Bottom: Immigrants with railroad tags pinned to their clothing, waiting to depart Ellis Island, 1926.

Opposite: Boarding a ferry to depart Ellis Island. Immigrants bound for destinations across the country took ferries to railroad terminals in Jersey City or Hoboken, while those going to New York City took the ferry to the Battery on the southern tip of Manhattan. There they would usually find a crowd of relatives, friends, baggage handlers, and boarding house runners.

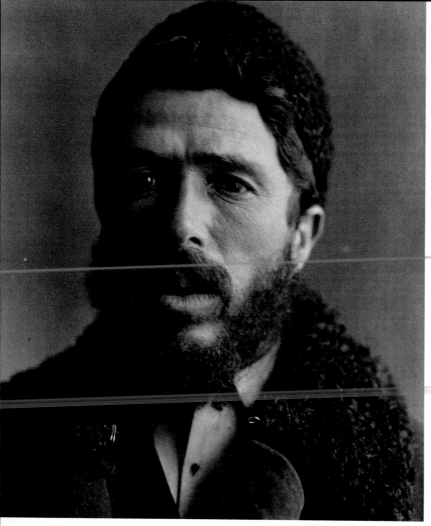

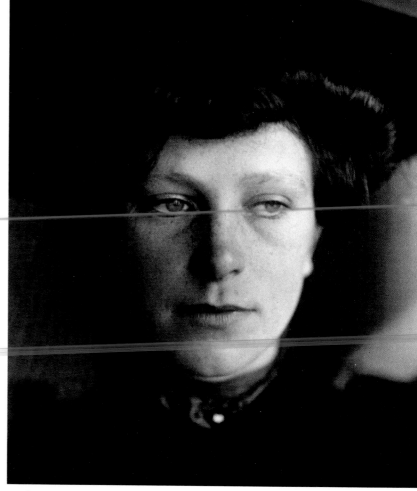

Ellis Island immigrants (destinations noted), ca. 1907:
Russian cattle dealer; Fargo, North Dakota
Hungarian wife; Chicago, Illinois

Irish servant; New York City

Austrian laborer; deported

Shepherd; Wyoming

Italian wife; New York City

Russian servant; Salem, Massachusetts

Swedish farmer; South Dakota

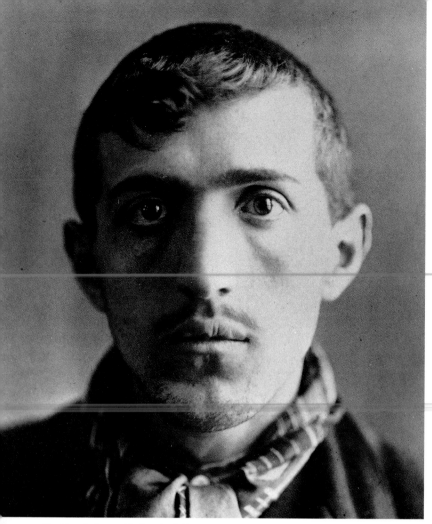

Italian laborer; St Louis, Missouri

Romanian domestic; destination unknown

Hungarian servant; Trenton, New Jersey

Russian student; New York City

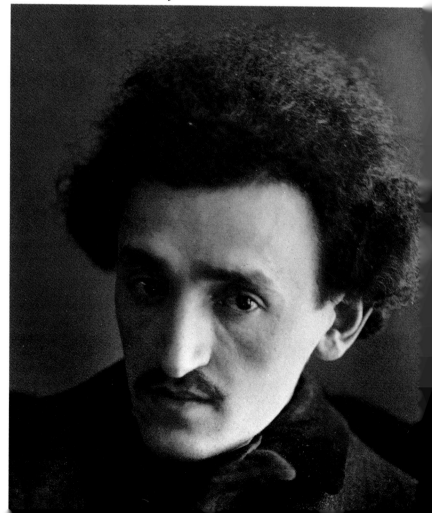

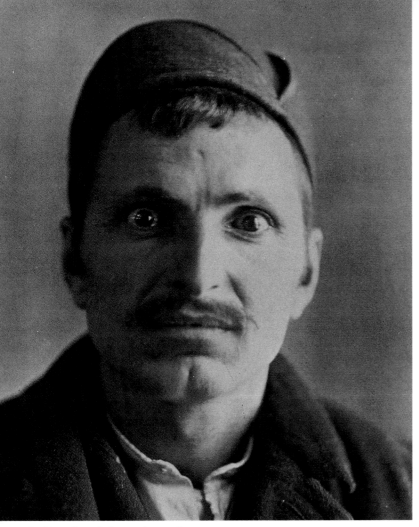

Serbian farm laborer; deported

Russian widow; Lancaster, Pennsylvania

Italian domestic; Lowell, Massachusetts

Hungarian farm laborer; Cincinnati, Ohio

Form 1508.

United States Immigration Service,
ELLIS ISLAND, NEW YORK HARBOR.

DETENTION CARD.

Name, Curren Vincenzo Sex, M M

Vessel, Ems

Date, Oct 12, 1899. M.

CAUSE OF DETENTION:

No ticket to Chicago

JAN. FEB. MARCH. APRIL. MAY. JUNE. JULY. AUG. SEPT. OCT. NOV. DEC.

Registry Clerk.

Form 1508.

United States Immigration Service,
ELLIS ISLAND, NEW YORK HARBOR.

DETENTION CARD.

Name, Abraham Rahal Sex, M 19

Vessel, La Acquitaine

Date, DEC 18 1899, 180, M.

CAUSE OF DETENTION:

to worcester mass

HOLD withdrawn

FOR MEDICAL EXAMINATION

JAN. FEB. MARCH. APRIL. MAY. JUNE. JULY. AUG. SEPT. OCT. NOV. DEC.

Registry Clerk.

Form 1508.

United States Immigration Service,
ELLIS ISLAND, NEW YORK HARBOR.

France

DETENTION CARD.

Name, Anna Dupont Sex,

Vessel, La Acquitaine

Date, DEC 18 1899, 189, M.

CAUSE OF DETENTION:

HOLD withdrawn

FOR MEDICAL EXAMINATION

EXAMINED:- DEFECT RECORDED.

Swollen cheek

JAN. FEB. MARCH. APRIL. MAY. JUNE. JULY. AUG. SEPT. OCT. NOV. DEC.

Registry Clerk.

Form 1508.

United States Immigration Service,
ELLIS ISLAND, NEW YORK HARBOR.

DETENTION CARD.

Name, Arbanas Michele 30 yrs Sex, M

Vessel, La Touraine

Date, Oct 29, 1899, M.

CAUSE OF DETENTION:

only $10

No ticket to Watsonville Cal

J. Raczkiewicz

JAN. FEB. MARCH. APRIL. MAY. JUNE. JULY. AUG. SEPT. OCT. NOV. DEC.

Registry Clerk.

Form 1508.

United States Immigration Service,
ELLIS ISLAND, NEW YORK HARBOR.

DETENTION CARD.

Name, Maffei Pietro Sex, 30

Vessel, La Champagne

Date, 11-2, 1899, M.

CAUSE OF DETENTION:

S.I. L.P.C.

JAN. FEB. MARCH. APRIL. MAY. JUNE. JULY. AUG. SEPT. OCT. NOV. DEC.

Registry Clerk.

Form 1508.

United States Immigration Service,
ELLIS ISLAND, NEW YORK HARBOR.

Hungary

DETENTION CARD.

Name, Pal Janos Sex, M 25

Vessel, Statendam

Date, Nov 15, 1899, M.

CAUSE OF DETENTION:

JAN. FEB. MARCH. APRIL. MAY. JUNE. JULY. AUG. SEPT. OCT. NOV. DEC.

Registry Clerk.

Immigrants who failed their initial inspection received cards recording reasons for detention. Of the cards above, all issued in 1899, two have medical stamps but most of the others mention a lack of funds or railroad tickets. The phrase S.I.-L.P.C. stands for "Special Inquiry–Likely to Become a Public Charge." Immigrants marked in this way had to convince a Board of Special Inquiry that they were able to earn a living and stay off the public dole. During Ellis Island's busy years, most of the excluded were L.P.C.s; many others were denied entry because they suffered from a contagious disease or were suspected of being contract laborers.

Held for Investigation

"They wanted to have their cards explained to them. This had been done ... many times before, but most of the newcomers seemed too ignorant and frightened to grasp the situation. Some had bad addresses, others had not money enough to take them to their final destination; still others had telegraphed to their American friends without receiving an answer; and all were anxious about their fate, stupefied, terror-stricken."

Abraham Cahan, "Two Love Stories," 1900

Ellis Island's tragic reputation as an "Isle of Tears" or a "Hell's Island" is based not so much on the experiences of the millions who were quickly inspected, registered, and sent on their way, but rather on the thousands of stories of aliens who were detained for further investigation. Approximately 20% of the those who came to the island were held up for one reason or another. Immigrants who had no money, or were suspected of being contract laborers, or seemed to fit the "likely to become a public charge" category were held pending a hearing before a Board of Special Inquiry.

A woman traveling alone was usually detained until immigration officials were sure she would be in trustworthy hands after she left the island. Women and children were detained until their husbands and fathers claimed them, or until they had a telegram vouching for their safety or railroad tickets that would take them to their loved ones, whether that meant a short hop beyond New York or traveling all the way to California.

One of the most common reasons for detainment was illness. Immigrants who appeared to be suffering from incurable contagious diseases like trachoma or favus, or seemed mentally incompetent, or had any physical defect that would make it difficult for them to earn a living would be detained for medical observation and sometimes deported.

Many of these immigrants had to be admitted to the Ellis Island hospital for observation and treatment. The 125-bed hospital, which opened in March 1902, sat on a separate island made of landfill and connected to the main island by a walkway. Even before the hospital opened, officials knew it would be too small to take care of the growing number of arrivals. It was soon overwhelmed with patients, many of whom had to be transferred to mainland hospitals. Within nine years, the Ellis Island hospital had to be expanded twice, eventually accommodating 275 beds.

The new additions, however, did not provide adequate space for the isolation and treatment of highly infectious diseases; immigrants so afflicted still had to be ferried to hospitals in New York City. Deaths caused by exposure to the cold were common. One doctor estimated that about 30% of the children suffering from measles died from exposure suffered on the ferry ride. A contagious disease hospital was completed in 1909, but the lack of equipment and lighting delayed its opening until 1911.

The new hospital, which occupied an entire third island made of landfill, embodied the latest theories about the treatment of

Mother and child await deportation in an Ellis Island dormitory, 1903. About 2% of those who came to Ellis Island were excluded and sent back to their ports of origin. Their return trip was provided free of charge by the steamship company that brought them. The immigrants could not recoup the cost of their original passage, a loss that meant financial hardship for many.

"One case haunted me for years. A young girl in her teens…was sent to the hospital for observation. I could imagine the effect on this girl, who had always been carefully sheltered and had never been permitted to be in the company of a man alone, when a doctor suddenly rapped her on the knees, looked into her eyes, turned her on her back and tickled her spine to ascertain her reflexes. The child rebelled—and how!"

Fiorello H. La Guardia, an Ellis Island interpreter, 1907–10

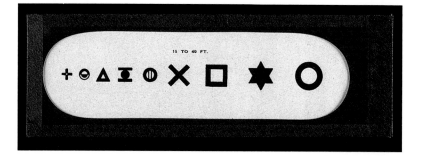

In 1914, two women doctors were appointed to the medical staff. Immigrant women were often frightened of the clinical routine on Ellis Island, especially of being examined by male doctors. Matrons were always present during these examinations, but the addition of female doctors alleviated a great deal of anxiety.

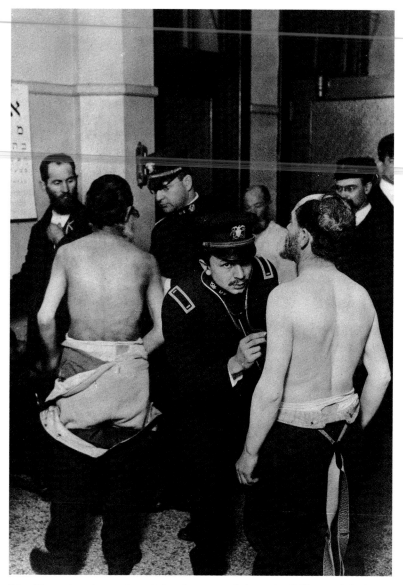

Top: To test immigrants' eyesight, doctors used charts in different alphabets. This eye chart of shapes was designed for illiterates.

Bottom: Doctors examining immigrants who had failed the line inspection. The man standing on the left has his lapel clearly chalk-marked "K," indicating a suspected hernia. Note the eye chart in the background with its Hebrew characters.

"**The nurses were there. 'Ladies in White' we used to call them. They were very nice. I mean, they talked to the children. They stroked their hair. And they touched their cheeks and held our hands. When they gave us our milk, sometimes, maybe if there was a pretty child, some nurses would kiss the child on the cheek. They were really very nice.**"

Elizabeth Martin, a Hungarian immigrant in 1920

infectious diseases. The distance between the islands as well as the spaces dividing the wards were calculated to control contagion. Most of the buildings were intended for the care of measles patients, but there were also separate isolation pavilions for those diagnosed with scarlet fever, diphtheria, and various combinations of infections.

The contagious disease hospital served mostly children afflicted by a gamut of typical childhood ailments, usually contracted during the ocean journey. In the close quarters of steerage, children sometimes contracted more than one infection. In addition, many children who arrived healthy at Ellis Island became ill during detention. Elizabeth Martin, who arrived from Hungary in 1920, recalled that all the children in her family caught measles while on Ellis Island. "My oldest brother, Emory, went down first and then it came down the line. Because all the kids were playing together in this one big place, so naturally if one had it the others would get it."

Going to a hospital placed a terrible strain on the entire family. While a child, a mother, or a father was recuperating, the rest of the family had to wait in the Ellis Island detention rooms. They received little information about their loved ones and were rarely allowed visits. For the hospitalized child, however, the experience seems to have been somewhat less harrowing. Asked to describe their hospital experience, people who immigrated through Ellis Island often mentioned the kind treatment they received as children. Bessie Akawie, who was 10 years old when she arrived from the Ukraine in 1921, remembered a favorite nurse: "Miss Hannah, she was so good. She would always bring me a present from New York City and she taught me English. By the time I got to New York, I knew how to speak English." Bessie spent eight months on the island.

Josephine Calloway, who arrived from Italy in 1922 at age 15, thought she would be deported because the doctors could not cure her illness. "But they found a cure for it," she recalled triumphantly. "So, they threw me a party. All the doctors got together and threw a party in Ward 18. That's the ward I was in."

John Titone, who traveled from Sicily as a nine-year-old in 1920, talked about his hospital stay as a diverting adventure: "Some people hate Ellis Island. I couldn't hate it. Even though they kept me there, I wasn't mistreated. We could play outside. We'd play ball, play tennis, and the food was good. The library was good. Once a week, you'd go to the movies. Who could go to the movies once a week in Sicily, you know?"

But many children as well as adults died on the island, and their

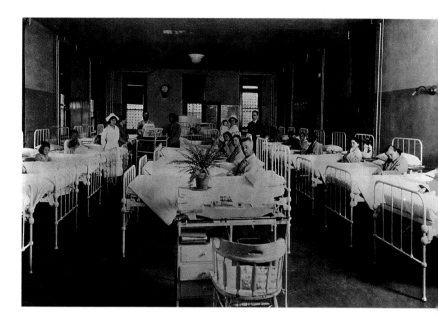

Top: Women's ward in the contagious disease hospital, ca. 1922. Ellis Island's medical complex of more than 15 buildings included a psychiatric ward, operating rooms, an X-ray plant, and a morgue.

Bottom: Walther Hayter sent this postcard to his sisters and brother, who were held in the Ellis Island contagious disease ward when they arrived from England in 1911. Once they recovered from their bout with smallpox, they joined their brother in Michigan.

"They found my grandmother had a black nail. She raised us, all the years, with that hand and with that nail. There was nothing wrong with it. And they held her back. They sent her back. They were stupid, to let an old woman, when she has her whole family here, to let her go home by herself. So we never saw her again. That was heart-breaking. I'm still crying over it."

Evelyn Golbe, a Russian Jewish immigrant in 1914

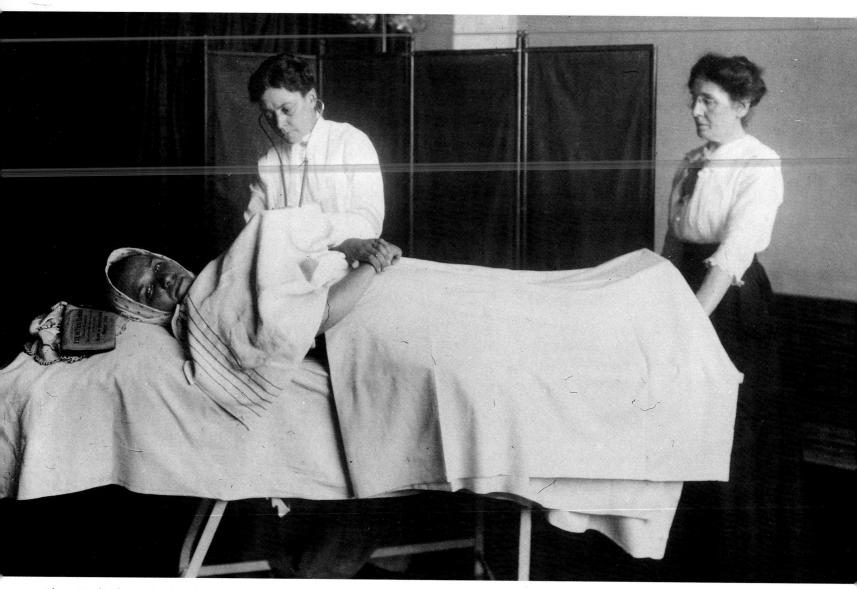

Above: Medical examination of a woman immigrant. The Ellis Island hospital, staffed with forty doctors, had to deal with every kind of medical disorder, from slight injuries to rare tropical diseases.

Opposite top: Undertaker's bill for Richard Moberg, a three-year-old from Sweden, who died of pneumonia on Ellis Island in 1920. Richard was laid to rest in Worth, Illinois. From 1900 to 1954, over 3,500 persons, including 1,400 children, died on the island.

Opposite bottom: Birth certificate for Sam Katz, one of over 355 babies born on Ellis Island. Perla Katz, from Poland, gave birth hours after arrival on Ellis Island. "A true son of America," his sister wrote, "Sam died on a German battlefield in World War II."

stories, despite the passage of time, evoke great poignancy. Martha Strahm, who arrived from Switzerland in 1920, told the following story about her two-year-old son: "Walter took sick and was admitted to the hospital. He was there six weeks and died on February 9, 1921. We were confined on Ellis Island those six weeks. Our days were very long days and only one of us could go visit our sick boy for five minutes once a week.... Our boy died at ten minutes after 11:00 p.m.... After all these years the picture in my mind is so clear when they took him down the hall wrapped in a sheet."

Immigration officials released Mrs. Strahm from the island without telling her what would happen to her son's body. In the ensuing years she thought constantly of Walter, never quite believing that her baby had died. Over half a century later, when the Ellis Island Immigration Museum was being developed, a daughter asked its researchers for some official confirmation of her brother's death, to set her mother's mind at ease. A researcher was able to find Walter's death certificate, which was sent to Mrs. Strahm, then over 90 years old.

Records dating from 1900 to 1954 show that over 3,500 persons, including more than 1,400 children, died on Ellis Island. Fortunately, the vast majority of the patients recovered and could be reunited with their families after an average hospital stay of one to two weeks. There were even occasions of great joy: over 355 new American citizens were born to immigrant parents in the Ellis Island hospital.

Over the years, U.S. Public Health Service doctors detained an increasing number of immigrants suspected of being mentally impaired. This attention to mental competence came at a time when state asylums and charity houses charged that their resources were being overwhelmed by immigrants suffering from various kinds of mental impairment. Public pressure was brought to bear on immigration officials to weed out suspected mental cases, lest they become burdens on society.

In the Ellis Island inspection line, doctors kept an eye out for immigrants whose behavior or attitude seemed to indicate mental instability. E.H. Mullan, an Ellis Island doctor, outlined some of the telltale symptoms: "facetiousness," "nail biting," "smiling," and other "eccentricities." Doctors also had to be sensitive to ethnic differences. "If an Englishman reacts to questions in the manner of an Irishman, his lack of mental balance would be suspected. The

"They asked us questions. 'How much is two and one? How much is two and two?' But the next young girl, also from our city, went and they asked her, 'How do you wash stairs, from the top or from the bottom?' She says, 'I don't go to America to wash stairs.'"

Pauline Notkoff, a Polish Jewish immigrant in 1917

"When my mother got up there he said, 'How much is five and five?' My mother looked at me. And she didn't know whether he was insulting her or what, a man asking a grown woman how much is five and five?"

Helen Nitti, an Italian immigrant in 1920

"My brother Saul had come down with diphtheria. He was quite sick and had lost a considerable amount of weight. And from there on, he was not the same child. At Ellis Island, when he was asked questions, he'd act as if he didn't know the answer. He was frightened by it. And for whatever reason they had, they said that he would have to go back."

Alex Eckstein, a Hungarian Jewish immigrant in 1926

converse is also true. If the Italian responded to questions as the Russian Finn responds, the former would in all probability be suffering with a depressive psychosis."

About nine out of every one hundred immigrants were suspected of being mentally impaired. They were quickly chalked with an X, removed from the line, and taken to another room for an examination. There doctors conducted a preliminary interview, asking immigrants about themselves, their families, where they came from, and other similar questions. Perhaps they would ask an immigrant to solve a simple arithmetic problem or count backward from 20 to 1, or complete a puzzle. Out of the nine immigrants held for this "weeding out" session, perhaps one or two would be detained for more testing.

For this next step, doctors used a variety of tests, some standardized as well as some that were developed on Ellis Island. One doctor who took a special interest in gauging intelligence was Howard A. Knox, who practiced medicine on Ellis Island from 1910 to 1916. He developed a number of puzzle and mimicry tests that were especially useful because they did not have to be explained through an interpreter; nor did an immigrant have to know how to read or write in order to solve them. Dr. Knox's memory test, for example, simply required the immigrant to tap a series of cubes in the exact order shown by the doctor. As the test progressed, the pattern of touches became more complex.

How reliable were these examinations? Dr. Knox's articles for medical journals indicate that Ellis Island doctors tried to be fair to the immigrants, giving them every benefit of the doubt. Immigrants had to fail the mental examination three times before they could be certified as mentally impaired, which mandated exclusion.

Other immigration officers, however, expressed some skepticism about the mental testing. Assessing normal intelligence among the immigrant population was extremely difficult because of the many variables that had to be considered. The immigrants' diverse backgrounds, languages, cultures, and levels of education and other factors affected their behavior in different ways. One doctor recalled that the process of identifying mental incompetence in the line inspection was "always haphazard," and that often fully competent people were held for examination. When this happened, the immigrant was nearly always piqued by the mistake, especially when it meant an unnecessary overnight stay on the island.

Above: Visual comparison test devised by Dr. Howard A. Knox to test illiterates over the age of 12. Immigrants had three chances to find the four sad faces within twenty seconds. Doctors timed their attempts with stopwatches. Dr. Knox explained that "if after three trials the subject cannot be made to understand what is wanted by the examiner or a competent interpreter, then the fact is evidence that he {the subject} is defective."

Opposite: Immigrants, clearly marked with Xs indicating suspected mental impairment, wait to be examined.

"**The whole experience was very frightening. They brought me up to a room. They put a pegboard before me with little sticks of different shapes and little holes. I had to put them in place, and I did it perfectly. They said, 'Oh, we must have made a mistake. This little girl, naturally she doesn't know English, but she's very bright, intelligent.' So they took the cross [chalk mark] off me so we were cleared.**"

Victoria Sarfatti Fernández, a Macedonian immigrant in 1916

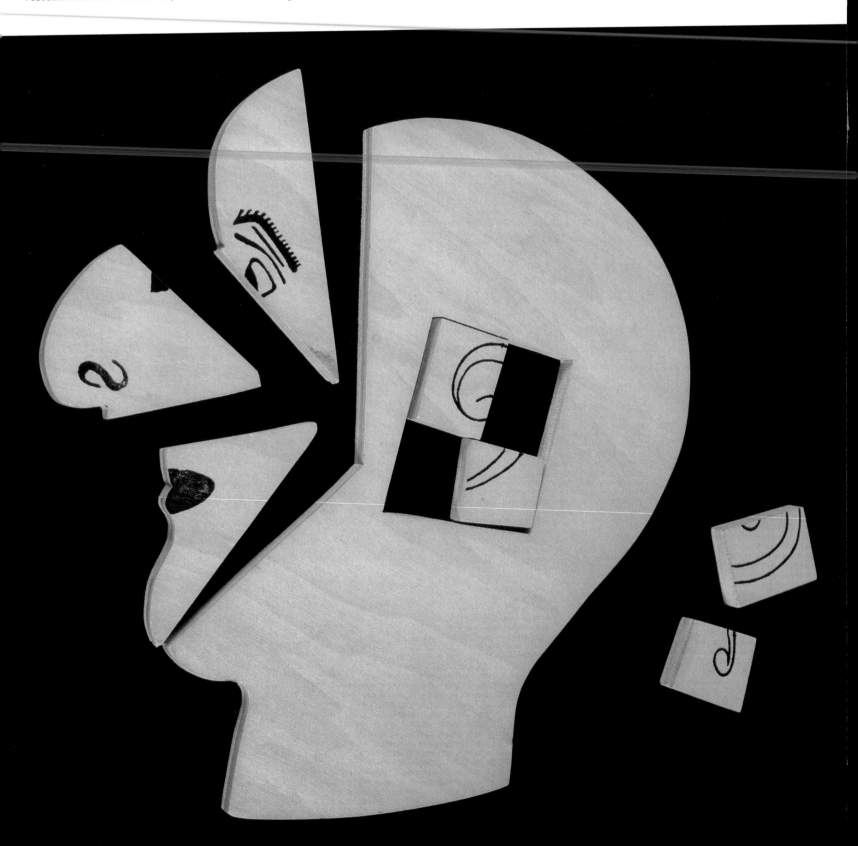

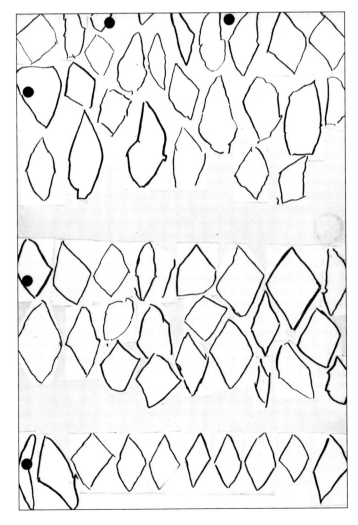

Top: Steamship puzzle used to test immigrants at Ellis Island by Dr. Howard A. Knox, ca. 1916.

Bottom right: Dr. Knox (center), with the help of interpreter Isaac Prussin, testing a suspected mental case, ca. 1916.

Bottom left: Diamonds drawn by illiterate Slavic and Italian men between the ages of 15 and 30. The top group was drawn by immigrants who had never held a pencil before; the middle diamonds by those who had never gone to school; the bottom row by those with less than a year of schooling.

Opposite: Feature profile puzzle, considered by Ellis Island doctors to be their most difficult test. Adults had ten minutes to assemble the pieces.

Board of Special Inquiry

About half of those held for investigation had to appear before a Board of Special Inquiry. Three boards were usually in session all day, every day, to hear what seemed to be an unending stream of tales of woe and hard luck. Each board decided fifty to one hundred cases every day. During the peak season of immigration—spring, summer, and early fall—a fourth board was added. Each hearing was conducted by three board members in the presence of an interpreter and a stenographer.

The boards were strictly administrative bodies, not legal tribunals, whose sole purpose was to decide whether an alien should be admitted to the United States. The Supreme Court had ruled as early as 1893 that aliens had no right to land and therefore no right to a legal hearing to decide their eligibility to land. The board's procedures, therefore, were uninhibited by due process. Immigrants whose cases were referred to the board were not allowed to confer with relatives, friends, or lawyers, lest they try to concoct a plausible story. Nor could new arrivals be represented by a lawyer at their hearing, although they could have relatives and friends appear and testify on their behalf. If the board rendered an unfavorable decision, the immigrant had the option of appealing the case, with the help of counsel, directly to Washington, D.C.

An appeal could take weeks or months, and in the meantime the immigrant had to wait on Ellis Island until a verdict was returned. These prolonged stays were by all accounts nerve-racking episodes. In 1922, British ambassador Sir Aukland Geddes toured the island and pinpointed the appeal system as the "very heart of the tragedy of Ellis Island.... For days some wretched creature is kept in suspense.... Days slip by, into weeks sometimes, before a decision is reached. When the doubt affects one member of a family, perhaps a child, the mental anguish must be excruciating."

The anguish of waiting, however, did not stop immigrants from pursuing every avenue of hope. It was almost impossible to reverse an unfavorable decision from Washington, but some immigrants tried by appealing to a federal court, whose verdicts were absolutely final. About 15 to 20% of the immigrants who had to appear before a Board of Special Inquiry were excluded, but nearly all who took their cases beyond the U.S. Immigration Service to the federal courts were turned down. Typical of these cases, the men, women, and children whose stories follow lost their appeals and were forced to return to their ports of origin.

On June 22, 1906, Slate Lewin and her seven-year-old son, Alter, underwent inspection on Ellis Island. The doctors diagnosed Alter as having severe curvature of the spine, which would affect his ability to earn a living. Slate's husband and daughter, who had immigrated years earlier, testified on her and Alter's behalf before a Board of Special Inquiry. The father and daughter asserted they would take care of the boy and he would not become "a public charge." The board, however, decided that the necessary medical care was beyond the family's means and therefore ordered the exclusion of the mother and son. To save his family from being separated, the father appealed the case to Washington, and then to a federal court. Both appeals were denied, and by July 17, Slate and Alter were under orders to return to their port of origin on the next available ship.

When Olga Samin, a seven-year-old girl from Syria, arrived at Ellis Island on June 19, 1906, the doctors discovered that she had the eye disease trachoma, which warranted deportation. Olga's father had immigrated in 1899, and her mother followed him in 1905. Olga had been left in the care of her grandmother, and her arrival in America would reunite the family. A Board of Special Inquiry, which heard Olga's case on June 25 and 28, ordered her excluded. It acknowledged, however, that the case was distressful since the father had been mistakenly advised that the child could be treated in the United States. The distraught parents' appeals to a federal court in Washington were of no avail. By July 17, the court had upheld the board's original decision, and Olga was ordered to return to Syria.

Mendel Feingold was held for examination before a Board of Special Inquiry on March 2, 1910. The board decided that Feingold was in violation of the Alien Contract Labor Law. Evidently, Mendel's brother, who had immigrated previously, had written to Mendel that his boss would give him a job, and sent him a steamship ticket to New York. During the hearing, the brothers were questioned separately. One said he had sent the prepaid ticket, the other said he had not. Their confusion did not help Mendel's case. He was ordered deported on the grounds that he had been promised a job and therefore was in violation of the contract labor law. For good measure, the Ellis Island board also deemed him "likely to become a public charge." Feingold's future was quickly determined. By March 11, his appeals to Washington and a federal court had been denied and his exclusion order upheld.

"'Ask them why they came,' the commissioner says rather abruptly. The answer is: 'We had to.' 'What was his business in Russia?' 'A tailor.' 'How much did he earn a week?' 'Ten to 12 rubles.' 'What did the son do?' 'He went to school.' 'Who supported him?' 'The father.' 'What do they expect to do in America?' 'Work.' 'Have they any relatives?' 'Yes, a son and brother.' 'What does he do?' 'He is a tailor.' 'How much does he earn?' 'Twelve dollars a week.' 'Has he a family?' 'Wife and four children.' 'Ask them whether they are willing to be separated; the father to go back and the son to remain here?' They look at each other; no emotion as yet visible. The question came too suddenly. Then something in the background of their feelings moves, and the father, used to self-denial through his life, says quietly, without pathos and yet tragically, 'Of course.' And the son says, after casting his eyes to the ground, ashamed to look his father in the face, 'Of course.'"

Edward Steiner, *On the Trail of the Immigrant*, 1906

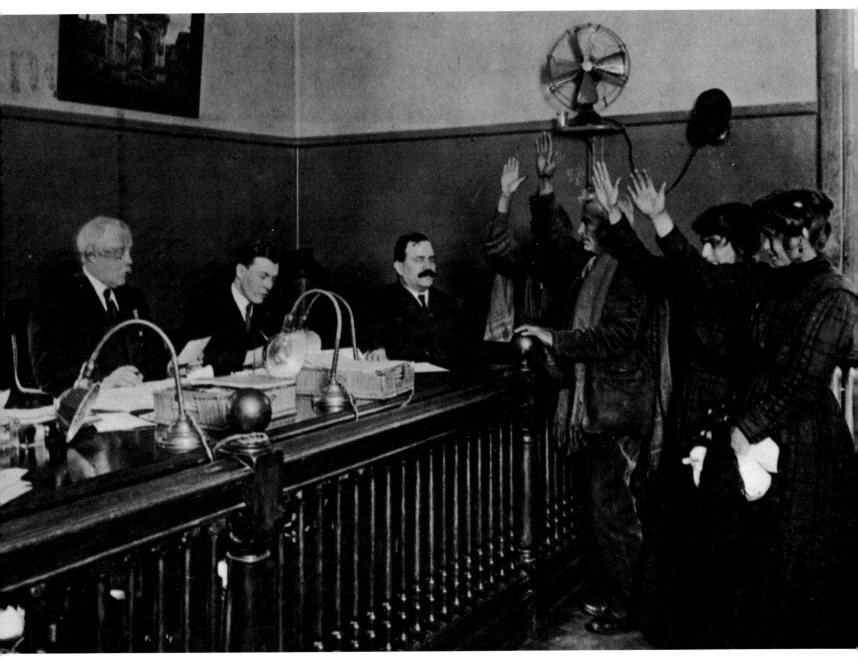

Italian immigrants before a Board of Special Inquiry, ca. 1911. Fifteen to 20% of the immigrants who appeared before such boards were excluded and ordered deported.

"The time that I spent on Ellis Island seemed like the longest waiting period for me because of the regimen. At the time it was a nightmare. They weren't unkind, but you had no communication with the people who took care of you. And you had no communication with the other people that were there because everybody was so full of their own fright."

Barbara Barondess, a Russian Jewish immigrant in 1921

Right: Mary Johnson, dressed in men's clothing and sporting a mustache, arrived at Ellis Island from Canada under the name Frank Woodhull. The truth was discovered in the inspection line. She was held for a hearing before a Board of Special Inquiry, during which she explained that as a woman she had limited opportunities: "Men can work at many unskilled callings, but to a woman only a few are open and they are the grinding, death-dealing kinds of work. Well, for me, I prefer to live a life of independence and freedom." The board decided that Mary Johnson had a valid point. She was admitted and allowed to proceed to her destination, New Orleans.

Below: Immigrants on the roof of the main building, ca. 1907. Periodically, detainees were led out of the crowded waiting rooms for a bit of fresh air.

Day In and Day Out

"How many more days do we have to be here? How many more days? That worried us."

Norman Adolf, a Czechoslovakian Jewish immigrant in 1920

An enforced stay on Ellis Island was never pleasant. Each new commissioner tried to improve the quality of life in detention, but during the peak years of immigration this was difficult, if not impossible. Dormitories and day rooms were constantly packed with people from diverse countries and cultures, speaking a babel of languages. One inspector recalled that in "those days we averaged about two thousand [detained every night]. In the detention room there were never less than nine hundred. It was an endless affair, like filling a trough at one end and emptying it at the other."

Such conditions, of course, were perfect targets for the sensational press. From Ellis Island's earliest days, newspapers frequently published horror stories about immigrants being forced to clean spittoons in the hospital, or locked outside on balconies as punishment, or herded about like cattle, or eaten alive by vermin. The more crowded the island became, the more outrageous the stories.

The worst conditions seem to have existed during the island's earliest days of operation. In 1902, when President Theodore Roosevelt appointed William Williams the new commissioner of immigration in New York, he told him that the immigrants on Ellis Island "were being improperly inspected, robbed, and abused." Roosevelt said that the place needed a clean sweep and gave his new commissioner the support he needed to rout out the entrenched powers of corruption. In addition to getting rid of crooked concessionaires, Williams also attempted to make Ellis Island a clean and efficient government facility. He had a great deal of work to do. On his first inspection of Ellis Island, he found that "immigrants were hustled about and addressed in rough language…until they were frequently both bewildered and frightened." The fact that the detention quarters were called "pens" made sense, he noted, "in view of their filthy condition."

But later, when the same accusations were being leveled against Williams's administration, he maintained that the immigrants themselves brought in dirt and vermin, and that filthy conditions in the detention rooms persisted despite several cleanings and scrubbings each day. He admitted that immigrants often had to sleep on the floor, but he explained: "That is not my fault…. There are not 2,000 beds on Ellis Island, and we sometimes have to detain 2,000…. Under the circumstances those that do not have beds, say 200, will have to sleep on benches."

Ellis Island was simply never equal to the task for which it was

Dinner in a detention room, 1903.

built. The huge jump in immigration that occurred during the first decades of the twentieth century overwhelmed the island's limited space and resources as well as its personnel. No matter how many improvements were made, detention meant living and sleeping in overcrowded rooms and sharing close quarters with people of vastly different backgrounds, levels of education, and personal habits.

The gravest burden for detainees, however, was the constant anxiety of not knowing how long they would have to stay or what would happen next. As time passed, some of the anxiety dissipated and tedium took its place. "I was so bored," said Inga Nastke, who came from Germany as a child. But, she recalled, the children generally found ways to amuse themselves: "We just made a lot of noise. Some talked in Russian, some in Hungarian, some in Italian, all kinds of nations. Somehow we got together and we chased one another. This kept us from literally going crazy with all that waiting."

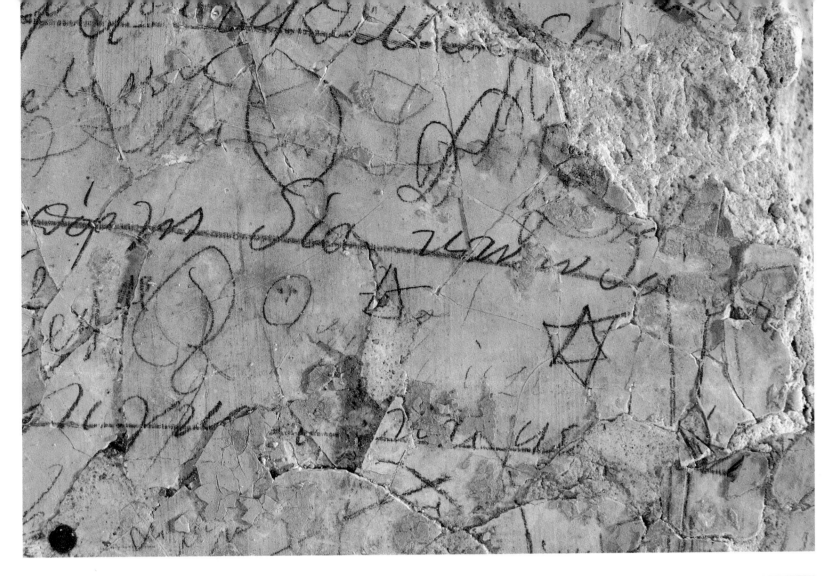

Graffiti fragments from Ellis Island's detention rooms, with signatures and inscriptions in Italian, Greek, and German.

"It was very sad, very painful," said Endre Bohem, who came from Hungary in 1921, "because I was so close and yet I was so far." His words convey something of the deep longing and angry frustration that must have been felt by all detainees as they waited at America's threshold to learn their various destinies. Detainees sometimes expressed their feelings by writing their signatures, dates of detainment, and other graffiti on the walls and doors of Ellis Island.

Periodic refurbishings over the years covered these graffiti with layers of paint. After Ellis Island shut down in 1954, however, the interior walls gradually peeled and shed their thick crust of paint, revealing once again a crowded surface of inscriptions and drawings—visible evidence of the island's past left by people who traveled through this place decades ago. During the restoration of Ellis Island's main building in the 1980s, conservators salvaged and preserved many of the graffiti.

"I left my mother in Italy. You cry for your mother all the time, so I wrote a letter to my mother from Ellis Island. Told my mother I got off, I got a job. And it made my mother strong."

Felice Taldone, an Italian immigrant in 1924

Above: Detained immigrants writing letters home, 1903.

Opposite: Detained children posing for photograph in rooftop playground of main building, ca. 1910. Seated in an "Uncle Sam" wagon and holding the stars and stripes, they have already begun the process of Americanization.

Nowhere were conditions worse than in Ellis Island's numerous dormitories, which were filled to capacity nearly every night. The main building had several dormitories, including two large ones located along the balcony of the Registry Room. When these could no longer accommodate all the detainees, the rest had to sleep in temporary wooden sheds constructed behind the main building. By 1910, the sheds had been replaced by a baggage and dormitory building made of brick.

Most of the immigrants slept in double- or triple-tiered bunk beds. The beds had no mattresses but consisted of wire mesh or canvas stretched across the bed frame. Immigrants were supposed to be issued two blankets, one to sleep on, another to provide cover, but often there were not enough blankets to go around, or immigrants would reject them because they were infested with lice.

By 1922, the bunks also had wire mesh enclosures. "They are arranged in wire cages," wrote Sir Aukland Geddes, the British ambassador who came to inspect Ellis Island on behalf of immigrants from England. "I am sure that it is necessary to encage the bunks to prevent thefts and even more unpleasant outrages. Yet I can understand a certain reaction of annoyed surprise on the part of those whose early experiences were of decent surroundings on being told to go to bed in a cage, even though the cage is necessary and provided for their protection."

After the quota laws were passed in the early 1920s, Ellis Island became far less crowded, allowing the commissioner of immigration, who at that time was Henry H. Curran, to get rid of the notorious bunks with their wire cages and mesh mattresses. He later wrote: "I have seen many jails, some pretty bad, but I never saw a jail as bad as the dormitories at Ellis Island, where nine out of ten of the immigrants had never committed any crime at all." Curran replaced the bunks with single beds and real mattresses and, for the first time, provided private rooms for families.

Top: Group of immigrants confined to one of Ellis Island's detention rooms, 1903.

Bottom: Dormitory room located on the Registry Room balcony, ca. 1908. During the day, the bunks were raised to convert the dormitories into waiting rooms.

"The first night in America I spent, with hundreds of other recently arrived immigrants, in an immense hall with tiers of narrow iron-and-canvas bunks, four deep.... The bunk immediately beneath mine was occupied by a Turk.... I thought how curious it was that I should be spending a night in such proximity to a Turk, for Turks were traditional enemies of Balkan peoples, including my own nation. For centuries Turks had forayed into Slovenian territory. Now here I was, trying to sleep directly above a Turk, with only a sheet of canvas between us."

Louis Adamic, a Slovenian immigrant in 1913

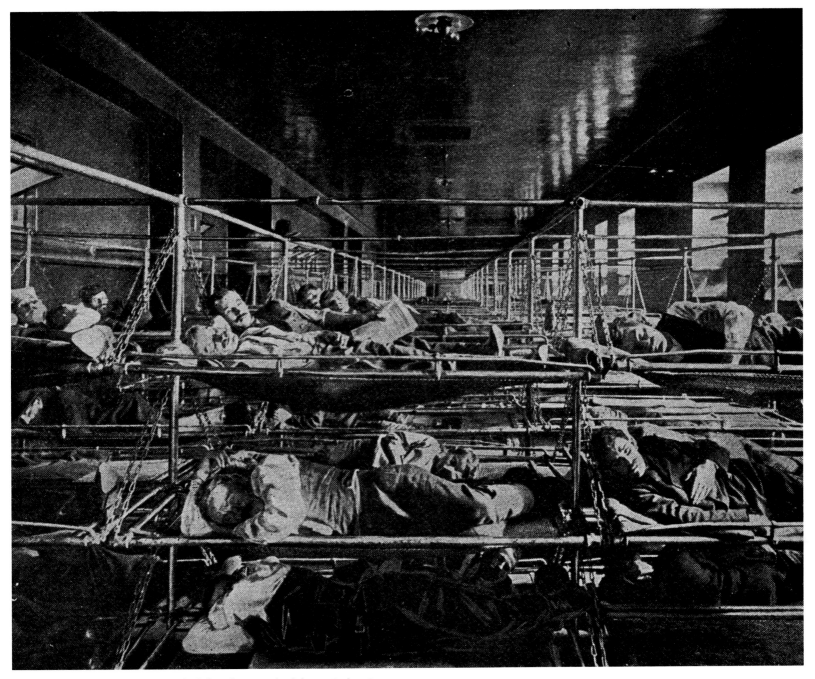

In 1907, Leslie's Weekly *published this photograph of the men's dormitory, located along the balcony above the Registry Room. This room had enough triple-tiered wire mesh bunks for 300 detainees. In 1908, the room was subdivided into seven smaller rooms, each one able to accommodate approximately fifty immigrants, thus increasing the dormitory's capacity.*

Overleaf: About 1,200 immigrants could be served at one seating in the Ellis Island dining room, ca. 1908.

"As for the food, we were hungry enough to eat the other food. But we couldn't eat the bread. Our Italian bread was so delicious. We couldn't understand this kind of soft, mushy bread. And we thought, oh dear God, is this the kind of bread we're going to have to eat in America?"

Josephine Reale, an Italian immigrant in 1920

"I remember the terrible rush that the immigrants would make into the dining room. It was generally set very beautifully. There would be dishes and forks and knives and a white napkin. But when the people went in, it was like chaos. There was no order. They would grab the butter. And if you didn't get there early enough, there was no butter left on the table."

Vartan Hartunian, an Armenian immigrant in 1922

```
                    Department of Commerce and Labor
IN ANSWERING REFER TO              IMMIGRATION SERVICE
NO.  31371

                                          OFFICE OF THE COMMISSIONER
                                               NEW YORK, N. Y.
                                          November 21, 1906.

Hon. Robert Watchorn,

     Commissioner of Immigration,

        Ellis Island, N.Y.H.

Sir:

        I have the honor to report that on Tuesday, November 20,

1906, the bill of fare in the immigrants' Dining Rooms was as follows

                         BREAKFAST
Coffee, with milk and sugar, and bread and butter.
     Crackers and milk for women and children .

                         DINNER:
Beef stew, boiled potatoes and bread.
        Smoked or pickled herring for Hebrews.
        Crackers and milk for women and children.

                         SUPPER.
Baked beans, stewed prunes, rye bread and tea,
               with milk and sugar.
     Crackers and milk for women and children.

        The food was well cooked.  Each immigrant received a sufficient

quantity and the help was attentive and obliging.  The rooms were

clean.

                    Respectfully,

                    SIGNED Joseph Murray,

                             Assistant Commissioner.
```

Each day the assistant commissioner of immigration inspected the dining room and reported his findings to the commissioner. A survey of several of these reports showed that the menu was often identical for days at a time. What immigrant fare lacked in variety, however, it made up for in quantity.

Detainees ate their meals in the Ellis Island dining room, which could seat 1,200 at a time. Reactions to the food varied, with many recalling that the meals were wholesome but bland. The dining room gave most immigrants their first taste of New World specialties such as ice cream, white bread, bananas, and corn on the cob.

The cooks tried to serve ethnic dishes as well but found it nearly impossible to please everyone's palate. Scandinavians refused to eat spaghetti, and Italians found oatmeal unappetizing. Immigrants generally liked the stewed prunes that were served on Ellis Island, but they objected to having them every day. For people detained for long periods of time, the recurrent prunes seemed to symbolize the monotony of their enforced stay.

The dining room was operated by a concession under contract to the U.S. Immigration Service. Its costs were charged to the steamship companies, which were required by law to provide food for detained immigrants. During Ellis Island's early, disreputable days, immigration officers were accused of detaining large numbers of immigrants simply to provide business for the concessionaire. Worse, the food was inedible. A 1902 report on Ellis Island charged: "The kitchen methods and methods of serving food to the immigrants are filthy and unsanitary in every way."

William Williams fired the corrupt food service concession and hired a reputable replacement that cleaned up the dining room and provided fair to good meals. "They had a nice dining room," said Ella Dowleyne, who arrived from Barbados in 1907. "And what a group of people, oh my goodness, never saw so many people at one time in my life."

In 1911, the food service was expanded to include a kosher kitchen to provide meals for the many Jewish immigrants arriving from eastern Europe. Otherwise they would not eat. The kosher kitchen seems to have been well run. "I loved the food," recalled Bessie Akawie, a Jewish immigrant from the Ukraine who was detained in 1921. "I became very friendly with the cook. Gee, I can still remember her. We had good food, potatoes, corn, lettuce. But the thing we liked the best was the ice cream."

In 1922, when the British ambassador was reporting on his visit to Ellis Island, he wrote: "The food is of good quality and well cooked. The dining room is the cleanest room in the building.... Tables are covered for each meal with clean paper 'cloth.'... I personally saw the dinner served. It was excellent."

"We got oatmeal for breakfast, and I didn't know what it was, with the brown sugar on it, you know. I couldn't get myself to eat it. So I put it on the windowsill, let the birds eat it."

Oreste Teglia, an Italian immigrant in 1916

"There was a man that came around every morning and every afternoon, with a stainless steel cart, sort of like a Good Humor cart. And the man was dressed in white and he had warm milk for the kids. And they would blow a whistle or ring a bell, and all the kids would line up, and he had small little paper cups and every kid got a little warm milk."

Donald Roberts, a Welsh immigrant in 1925

Fork and bowl once used on Ellis Island. The "H.B." stands for Harry Balfe, who operated the food service concession from 1905 to 1908. Balfe was contracted to provide meals at the following costs: breakfast, 5.5 cents; dinner, 11 cents; and supper, 8 cents.

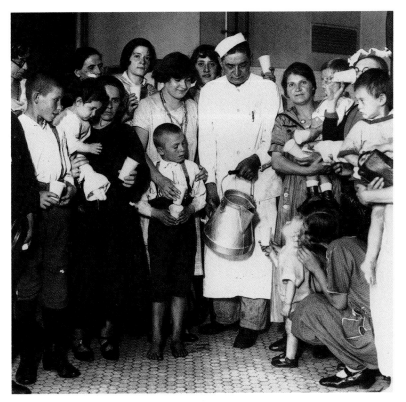

Women and children were served snacks of warm milk and crackers every afternoon and evening. The news service caption for this photograph, published in 1925, reports that these women and children had "knocked in vain at Uncle Sam's door" and were waiting to be deported.

"It was Passover and some Jewish people came. They said, 'How many Jewish people are here? We have a kosher meal for you.' And we came to the table. And there were people from the HIAS [Hebrew Immigrant Aid Society] who were attending to everything, telling everyone where to sit and serving and all that."

Fannie Friedman, a Ukrainian Jewish immigrant in 1921

Immigrant Aid Societies

Above: Salvation Army worker distributing donuts to immigrants, ca. 1920.

Right: Passover seder for Jewish immigrants and staff, ca. 1920.

Opposite: Christmas celebration, ca. 1906. Robert Watchorn (on the far right), commissioner of immigration from 1905 to 1909, attended this event, organized by immigrant aid societies stationed on the island. The government offered few social services, but Watchorn actively encouraged the work done by private agencies that gave immigrants help and advice.

At a time when the government offered few social services, the burden of helping new arrivals make their first adjustments to life in America was shouldered by various ethnic and religious organizations. Over forty immigrant aid societies had representatives on Ellis Island. The Hebrew Immigrant Aid Society (HIAS) and the Society for the Protection of Italian Immigrants were among the most important, but there were also divisions of the Salvation Army, the YWCA, and the Daughters of the American Revolution, among others.

Representatives from these societies acted as interpreters for the immigrants, gave them clothing and money, and helped them unsnaggle bureaucratic tie-ups, locate lost luggage, and contact friends and relatives. The support and personal care they provided brought a modicum of calm to many situations that were fraught with high emotion.

The societies also did their best to ease the sheer boredom of detention. They organized music programs, religious services, Christmas parties, Passover seders, and other holiday celebrations. Children greatly enjoyed these events, especially when it meant receiving a toy, an orange, some candy, or other present. Elizabeth Martin, who arrived from Hungary in 1920, vividly remembers a Christmas party complete with red and green decorations and a Santa Claus "with a big white beard." Helen Cohen, from Poland, recalled hearing Enrico Caruso in concert on Ellis Island: "The real Caruso! He gave the concert, and it's still ringing in my ears. He was just out of this world."

The social workers on Ellis Island were sensitive to the immigrants' special agony of leaving the homeland and venturing into an uncertain future. But they also encouraged their charges to start the assimilation process soon. Looking American seemed to be the inevitable first step. Well-meaning social workers often took detained women in hand and gave them outfits of American clothes. A visit to the social services second-hand clothing closet might yield a woolen coat and wide-brimmed hat to replace a shawl and kerchief. Immigrant women, however, were not always easily convinced. While some welcomed the American fashions, many others found them too startling and quickly changed back into their own familiar clothes.

Ellis Island also drew an assortment of do-gooders and proselytizers who distributed Americanization tracts, prayer books, or Bibles. They thrust their material at the immigrants as they were leaving the island or waiting in the detention rooms. Bible missionaries were so zealous in this effort that they were reprimanded by the immigration commissioner. "A great many of our immigrants are Hebrews," he explained, "who are on their way from one persecution by one style of Christians, and when they have Christian tracts—printed in Hebrew—put in their hands, apparently with the approval of the United States government, they wonder what is going to happen to them there."

Most of the social workers on Ellis Island, however, came there to work with the immigrants and give them whatever practical assistance they needed. One of their most useful services was finding work for new arrivals. Immigrants who did not know English were easy prey for unscrupulous labor brokers, who exploited their own countrymen, gulling them into accepting backbreaking jobs for meager pay. To bypass these predators, who prowled the Battery looking for recruits, social workers escorted their charges from Ellis Island directly to the safety of a society's employment office.

Many of these societies also ran homes where single women could live until they found suitable employment and were safe from being entrapped in prostitution, a common fear at that time. Since Ellis Island officials rarely let unescorted women off the island, the representatives of the homes who vouched for the women's protection saved many of them from being excluded and sent back to their homelands.

Above: "Saving Heartaches with a Dash of Powder and a Comely Skirt" reads the headline over this photo, published in a 1926 article about Ludmila K. Foxlee, a YWCA social worker on Ellis Island. One of her chosen tasks was "to beautify immigrant women for the dramatic meeting with husbands" after years of separation. The article explained that "10 or 15 years in America make a good deal of difference in a man's ideal of womanhood."

Opposite: One of the "1000 Marriageable Girls" who arrived at Ellis Island on September 27, 1907. They had booked passage independently, but the coincidence of so many single women traveling on one ship caused a great media sensation. Their arrival prompted many offers of marriage, but the women had their own ideas: "It's a Pittsburgh millionaire for me," said one.

Isle of Hope/Isle of Tears

"By the time we came to New York, somehow the experience on Ellis Island had aged us. We didn't want to sing anymore. We were all grown up. I was there almost a year. Eight months was a long time."

Bessie Akawie, a Ukrainian Jewish immigrant in 1921

"Ellis Island was a purgatory," remarked Samuel Nelson, a Russian Jewish immigrant in 1905. "Something you had to go through."

After all the waiting and interrogation, most of the detainees were given permission to land. But a significant number, approximately 250,000 during the years 1892 to 1924, were excluded. To be turned back at this point and forced to return to a port of embarkation caused extreme distress. Many immigrants had sold nearly everything they owned to pay for the journey to America. They would go back to the old country worse off than they were before. Others could expect to find religious persecution or political harassment. But the greatest heartache was the separation of families—some members allowed into America while others were turned away. Sometimes these families would never be reunited again. These were the terrible fates that weighed so heavily on the minds of the immigrants during detention.

For those who were admitted, however, the frustration and agony of waiting ended in joyous relief. Once given permission to land, they tried to put Ellis Island behind them. The weary newcomers quickly gathered their belongings in the ground floor Baggage Room and went out to the ferry slips. Most still had long journeys ahead of them, but as they left the island, carrying their makeshift luggage, bundles, and babies, they must have felt heartened. The goal for which they had come so far had been achieved, and they were about to embark on new lives in America.

Above: Women denied admission to the United States, 1903.

Opposite: Saved from exclusion by an appeal to Washington, 1903.
Overleaf: Immigrant baggage in front of the main building.

Treasures from Home

"So preparations were made for the journey—clothing was sorted out which would be taken along, packed in the suitcases; treasured photographs of Mom and Dad when they were 25, carefully packed; some silver, which Mom treasured and wanted to take; and then lastly the food."

Maria Oogjen, a Russian immigrant in 1923

They each brought something. In addition to their hopes and dreams, they packed up whatever material things they thought they might need in their new homes, and bundled them into an assortment of trunks, valises, baskets, or sheets. Some had long overland journeys across Europe to the nearest seaport, and had to anticipate carrying their things on and off trains, into and out of stations, all the while keeping track of tickets, money, passports, and children.

Most brought a mix of the functional and the familiar: Bibles and prayer books, family documents, and handmade linens, dresses, underwear, and socks. They also packed their native costumes, beautifully stitched and embroidered. Some could fit all they owned into a little suitcase; others had to make careful choices, selling most of their belongings to finance the journey and perhaps giving a few pieces to friends and relatives left behind. The rest, whatever they could manage to carry, they took with them.

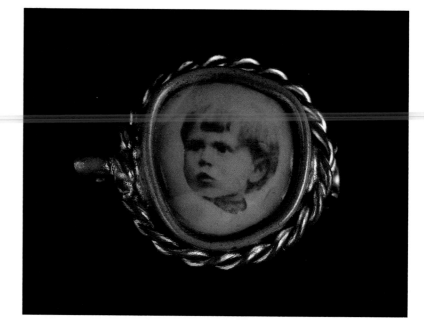

Above: Pia Miorelli Ischia, who came to the United States in 1924 from Arco, Italy, wore this locket to remember her baby daughter Lina, who had died six years previously. A photograph of the child decorates the cover, while the small container held a lock of Lina's hair as well as a necklace and medal that once belonged to her. A poignant note in Italian tucked inside the container reads: "Hair and medal of my adored Lina—Died 3–6–1918."

Opposite: All immigrants brought clothing and apparel, much of it handmade by the women in the family, for everyday wear as well as for special occasions. Some of these clothes were worn by new arrivals when they passed through Ellis Island.

"What did we take with us? Our clothes, our pillows, our big, thick comforters made from pure goose feathers—*not* chicken feathers—and a barrel of pickles."

Fannie Shoock, a Polish Jewish immigrant in 1921

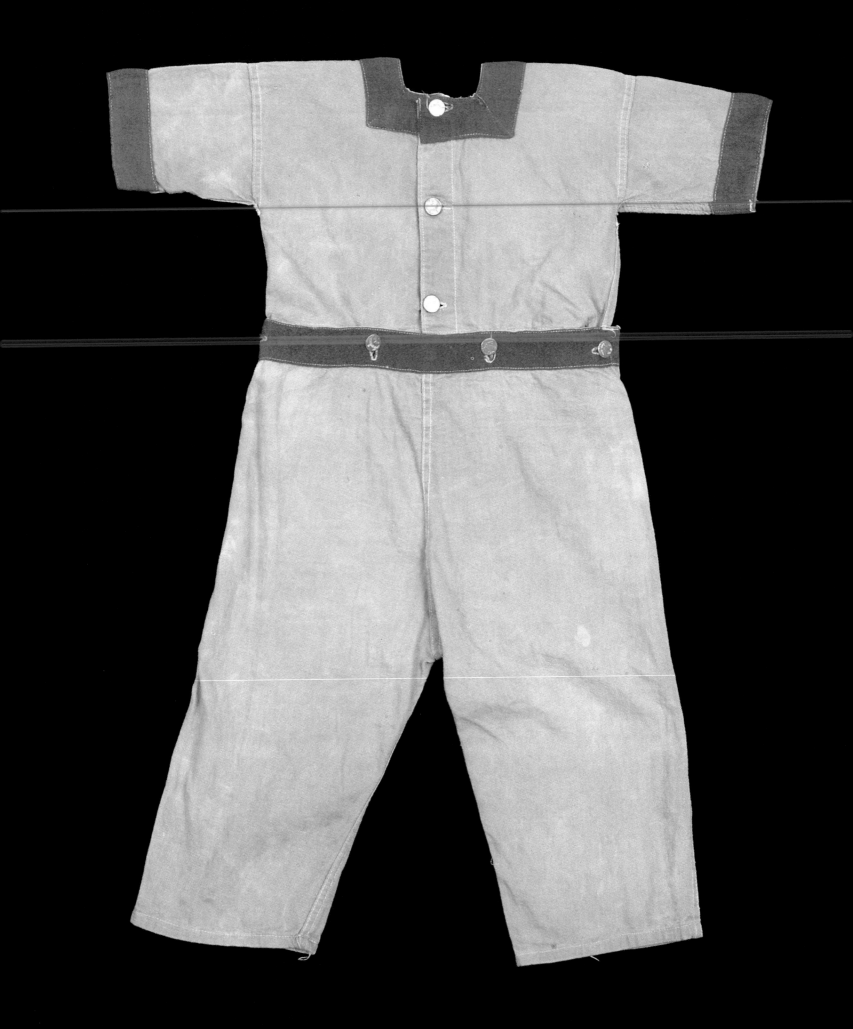

Opposite: Suit worn by John L. Thomas on March 30, 1925, when he arrived at Ellis Island with his mother and sister. John's mother had been to America before, sometime around 1912, but had returned to Austria to marry. The belongings carried to America in 1925 included two little forks for the children and a pair of shoes for John.

Above: Handmade black flannel vest with cotton cockades, brought to the United States in 1920 by Apolena Pribilova Joch, a Moravian woman. Farm wives commonly wore vests like these on important occasions. The decoration indicated the woman was married.

"I had a small steamer trunk for a start. One of those small ones that you can push underneath a bunk. I didn't bring very much clothes, just a work suit and my best suit. And I had this pound of butter wrapped up. I guess somebody told me to take it to somebody who'd like Irish butter. It was good butter my sisters made."

Joseph Patrick Fitzpatrick, an Irish immigrant in 1910

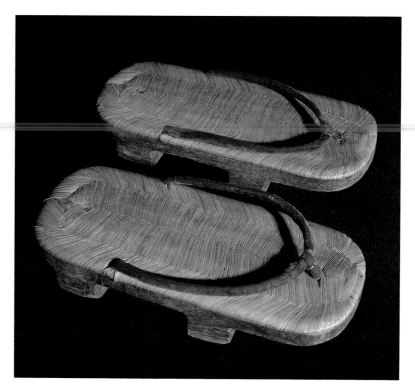

Above: Hatsu Odagiri arrived in San Francisco in January 1920, from Japan, wearing these wooden shoes (geta) as well as a traditional kimono. She and her 12-year-old son were joining her husband, Kichishiro Odagiri, who had immigrated earlier. During the peak immigration years, around 300,000 Japanese came to the United States and settled, primarily in California. Life in the adopted country was a bittersweet experience for many. Along with more than 110,000 other Japanese Americans, the Odagiris were forced from their home during World War II and sent to an internment camp.

Left: Skirt and jacket worn by Marie Eanello Macaluso, an Italian immigrant, during her journey to America around 1913.

Opposite: Man's shirt and vest worn by Volodymyr Lelet, who left the small Ukrainian town of Kosiv in 1913 to come to America. The embroidered linen shirt and vest were part of the folk dress of the Hutzul region of the Carpathian Mountains.

"I arrived in New York in 1921—all my belongings consisted of an additional change of underwear and two books."

Abraham Burstein, A Russian Jewish immigrant in 1921

"My mother had her trunk just chock full of stuff, all our clothes and a lot of food that my grandmother liked, all kinds of cheese and sausage."

Margaret Lehan, an Italian immigrant in 1911

"My parents managed to get us a new pair of shoes, a new outfit, besides the old. But you didn't take too much. You didn't have a valise. You just had one of those sacks, that was all."

Marianthe Chletsos, a Greek immigrant in 1910

Top: Rosaria Marino Ciocco made this beaded purse on the occasion of her engagement to Frank Ciocco in 1874. Flowers, little animals, and love birds are woven into the beaded design. The Cioccos emigrated from Italy in 1898.

Bottom: Fourteen-year-old Ellen Whaite Pierce packed these clogs in 1920, when her family left England and sailed for New York. Clogs were the traditional footwear of her native Lancashire. The Pierce family settled in St. Maries, Idaho.

Top: This regal-looking fan, made of carved ivory and paper decorated with a colorful court scene, was brought from Spain, ca. 1890. The fan belonged to an elaborate Aragonese costume that included a full-length black skirt, moire blouse, and lace mantilla.

Bottom: Apolena Pribilova Joch brought this festive costume with her when she left Moravia in 1920.

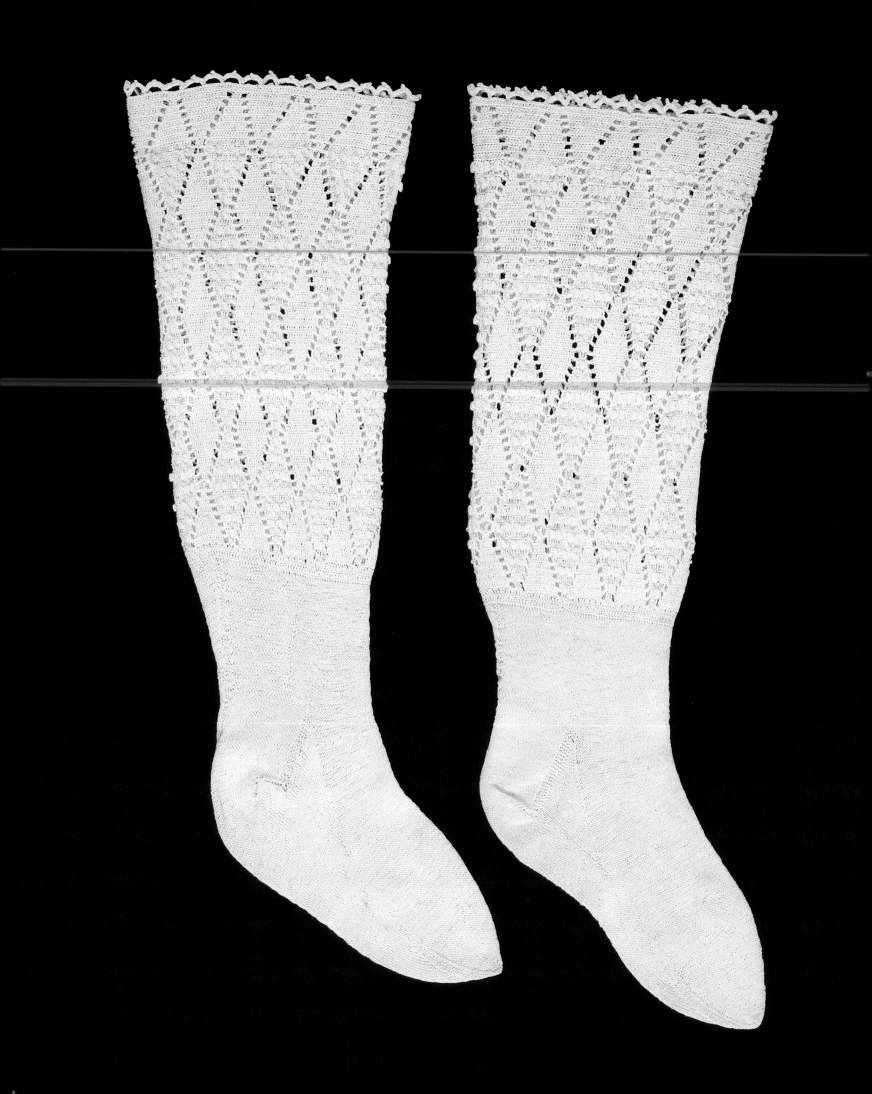

"Most dear to me are the shoes my mother wore when she first set foot on the soil of America. You must see these shoes to appreciate the courage my parents had and the sacrifices they made giving up family and security to try for a better life, but not knowing what lay ahead. We came to this country as many others did, POOR! My mother's shoes tell a whole story."

Birgitta Hedman Fichter, a Swedish immigrant in 1924

Opposite: Pair of crocheted socks brought by Henrietta Jatasciore, who immigrated from Chieti, Italy, in 1892.

Above: Hightop shoes worn by Elin Maria Hedman in 1924, when she and daughter Birgitta arrived at Ellis Island.

Birth certificate issued to Hendel Herzlinger, an Austrian Jew who immigrated around 1899.

Many immigrants carried letters of introduction and credentials, witnessed and verified by the proper authorities. The documents proved that the newcomers were upright citizens, had paid their taxes, had served in the military, or had graduated from school. Some families, like the Ishmaels, can trace an entire story with the documents they have saved. Percy Ishmael, who came from Barbados in 1919, carried his passport and a letter of recommendation from his church in Barbados. A year after settling in America, he petitioned the British Consul General for permission to marry Miss Eliza Griffith, who then obtained a passport to come to the United States. By the 1930s, as a family with two daughters, the Ishmaels had added citizenship papers to the family archives. But their real legacy, according to daughter Rose Ishmael Tully, is their descendants, who "became teachers, supervisors and managers in government service and leaders in private industries."

Documents usually helped to ease the immigrants' passage but sometimes they were not enough. When Anna Schiller Griasch, age 14, arrived at Ellis Island with her younger brother, she tried to present her papers to immigration officers but was pushed aside. "We're not supposed to be here," she tried to explain. "I have papers here from my people." The youngsters spent ten confused and harrowing days in detention before a telegram from their parents in Chicago won their release.

Nagykikinda r. t. város rendőrkapitányától.-

3140 szám
rk. 1909

Hatósági bizonyitvány

Nagykikinda r. t. város rendőrkapitányi hivatala részéről hivatalosan bizonyíttatik,
hogy 161781/909 számú útlevéllel Amerikába ki-
vándorolt kiskorú Schiller Anna és Schiller Ádám
helybeli lakosok bejelentett kisérője Anschau Zsu-
zsanna amerikai lakósnő volt, kinek is e czél-
ra a rendőrkapitányi hivatal által 136/909 útl. szám
alatt hatósági bizonyitvány állíttatott ki.-

Miről ezen bizonyitvány - a gyermekek nagy-
atyja - Pfendt János helybeli lakós kérelmére ki-
adatik.-

Nagykikindán 1909 évi augusztus hó 10én

Rajsau
rendőrkapitány

Községi bizonyítvány.

Alólírott Község elöljárósága hivatalosan bizonyítja, hogy

Kinner Dávidné, orbaufkémi lakos két fiu gyermekével, valamint szülei Taub József és neje Grünberger Róza, Amenhálea fiyéhez, vándorel ki, itt semmi nemü köztartozással nincs hátrálékban. Bizonyítja továbbá, hogy Kivándorló víz- és feletrenünje sajáb tulajdonát képezi és azt saját használatára szükséges, annak külföldre vitele ellen akadály fenn nem forog.

Banffihán 1920. febr. 24én

Horváth József
biró

Church certificate issued to the Wikstedt family, who immigrated in 1902. The document says: "Karl Wikstedt, born June 1, 1874, in Pori, Finland, a member of the Lutheran Church, has received his smallpox inoculation and has taken Communion in the Church, and enjoys citizenship in the Church, with his wife, Maria, born October 16, 1871, and his daughter, Kaarin, born November 30, 1901, for the trip to America. Witnessed, October 20, 1902."

Above: Palestinian identification card of Joshua David Lowenfish.

Right: Marriage certificate of Miriam and Felix Lowenfish.

Shortly after World War I, Miriam and Felix Lowenfish and their three sons, Martin, Joshua, and Arthur, left Poland for Palestine. The oldest son, Martin, had immigrated first to avoid conscription, and was followed by the rest of the family. In 1923, they came to the United States so their sons

CERTIFICATE OF MARRIAGE.

Pursuant to Act 6 and 7 Gulielmi IV., Cap. 86.

189**6** MARRIAGE solemnized at *St Mary of the Angels Batley*
in the District of DEWSBURY, in the County of York.

No.	When Married.	Name and Surname.	Age.	Condition.	Rank or Profession.	Residence at the time of Marriage.	Father's Name and Surname.	Rank or Profession of Father.
87	Twenty fifth May 1896	Thomas Horkan	26 years	Bachelor	General Labourer	Melton Street Batley	Thomas Horkan (deceased)	General Labourer
		Mary Anne Bones	23 years	Spinster	—	Cross Bank Road Batley	John Bones	Tanner

Married in the *St Mary of the Angels* according to the Rites and Ceremonies of the *Roman Catholics* by *Certificate* by me.

This Marriage was solemnized between us, { *Thomas Horkan* / *Mary Anne Bones* } In the Presence of us, { *John Horkan* / *Bridget Bones* } *Chas Gordon* R C P *Benjamin Whitaker* Registrar

I, the undersigned, Registrar of Marriages for the District of DEWSBURY, in the County of York, do hereby Certify that the foregoing is a true Copy of an Entry in the Register Book of Marriages for the said District. And I further Certify that the said Register Book is now lawfully in my custody.

Witness my hand, this *Twenty Seventh* day of *May* 189**6**

N E Whitaker Copy Registrar.
24 May 1896

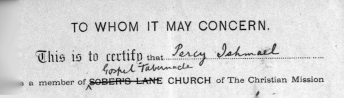

when she resigned.

During the time she was in the Service *her conduct was*

satisfactory in every respect.

Date-Stamp.

NEWCASTLE-ON-TYNE
DE 22

J. W. Pickwett

Jr.

for Postmaster.

[7613] 53130/158 4000 2/16 v 1655 G & S

La Cugna *a rejo Giuseppe di Sebastiano*

la Croce al Merito di Guerra

Roma   addì 3 agosto 1923

Il Ministro

B Mussolini

Hely's Limited, Printers, Dublin.

(Boy's Indenture).

TO WHOM IT MAY CONCERN.

This is to certify that *Percy Ishmael*
Gospel Tabernacle

is a member of ~~SOBER'S LANE~~ CHURCH of The Christian Mission

"Greetings from Sweden" reads the legend on this dried oak leaf, brought to America by Amanda Karlson in 1891. The leaf's design includes Sweden's traditional coat of arms.

"My mother brought her candles, the ones you use on Friday night. She brought her Bibles. She brought the things that were near and dear to us which were not very important to anybody but us. To us, they brought back memories."

Sam Auspitz, a Czechoslovakian Jewish immigrant in 1920

Most immigrants came to America armed with their faith. Holding fast to traditional religion gave new arrivals the moral guidance and strength they needed to cope with the demands of living in a new world. Religion governed daily prayer as well as celebrations of life's major events—birth, coming of age, and marriage.

The sacred items the immigrants brought with them reflect an enormous diversity of religions and forms of worship. Among their belongings they packed medals, rosaries, prayer books, and other religious objects. Loduvina de Conceicao Camara, who came from the Azores in 1895, packed a tiny bone-bound missal she had carried on her wedding day. She also had two black mantillas for church ceremonies and funerals and sacred figurines set up each year at Christmas.

Marcele Grucis Visbaras arrived in New York in 1914, carrying one of the first Lithuanian prayer books to be published after a czarist ban on Latin orthography and script was lifted in 1904. The Perdikis family, who emigrated from Cyprus in 1921, packed icons of St. Helena and St. Nicholas painted in the Byzantine tradition. Many eastern European Jews, persecuted for their faith in the old country, adhered to traditional Sabbath and holiday observations. The Weinkle family, immigrants from Russia in 1890, carried a ram's horn (*shofar*) used on the Jewish high holy days of Rosh Hashanah and Yom Kippur.

The determination to preserve their religious heritage and maintain continuity with the homeland led immigrants to form close-knit congregations and build churches and synagogues. Each ethnic group wanted its own place of worship, where members of the congregation could hear sermons in their native tongue, celebrate their own religious holidays, and sing the same hymns they had known in the old country. "The first thing we do whenever we move," said Elizabeth Smith Nimmo, an English immigrant in 1920, "is go looking for a church and make friends." Spiritual life was not simply a matter of worship; most congregations were dedicated to performing good works. Visiting the sick, helping the poor, sending money to missionaries, raising funds to build a new church or school, these were activities that built strong, cohesive communities.

Top: Wedding clothes, christening outfit, prayer books, rosaries, and other artifacts of spiritual life.

Bottom: Beaded wedding shoes of Candida Arena, who married Michelangelo DiVittorio on February 5, 1907, in Trabia, Sicily. A few years later, Michelangelo left for America. After settling in California, he sent for his wife and five-year-old daughter Giuseppa, who arrived at Ellis Island in 1913.

Wedding dress worn by a young bride in Harput, Armenia. Around 1890, she accompanied her husband to Worcester, Massachusetts, which had a large Armenian community.

Gizella Mudry was married in this wedding dress shortly before she left her native Hungary to come to America in 1900.

In 1909, Michael and Helena Papieski Przybylski emigrated from Poland. Among their most cherished possessions was this image of the "Black Madonna," which they carefully wrapped in down quilts and packed in a wicker basket for its trip to America.

Statues of Jesus Christ and the Madonna brought by Anna Marfica Mielak, who emigrated from a farm in the Cracow region of Poland in 1885. She settled in Columbus, Nebraska.

"When we left Cyprus, my people being extremely religious, they made sure that all the icons were brought with us."

Harold Perris, a Greek Cypriot immigrant in 1921

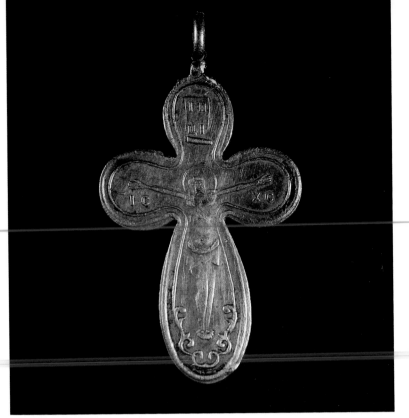

Above: Ten-year-old Tessie Argianas embroidered this image of a cross entwined with flowers shortly before she left Greece with her mother and sister in 1914.

Top right: John Stetzky wore this crucifix on a chain when he emigrated from Russia in 1907.

Bottom right: Hanukkah menorah brought by Benjamin Mintz from Poland around 1890.

Opposite: In 1900, Harris Kaminsky came to America from a suburb of Vilnius, Lithuania, then part of the Russian empire. Among his belongings was this pouch, which contained his phylacteries (tefillin). The pouch is embroidered with his initials and flowers. He also brought prayer books and his wedding vest.

"My father brought a prayer shawl and phylacteries, which went with every Jew that came from Europe at that time."

Seymour Rexite, a Polish Jewish immigrant in 1920

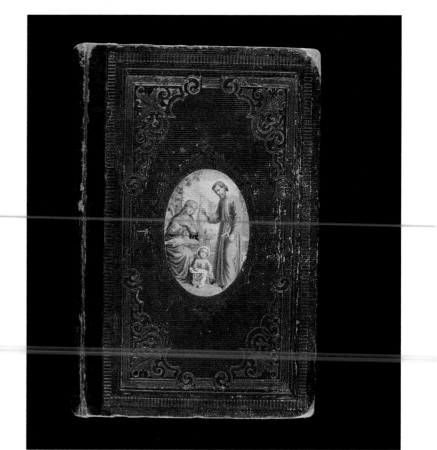

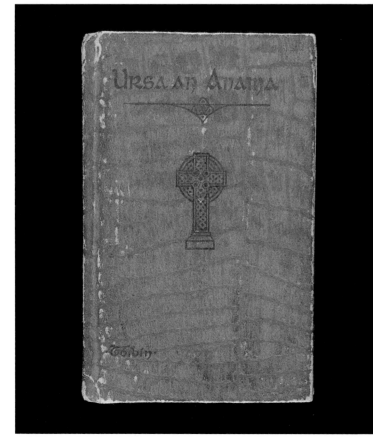

Top: Hebrew prayer book of Nathan Hofstetter, Galicia, 1896.

Bottom: Gaelic prayer book of Catherine Cawley Ford, Ireland, 1928.

Top: Missal of Frances Grubesic Kovacevich, Croatia, 1905.

Bottom: Hebrew prayer book of David Singer, Poland, 1921.

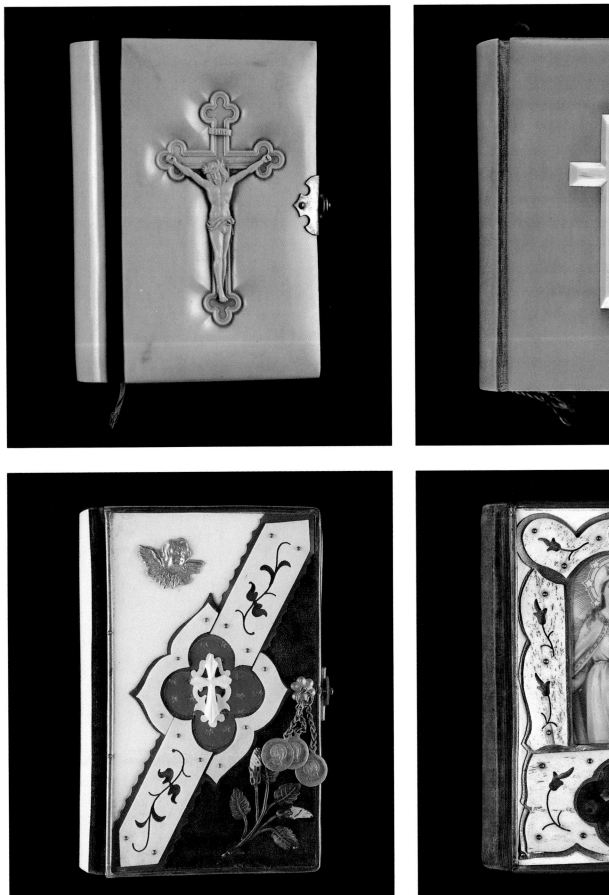

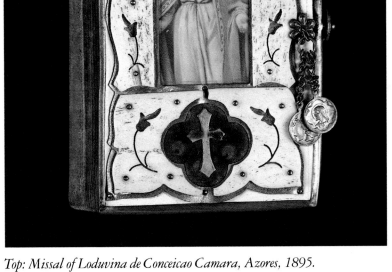

Top and bottom: Two prayer books of Michael and Helena Papieski Przybylski, Poland, 1909.

Top: Missal of Loduvina de Conceicao Camara, Azores, 1895.

Bottom: Prayer book of Marcele Grucis Visbaras, Lithuania, 1914.

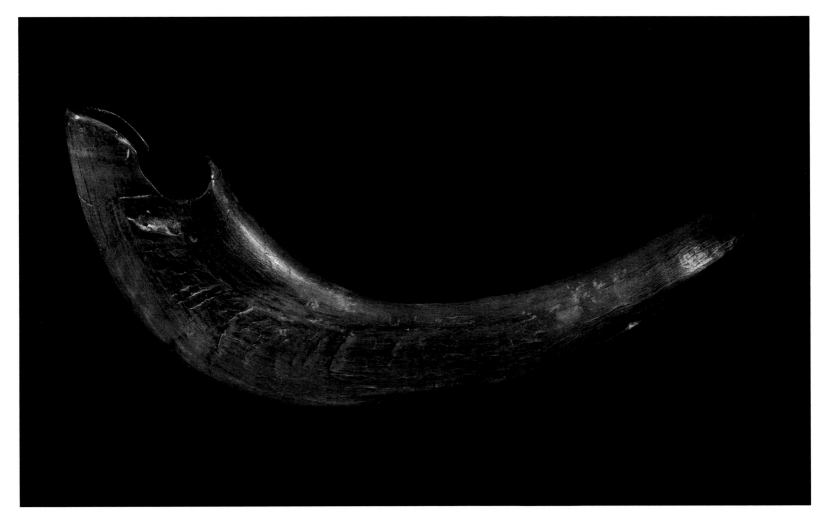

Opposite: Handpainted Easter egg, brought by Olga Bobek Silha from Bohemia in 1906.

Above: This ram's horn (shofar) belonged to Marcus Joseph Weinkle, born Mordcho Yosef Vinikovsky, who arrived from Russia in 1890. The shofar is sounded on Rosh Hashanah and Yom Kippur, the Jewish high holy days.

"My mother took an awful lot of things with her—linen tablecloths and a lot of things that she could carry. Bedclothes and stuff like that. She had big bundles—she just had them tied up in bundles. All she could carry."

F. G. Gregot, an immigrant from Lithuania in 1914

"When I was a little boy I would hear stories of how my family travelled to America from Grodno, Russia. The older relatives told of how the family had nothing to bring with them, and of leaving Grodno with an empty suitcase they borrowed so no one would know they had no worldly possessions."

Joel Greenberg, grandson of Rose Greenberg, a Russian Jewish immigrant, ca. 1915

A spinning wheel, musical instruments, and handmade textiles are among the treasured remnants of family life that have survived years of use.

The great sacks that immigrants carried with them usually contained an assortment of domestic goods, the essentials for setting up housekeeping and a new home. Everyday items included dishes, pots, tablecloths, napkins; for holidays there were special linens, candlesticks, musical instruments, and other prized possessions that would help make life more comfortable and create a sense of home in an unfamiliar place.

Mary Louise Mills, who arrived in 1925, wouldn't leave Scotland without the teapot given her by Sir Thomas Lipton, the tea manufacturer, in Glasgow. She must have wrapped it very carefully to survive the long journey. Tong Ly Jue and his bride Jeang Quai Sen also brought a favorite teapot, when they emigrated from China. It came with a padded wicker basket to keep the tea piping hot.

Maria Ferrera Folgarelli packed a bottle of "bellyache" medicine given her by her mother in case she got sick during the ocean crossing. Anna Gröf, from Norway, bought a spinning wheel to bring with her just before she left Oslo in 1894. And Charles Magill's father gave him a donkey-shoe good luck charm before he left Carncastle, Ireland, in 1929.

Pearl Pohrille's mother, who left Germany in 1921, packed up all the wares of her kosher household: two sets of dishes, dishtowels, and cutlery for meat and dairy. But at the port of embarkation the steamship company fumigated all the passengers' baggage with steam and ruined most of their things. "It was a shambles," Mrs. Pohrille recalled. "But my aunt reassured Mother that it could be replaced. And it was."

Francisco de Albuquerque Silva, who emigrated from Portugal in 1919, brought his most cherished possessions—his books. His daughter wrote: "He loved books! When he was to receive his diploma from grammar school, my dad asked my grandfather to buy him a pair of shoes, but my granddad needed money for more important things and told my dad there would be no shame going barefoot to receive his diploma." Her father did not attend the graduation, but when he returned to Portugal in 1926 to marry, he made a special trip to his old school to pick up the diploma he had earned years before.

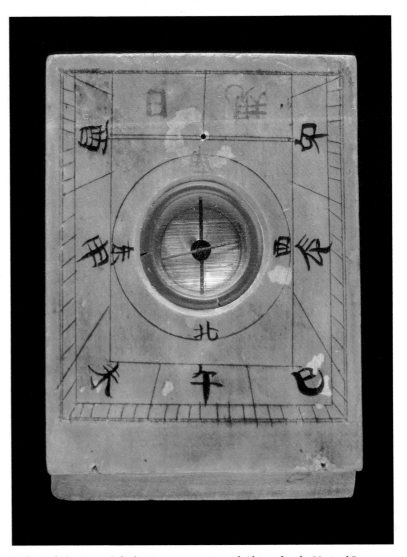

When Philip Lowe left the Canton province of China for the United States in 1924, he brought this compass so he could "find his way in America." He later became a photographer and opened his own studio in San Francisco's Chinatown.

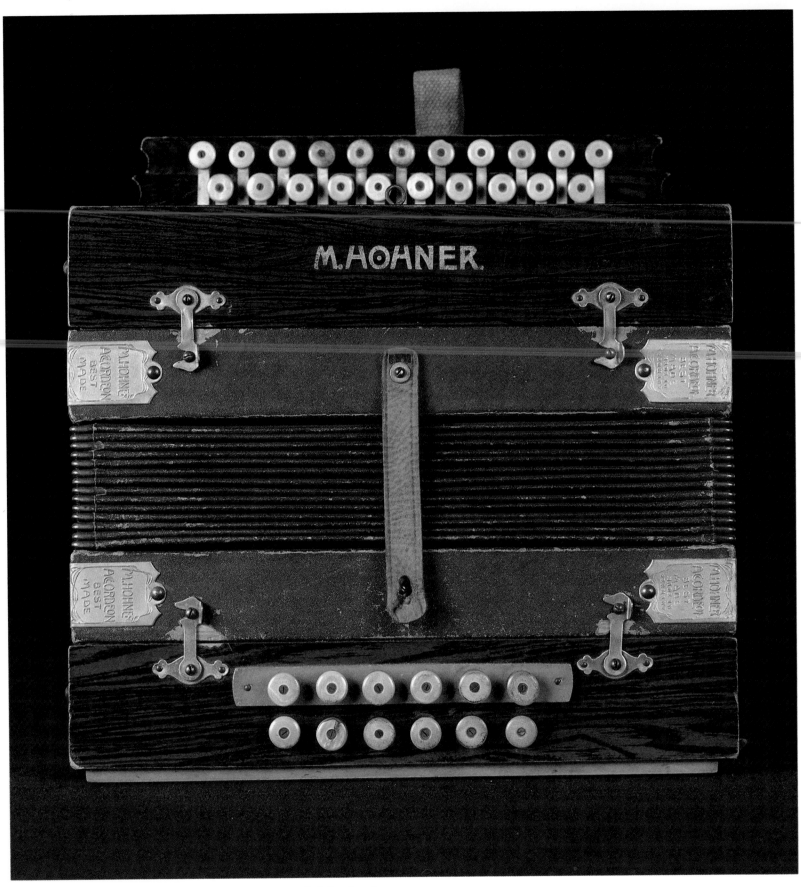

Robert Erzy Buraczewski's Hohner accordian was among the belongings he packed when he left Poland to come to America around 1915.

When Christian and Marthina Pettersen emigrated from Norway with their two-year-old son in 1893, they carried the wherewithal for establishing a new home: a zither (above), a sewing machine and instruction booklet, and the family Bible.

"This is the teapot that Harry's father brought from China. He had it inside a basket. The basket is padded to keep the tea warm, to keep the tea hot in fact. They heard that in America, they don't have teapots. And they don't know how to keep their tea hot for long. So, he brought this with him."

Mary Jue, daughter-in-law of Tong Ly Jue, a Chinese immigrant, 1880s

Above: Teapot of Tong Ly Jue, who emigrated from Canton, China, to California during the 1880s.

Opposite: Mathias and Katherine Henges, a German couple who lived in St. Petersburg, Russia, brought this samovar in 1910.

Морозъ и солнце
День чудесный
Еще ты дремлешь
другъ прелестный

"I have a linen bed sheet that is richly embroidered in cutwork, which is typical of Danish needlecraft. The only time the sheet was used was when my mother gave birth to all of us babies in our farm home, because she wanted the doctor to see something beautiful she had brought from her native land."

Evellyn S. Huyser, daughter of John and Anna Andersen, Danish immigrants in 1905

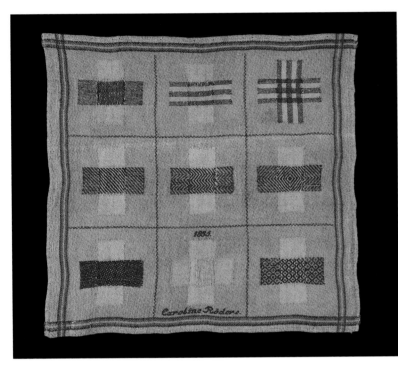

Above: Sampler sewn by Caroline Roders in 1885, when she was a schoolgirl in Bremen, Germany. It was among the prized possessions her family carried to America in 1888.

Opposite: This dresser scarf belonged to Sara Orlov. During World War I, she and her three-year-old daughter managed to travel from Russia to Sweden and then on to England, where they boarded a ship for the United States. They were to join Sara's husband, who had emigrated several years before. The Russian inscription reads: "Frost and sunshine/Make for a radiant day/And you are dreaming/About a lovely friend."

Top: Handmade lace table centerpiece brought from Denmark in 1929 by Helga Langberg.

Bottom: Towel, part of a trousseau handmade by Esther Borochowitch Kaminsky while living with her parents near Vilnius, the capital of Lithuania. When she and Harris Kaminsky married in 1898, they were both 24 years old. Two years later, he left for America, and in 1903 she followed him with their three-year-old daughter. On the eve of her departure, Esther's mother told her not to be sad at parting but to be happy about joining her husband. She and her mother would never see each other again.

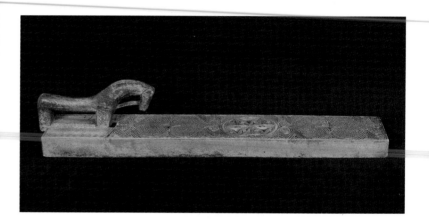

Top: These bone-handled utensils, brought from Germany in 1921 by Pearl Pohrille, were damaged during routine fumigation at the port of departure.

Bottom: This copper pot for making gefilte fish originally belonged to Yetta Fiscus Voichick, who emigrated from Poland in 1909. In 1927, she gave the pot to her daughter-in-law Stella, who, according to her daughter, continued the Voichick tradition of making good gefilte fish.

*Top: Mangle board (*mangletre*), a cold iron for stretching and pressing woven material, especially linen, from Norway, ca. 1890. Fabric was rolled onto a wooden pin, sprinkled with water, and rolled back and forth with the mangletre.*

Bottom: When Jane Magill left Ireland in 1907, her mother, Annie Connolly Magill, gave her this glass plate, which bears an excerpt from the Lord's Prayer. The plate originally belonged to Annie's mother.

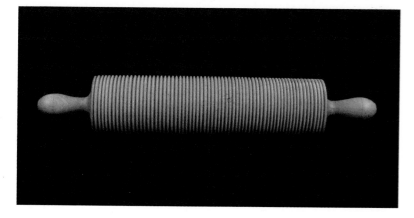

Top: This incised wooden press, used for making kahtah *(Turkish bread), was part of the varied cargo brought by the Semerjians, an Armenian family who left Turkey in 1921.*

Middle: This cabinetmaker's plane and grooving tool belonged to Karl Steitz, who emigrated from Germany around 1919.

Bottom: Rolling pin brought from Norway by the Underdahl family, ca. 1890. It has deeply cut parallel grooves for making lefse, *a traditional bread.*

Child's top brought by Francisco de Albuquerque Silva from Portugal in 1919.

Helen Ruby carried a favorite doll when she came to the United States from Austria around 1918.

"My mother brought candlesticks. You know, those were the things that you brought. And generally you bring the down feather bed which you just don't want to let go of. It's expensive and it's dowry."

Anne Littman, a Ukrainian Jewish immigrant in 1913

"I didn't have anything with me—only a small bottle of cognac my father gave me in case I got seasick."

Charles T. Anderson, a Swedish immigrant in 1925

Above: Playing cards brought from Austria-Hungary in 1910 by Josefine Schild, who also packed a brown shawl, a photograph album, and a diary with pressed flowers.

A story of a long delayed family reunion lies behind this handloomed wool blanket. In 1912, Katherine Stollmayer, age 18, left Arad, Hungary, to join older brother Joseph in Pittsburgh. She found work as a governess with a wealthy family. In 1924, she married John Schmidt, another native of Arad, and they had a child, Edward. In 1925, Katherine sent for her parents, Anton and Helen Stollmayer, who deeply missed their children. Among the belongings that the elderly couple carried with them on their journey from Hungary to America was this blanket, kept and preserved through generations, linking the old country with the new.

Opposite: James Reginald Ferguson, who came to the United States from Guyana around 1914, brought this coconut to remind him of his tropical homeland. Like many immigrants, he came to America via a circuitous route. His father, who owned a large store in Georgetown, Guyana, had sent James to Oxford University in England. Around 1914, the young man came to America with his souvenir coconut, four silver dollars, and his proudest possession—a British passport. He intended to stay just long enough to make some money and then return home. Instead he married a woman from Tennessee, Mae Singleton, and they settled in New York City, where their grandchildren and great grandchildren still reside.

Overleaf: Pillow cover made from silk rectangles that came in cigarette packages. This unusual item belonged to Gérard and Eugenie Gagnon Chénard, French Canadian immigrants who settled in New Hampshire in 1923.

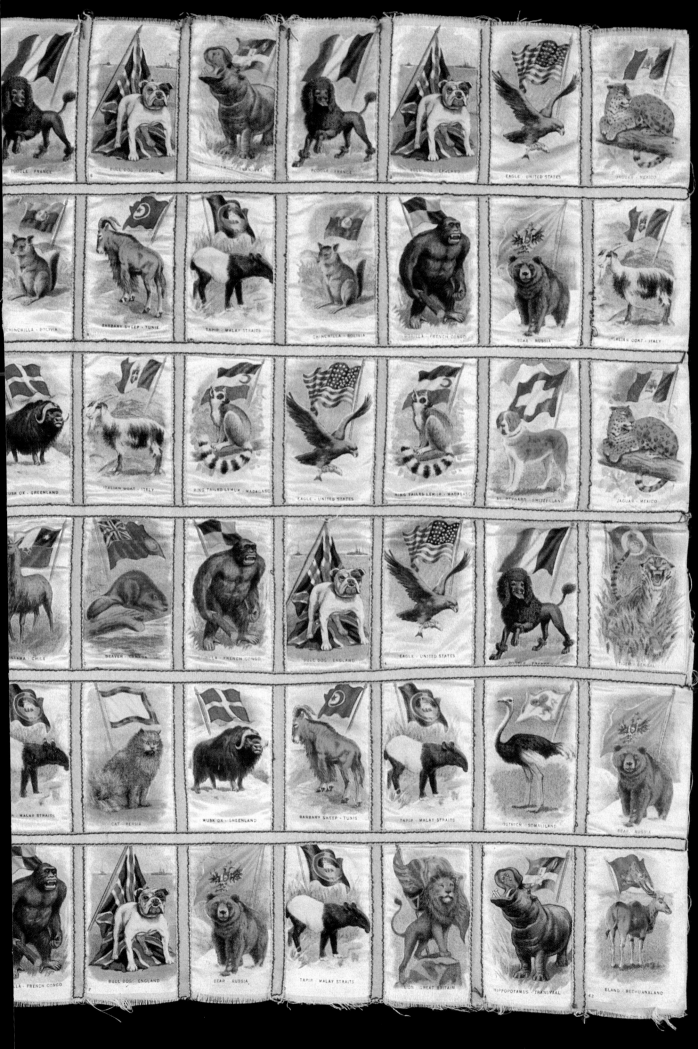

Family photographs were the most portable and easily saved mementos. These images, pressed into albums or displayed in the home, provided the most visible and direct connection with life in the homeland. Some of the photographs are well documented, accompanied by stories of triumph and tragedy—a difficult journey, a narrow escape, an untimely death, or a hard-won success. Other portraits can be only sketchily identified, the histories of their subjects obscured by the passage of time and failing memory. Nevertheless, the faces in these aging photographs convey a certain nobility as well as the determination and courage needed to pull up roots and travel to an unfamiliar world.

Marthina Pettersen, who emigrated from Grimstad, Norway, in 1893, carried this photograph of her sister (seated) and two nieces. Marthina settled in New York City with her husband, Christian, and two-year-old son, Abraham.

*Imkeri and brother Risto Sjöman in Pori, Finland. The children's widowed
mother had immigrated to Fitchburg, Massachusetts, in 1912, and brought
her children over later. Imkeri was nine years old when she left Finland in
1914. Risto joined them in 1916. Imkeri, who became Ingrid in America,
recalled that "Fitchburg had a regular area where everything was Finnish,
so that's why so many of them went to Fitchburg. There was plenty of work*

*Gertrude Itak Decker was five years old in 1907, when she came to the
United States from Austria-Hungary. The youngest in her family, she
traveled with parents Eva and Joseph, brothers John, Michael, Frank, and
Joseph, and sister Eva. They were on their way to join three older children*

Lilly Hollander Hovsepian, born in 1906 in Budapest, Hungary, posed for this portrait before immigrating to the United States in 1912. The photograph, the dress she is wearing, and a set of children's blocks were among the things she brought to America.

Pauline Baum Nismann is five years old in this photograph, taken shortly before she emigrated with her mother from Bialystok, Poland, in 1912. Their departure was a perilous escape from government officials. Her mother could not afford to pay a fine for selling foreign goods. Afraid she would be arrested, she hid with relatives until passage to the United States could be arranged. Pauline wrote: "Since our departure was so harrowing, we didn't salvage much, and there really wasn't all that much to salvage."

Agnes + Otto Hamer
Hamburg 1900

Top: Agnes and Otto Hamer, sister and brother, came from Hamburg,
Germany, as teenagers in the 1890s. They settled in Chicago.

Bottom: John and Ruica, cousins left behind by Ruth Brancu Watka in her
village of Pesac, Romania, when she came to America, around 1908.

Bella and Zelman (later Solomon) Reichman emigrated from Poland in 1923. Zelman was a cantor, but when he came to America he earned his livelihood from ritual slaughtering and from performing wedding ceremonies.

Vilhelm Ragner Hedman, a Swedish carpenter, immigrated to Vermont in 1923. The following year, his wife Elin and daughter Birgitta joined him. "He was the courageous adventurer," his daughter recalled, "looking for a better life for his family. My father never returned to Sweden, as we were here only six years when he died in 1930 at the young age of 39."

Sonya Jochenson Burlant when she was 16 years old and living in Uscilug, Poland, 1919. She married Nathan Burlant, who went to the United States in 1927, leaving Sonya with their newborn son Paul. Nathan settled in New York City, bought a horse and wagon, and made his living peddling seltzer and soda door-to-door. Two years after his arrival, he was able to send for his wife and son.

*The Reverend Mark E. Petrakis, wife Stella, and children (clockwise)
Barbara, Manuel, Tasula, and Dan. Parents and children alike give the
camera a level and steady gaze in this portrait taken on the eve of their
departure from Crete in 1916. They were on their way to Utah, where their
father would serve as priest for a congregation of immigrant Cretan coal
miners. The family's American-born son Harry wrote, "All of life, my
father often said, was a miracle we must try to deserve each day. And the
greatest miracle in his life, he told us, was to have brought his family to*

*Abraham Shavinovitz, from Kadzidlo, Poland, came to New York in
1905 and worked as a buttonhole maker on the Lower East Side. He stayed
in America for seven years and managed to bring over his oldest son, Isadore,
who brought over his brother Henry. When Abraham returned to Poland,
his sons remained in the United States and were later joined by two more*

SECESSIONS-FORMAT

Left: Onni Koskinen in 1917, dressed in his Finnish naval uniform. In 1928, he immigrated to the United States with wife Laila Wilhelmina and sons Eero and Esko. They sailed to New York on the White Star Line's S.S. Majestic, and then traveled to Onni's brother's farm in Roxbury, Connecticut. Later the family moved to Teaneck, New Jersey, where Onni found work as a mason.

Middle: Michel Dorogoi before he left Latvia in 1914. He settled in Tennessee and changed his name to Michael Brown.

Right: Rudolph Wolf at age 20, in Czechoslovakia, 1904. When he was 27, Wolf worked his way to the United States as a waiter. He met his future wife, Maria Theresa Spaller, in Vienna and sent for her once he had settled in New York City. In 1913, two years after his arrival, she followed to marry him. Wolf, who became a citizen in 1924, made his living as a chef and baker. He and Maria had one daughter and three sons.

When Antoinette Musico left her Italian home in 1907, she carried photographs of her friends, including the one shown above.

Top: *Abraham and Shushan Hartunian with their five children in Marash, Turkey. The Armenian family immigrated to the United States in 1922 to escape persecution by the Turks. They settled in Philadelphia.*

Bottom: *The Kiyonaga family of Hiroshima, Japan, sent this portrait to 18-year-old daughter Isayo in California. She had left home in 1918 to join her husband, Eiichi Yoshida.*

Top: Willy Clemmensen, the boy on the right, came to the United States as a ship's cabin boy when he was 16 years old, ca. 1915. Here he is pictured with his family in Denmark.

Bottom: Mathias and Katherine Henges and children, ethnic Germans who lived in Russia where Mathias was a supervisor in a glass factory. They immigrated to America in 1910.

When Wai Murata's parents emigrated from Hiroshima, Japan, to start a new life in America, they left their little daughter in the care of her grand-mother. Five years later, in 1916, they sent for Wai, who at age 11 sailed unaccompanied to Seattle on the Mexico Maru. *She joined her family in Colorado, then later married George Konishi, another Japanese immigrant. They lived on a dairy farm in Fort Lupton, where they had fifteen children.*

Celia Adler traveled from Russia to the United States in 1914. Her sister, who had immigrated earlier, convinced her to cut her long braids so she would "look more American." Embarrassed by the new look, Celia made a special hat to hide her short hairdo.

BELA VALENTINE ANDREW
FIUME HUNGARY 1912
JUST BEFORE SAILING TO AMERICA.

Bela, Valentine, and Andrew Solyom in Fiume, Austria-Hungary, before sailing to America in 1912 to join their father in Illinois. The brothers wore new travel suits their mother made for them from the same bolt of cloth. "It took mother six months to get the family ready to leave," wrote their oldest son years later. "Finally the great day arrived.... Goodbyes were said to our many friends as we boarded the SS Carpathia.... The three Solyom boys were all over that great ship, and found particular favor with the captain, who often gave us candy in the pilot house."

Minna Warrett, who came to the United States around 1912, cherished this photo of her friends back in Kamenets Podolskiy, Ukraine.

Two-year-old Maljan Chavoor, son of Assyrian parents who lived in
Harput, Turkey, ca. 1913. Following World War I, Maljan's grandparents, who had emigrated in 1905, sent money to his widowed mother to
bring her children to America. Maljan, his two sisters, and mother spent two
difficult years on the road. Arriving in New York in October 1922, they
were detained on Ellis Island for three weeks because one of the sisters was
blind. A successful appeal to Washington, however, gained their admission
to the country, and they were allowed to proceed to their final destination in
California. At long last, they were reunited with Maljan's grandparents
and other family members.

Maria Valvert Goussé and year-old daughter Marthe in Antwerp,
Belgium, prior to emigration in 1909. The baby died of diphtheria in 1911,
after a year in the United States.

> **"The teddy bear was part of Switzerland. It really was. It was part of Frutigen. It was part of everybody over there. And that's probably why I never wanted another doll. He was just it."**
>
> Gertrude Schneider Smith, an immigrant from Switzerland in 1921

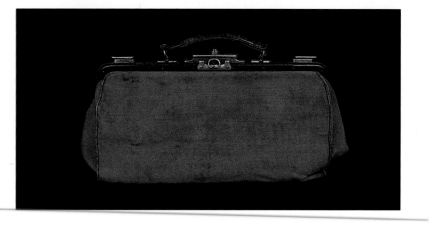

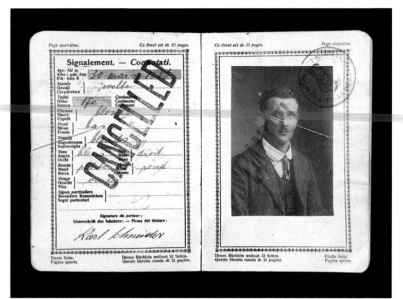

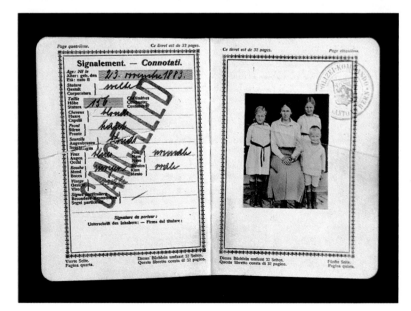

Top: Johann Carl Schneider's passport.

Bottom: Marie Isler Schneider and children's passport. Gertrude and Raymond are on the right and Margaret is on the left.

Gertrude Schneider Smith came to the United States in 1921 with her mother, brother, and sister. They were rejoining father Johann Carl Schneider, who had left their village of Frutigen in Switzerland the year before. "My father was what you would call a protestor," Mrs. Smith said. "Because he didn't like the way the workers were treated. He was sort of put on a blacklist, and he couldn't get a job. Someone said to him, why don't you try America? America is the land of golden opportunity." So Johann Schneider borrowed some money, packed up his belongings in a small canvas satchel, and set sail from Le Havre, France. After a stormy two-week voyage, he arrived at Ellis Island and then went to upstate New York, where he found work on a dairy farm.

When the rest of the family followed him, they packed up their household belongings, a feather bed, photographs, and, for Gertrude, a teddy bear. "He was in the trunk, though. I didn't have him to hug during our trip over here." What else did they take with them? "Whatever we wore on our backs, plus some really good clothing like the pinafores Mother put on us when we landed in New York—so we'd look pretty for my father when he came to pick us up."

Of their stop at Ellis Island, Gertrude remembers: "It was a huge place and it seemed so dark. It was very scary because we knew no English at all. They were giving us directions, but what they meant, we had no idea. We finally ended up in a huge hall, where there were big tables and benches. And we had to wait there until my father came after us."

The Schneiders eventually settled in Connecticut. When the children attended school, they Americanized their names: Werner became Raymond and Trudi became Gertrude. Their father changed his middle name from Karl to Carl. Getting accustomed to their new home was difficult at first, especially because they were homesick. "I felt that I would never see anybody again," recalled Gertrude. "Because it was so far away. And to hear my parents talk, it seemed like it was the end of the earth."

Top: Canvas satchel carried by Johann Carl Schneider on his journey to New York in 1920.

Opposite: Gertrude Schneider Smith's teddy bear, given by an uncle to console her after her favorite porcelain doll broke.

"I was born to be the rebel in my family," Nathan Solomon wrote about his decision to come to America. "I asked my family to leave and to establish a candy, cake, and biscuit factory, our going business, in any country where the Jew has equality. They rejected my plea."

In 1923, Nathan Solomon, born Naftuly Salamon, having determined to escape the anti-Jewish sentiment in his homeland, left his beloved parents, sister, and four brothers in Sambor, Poland. He was 23 years old when he sailed on the R.M.S. *Mauretania* to New York. But before he could start his new life he had to go to Ellis Island to undergo inspection.

"The physician took his time," he recalled. "He inspected my eyes and said, 'Uh oh, trachoma.'" While Solomon was detained on the island, the Hebrew Immigrant Aid Society appealed to New York City Congressman Samuel Dickstein to intervene on his behalf. The young immigrant was released after three weeks, and soon after found a job as a certified candymaker at $27 a week. In 1926, he and a cousin opened a small dairy store, and within three years Solomon owned five of his own stores.

During the 1930s, when Nazism was on the rise, Solomon tried to bring his family over to the United States. Because of the quota system enacted in the early 1920s, however, they could not get permission to enter the country. The restrictions on immigration had tragic consequences for the family. During the Holocaust, Solomon's parents, sister, brothers, aunts, and many cousins perished.

In 1931, Nathan Solomon became a citizen, and in the following year he married Irene Oransky, who had emigrated from Kiev at the age of six months. They had a long and happy marriage and prospered in America. In his later years, Nathan Solomon wrote two books of poetry dedicated to his relatives who lost their lives in Poland. Nathan and Irene Solomon leave an important legacy to their two children, five grandchildren, and two great grandchildren. "My father is tremendously in love with this country," explained his son, Solomon S. Solomon, "and the fact that it gave him freedom. This love was intensified by the fact that his whole family was wiped out in Auschwitz. He fostered that love of country in my sister and myself."

Above: Nathan Solomon's family—mother, sister, brothers, aunts, and cousins—in front of their candy store in Sambor, Poland. All died in the Holocaust.

Top: Nathan Solomon, ca. 1921.

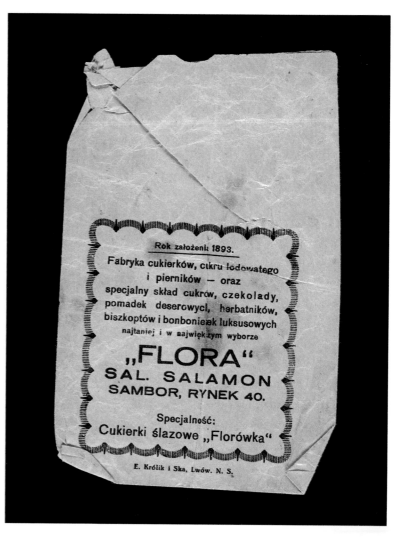

Top: When Nathan Solomon came to the United States, mother Gelle Solomon gave him this beater, called czepaczka *in Polish, and reminded him to use it to beat his pillows and quilts every Friday morning in preparation for the Sabbath.*

Bottom and right: Nathan Solomon brought his family's candy recipes, handwritten by his mother in Yiddish, and a bag of candy when he immigrated in 1923. The Salamon family had owned and operated a candy business, "Flora," since 1893. The family history in Poland can be traced back 200 years.

"In Croatia I enjoyed my godparents as really my real parents. They never talked about my mother and father in America. So, in other words, I didn't know that there was somebody in America. I didn't even know where America was or heard of America. Nothing."

Louis Zauneker, an immigrant from Yugoslavia in 1923

Top: Louis (Lajos) Zauneker's passport.

Bottom: Crocheted doily brought by Joseph and Klara Vukan.

Louis Zauneker's journey to America was delayed for nearly twelve years. His parents, Joseph and Klara Vukan, had emigrated separately from Croatia to Pennsylvania, where they met and married. In 1911, they decided to return home to introduce each other to their respective families. While in Europe, their son Louis (Lajos) was born. To celebrate the great event, "they had a big get-together," said Louis. "They brought baby gifts, wedding gifts, and farewell gifts." The following year, Joseph and Klara returned to the United States, leaving their baby in the care of his godparents. The separation was supposed to be brief, but soon after the young couple arrived in Pennsylvania, the father died of tuberculosis. Tragedy was followed by other troubles, and many years would intervene before Louis and his mother could be reunited. While the outbreak of World War I closed all shipping lanes to Europe, the child remained with his godparents, who he came to believe were his real parents. Meantime, his mother remarried and moved to Ohio.

Finally, in 1923, Klara was able to return for her son. Louis described their meeting: "One day, I was coming home from school, and a lady was coming toward me, dressed beautifully. When she came near us, she asked, which was Louis, and they pointed to me right away. And she came over to me, and she says, 'You're my son, I'm your mother.' And I said, 'No you're not' and just kept pushing her away. Well, when somebody comes out of nowhere and says, 'I'm your mother,' you can't believe it.

"When they came with the horse and buggy to take us to Germany to catch the boat, all of my neighbors, everybody came over. They were crying that we'll never see you again. You're leaving us and all that. That's all I had to hear. So I was crying. My godparents were crying. Everybody was crying.

"When we pulled in to New York we saw the Statue of Liberty. Everybody went on top deck. And of course we were happy. I remember that we were standing there listening to the music, and a lady came up and took my hat off and told me that I should hold it in my hand, because I should be proud that I'm in America."

The last leg of their journey was a train ride to Cleveland, Ohio. Lajos became Louis Zauneker, taking his stepfather's family name.

Top: Dresser scarf embroidered "Jo reggelt!" (Good Morning!), one of the wedding presents given to Joseph and Klara Vukan during their visit to Croatia in 1911.

Bottom left: Klara (Vukan) Zauneker traveled with a U.S. passport when she returned to Yugoslavia in 1923.

Bottom right: Louis Zauneker and mother Klara outside their Cleveland ice cream store, 1924.

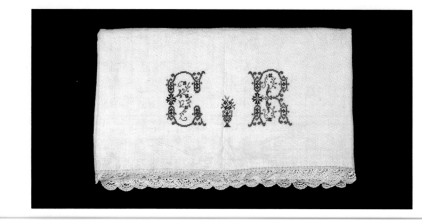

Alba Stramesi Fiorentino's father Giovanni immigrated to the United States in 1901. He went to Northampton, Massachusetts, to work in the Belding Silk Mill, where his brother Paolo already had a job. Mrs. Fiorentino recounted her parents' story. "My father came from Biella, Piedmont, which is in the northern part of Italy, at the foot of the Alps. And there he met my mother Rosina Comoglio and proposed marriage to her. She thought she could accept but she wanted to think it over. So he came to America and he wrote her letters. He made hearts and told her how much he loved her. He hardly knew her. He kept writing to my mother to have her come over to America and get married. And finally she agreed to come. So, in 1903, she sailed in steerage. It was so filthy and dirty, and the food was horrible. She ate nothing but water and lemons. And here she was, knowing that she would arrive and have to get married or be returned to Italy. She had to get married right then and there on Ellis Island after they had examined her to see if she was in good health."

Rosina Comoglio arrived at Ellis Island with a trunk. "In the trunk she had her trousseau, all her dresses, all these very fine things. She must have started working on these things when she was very young. My mother had one passion in life, and that was sewing. She loved to sew. She would lose herself in sewing. It started in Italy. They would sit there in that little circle of people, about ten, twenty of them. They would sing songs, they would tell stories." Mrs. Fiorentino pointed to one of her mother's towels, embroidered with her initials. "You must always embroider in your name," she explained. "Your single name, not after you're married. Because these are yours."

The Stramesis settled in Northampton's Italian ward, where they raised their two daughters, Alba and Rita. Giovanni had ten acres of land, which he farmed at night after working all day as a weaver in the local mill. Despite all the hardships, "we learned to enjoy life," recalled Alba, "to have a vivid imagination, and to believe in people. And yet keep one eye open. You know what I mean?"

Marriage Contract.

We, Giovanni Stramesi residing at 84 Williams St - Northampton Mass. and Rosa Camoglio residing at Ellis Island ex SS. La Touraine hereby agree to marry and become husband and wife, and to assume the marriage relation and the obligations thereto pertaining.

Executed in duplicate at Ellis Island, County of New York, State of New York, on the first day of August 1903.

Stramesi Giovanni
Comoglio Rosina

Signed and delivered
in the presence of:

Name, Frederick C. diGiovanni
Residence, Springfield ave. Cranford N.J.
Name, Elizabeth A. FitzGerald
Residence, 307 Hicks St. Brooklyn N.Y.

State of New York,
County of New York, ss.:

On this first day of August 1903, before me personally came Giovanni Stramesi and Rosa Camoglio known to me to be the individuals described in and who executed the foregoing instrument, and severally acknowledged that they executed the same with a full understanding of its contents and purport; and on said day also personally before me came Frederick C. diGiovanni and Elizabeth A. Fitzgerald known to me to be the individuals whose names and addresses are subscribed to the said instrument as witnesses, and severally acknowledged that they witnessed the execution of said instrument and subscribed their names and addresses thereto in the presence of the parties to the same.

Notary Public, New York County

Top left: Embroidered linen sheet made by Rosina Comoglio for her trousseau.

Top right: Key to Giovanni Stramesi's house in Biella. He kept it in case he ever returned to Italy.

Bottom right: Marriage contract between Giovanni Stramesi and Rosina Comoglio, 1903. Her residence is listed as Ellis Island.

Above: This 1924 photograph shows Mary Kudrna Garba wearing an outfit her mother made for her. She brought this costume with her from Czechoslovakia.

Left: Sampler made by Mary Kudrna Garba as a school project and presented to her father, whom she met for the first time in Pennsylvania.

In December 1912, Frank Kudrna said goodbye to his wife Anna (who was pregnant with their second child) and son Jan, and journeyed from their home in Sardice, Czechoslovakia, to America. He would not see his family again for ten years. World War I closed down most European ports from 1914 to 1919, and after the war, the First Quota Act restricted immigration from eastern Europe to the United States. By 1923, however, Frank Kudrna, who worked in a Pennsylvania steel mill, had arranged ocean passage for his wife, son, and daughter Mary, whom he had never seen.

Anna packed up her household belongings in a large wicker suitcase and came. Her daughter later wrote about their journey on the *Orbita*, "I became the ship's pet, and could go anywhere." Dressed in elaborately embroidered native clothes, she was a favorite subject for amateur photographers traveling in first-class. She also recalled the excitement of meeting her father for the first time. "We got off the train in Leetsdale, Pennsylvania, and some people were walking. And they said, 'Oh, so you're Frank Kudrna's wife and children.' They were so excited, because everybody knew we were coming. So they took us where he lived. And when he came, well, I kind of looked at him, and he looked at me."

Haig Semerjian, born Haigazoon Semerdjian, an Armenian, lived in Konya, Turkey, with his wife Virginia (Verghin) and their four children. He and his brother owned a prosperous shop selling fabrics, especially for women's gowns. His brother often traveled to Europe and England to select and purchase material. The Semerjians had a tranquil life and enjoyed being part of a close-knit, extended family of grandparents, aunts, uncles, and many cousins.

Their lives changed radically, however, in 1915, when a new wave of violence broke out against Armenians living in Turkey. For a time the Semerjians remained in Konya. Haig helped distribute American relief funds to Armenian refugees and opened his home to those in need. His courtyard was often crowded with people seeking or distributing aid and advice.

Eventually, the Semerjians were forced to leave their home. They made their way to Constantinople (today's Istanbul), where they waited for other family members to join them before they left for America. Some of their closest relatives, however, could not escape the violence that was sweeping the Turkish countryside. Virginia's parents and younger brother were among the more than a million Armenians who perished.

In 1921, having waited over a year, Haig, Virginia, and their four children, as well as Virginia's sister and her family, left Constantinople and took a small boat to Piraeus, Greece. They waited about two weeks for the Greek ship *Alexandria* to take them to the port of New York. Daughter Alice, who was seven years old at the time of the journey, recalled little of their stay on Ellis Island, except a brief vignette: "On our last day on Ellis Island, my mother and I took a last walk around the main hall. I panicked when I became separated from her. When I came upon her, she was in conversation with two young Black women dressed in colorful robes and turbans. It was my first sight of Black people. More amazingly, my mother was talking to them in English!"

Released from Ellis Island, the Semerjians took a train to Philadelphia, where they settled. They brought many cherished items with them, among them silk scarves passed down through Virginia's family, a book she was awarded in school for oratorical excellence, school notebooks, jewelry, and Bibles, including the one Virginia carried on her wedding day in 1909.

Above: Child's dress, ca. 1912. Marjorie Semerjian wore this as a little girl and then passed it along to Alice.

Opposite top: Virginia and Haig's wedding portrait. Virginia was valedictorian of her graduating class at the American School for Girls in Talas, Turkey. Her speech greatly impressed Haig's mother, who decided that Virginia was the right woman for her son. She initiated negotiations, and the two were married in July 1909.

Opposite bottom: Portrait of Alice and Marjorie, the older Semerjian daughters.

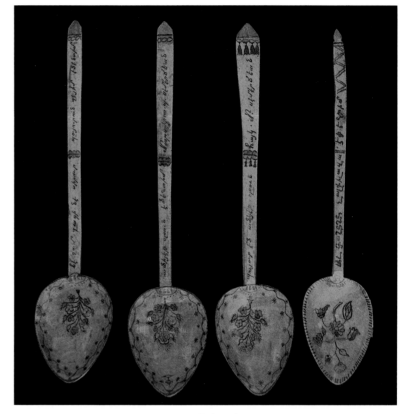

Lacquered wooden spoons painted with family names by Haig Semerjian as a boy.

233

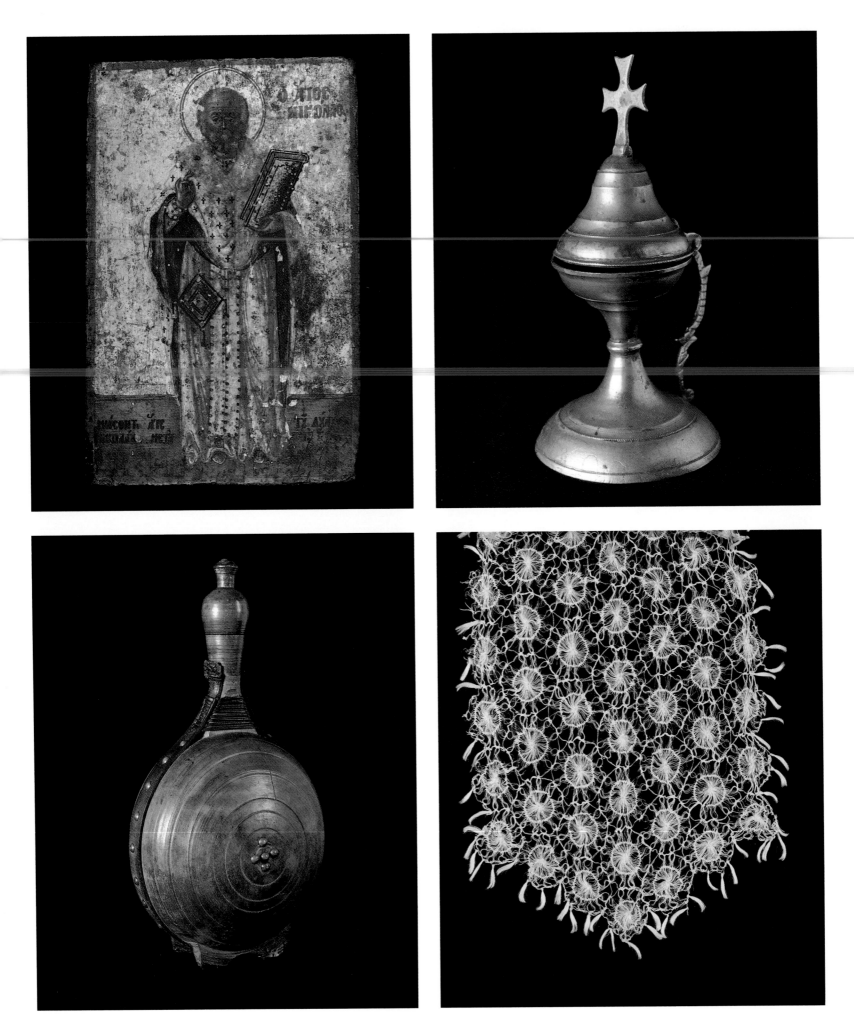

In 1921, Harold Perris, born Iparhos Perdikis, came to the United States with his parents, Alexandros and Ellas, aboard the S.S. *Themistocles*. The family settled in Yonkers, New York, where Alexandros opened a restaurant. Harold, who was 16 years old when he immigrated, described some of the belongings that his parents brought from their home in Larnaca, Cyprus—religious and household objects of a family life rooted in the traditions of the Greek community. Their *thimiaton*, topped with a cross, was part of a daily ritual. "Three times a day, my mother would take three leaves, lift the top, put the leaves in there, burn them. And when they stop burning they produce a very beautiful aroma from the olive tree. The olive branch is the sign of peace, so she did that three times a day in our home to keep peace in the family and tranquility." The icon of St. Nicholas, he said, "could be in my family for about two, three hundred years. When the painting is done as a whole figure, it belongs to the Byzantine era."

His mother's shawl typifies the delicate handicrafts practiced by women. "She washed the wool and then she spun it. And from that she made this wonderful shawl. I had a premonition that that shawl was going to be a masterpiece. So I made sure that I kept it well."

Harold led a full life in New York. "From that beautiful city I got my dreams," he said. "I watched the signs on Broadway of the dancers and show people. And I sat down one day and I said, why should I wash dishes? So, after I worked and started making money, I went to a very wonderful dance teacher, and I said, I want to be a dancer." Harold eventually became part of a dance team, Perzade and Jetan, and performed in vaudeville theatres and nightclubs throughout the country.

Photo of Harold Perris as a boy, ca. 1916.

Opposite top left: Icon of St. Nicholas, painted in the Byzantine tradition.

Opposite top right: Thimiaton, *used for burning olive leaves.*

Opposite bottom left: Wooden flask for water or wine. A gift from an old friend, it expressed thanks for Alexandros Perdikis's help at a time of need.

Opposite bottom right: Shawl made by Ellas Perdikis.

Above: Jenny Mirelowitz and her children, Mary, Harry, and Hyman, in Vilnius, ca. 1904.

Right: Barnett Mirelowitz, in a Russian uniform, and his son Hyman, ca. 1900. "He was indoctrinated into the army," his grandson said, "and served his time and then was released. He was a very stern man. He was quick to remember the hard years in escaping the pursuit of the Cossacks."

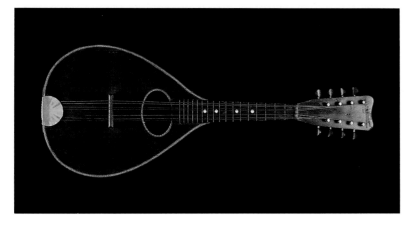

Barnett Chadekel, a former soldier in the Czar's army, lived with his wife Jenny and their three children in Vilnius, Lithuania, until 1909, when pogroms against Jews forced them to flee. A grandson, Stanley Mirel, recalled that his grandparents had to change their name to escape the authorities: "My grandfather came from a very wealthy family," he said. "They had factories where they manufactured glass in Vilnius. While in flight from the persecution, they adopted my grandmother's maiden name. That's why our name has been Mirelowitz since they came to the United States." The family made its way to Hamburg, Germany, then boarded the *President Grant* to New York.

"They were a very handsome couple," Mirel continued. "When they came to this country, they lived down on the lower end of Manhattan, and eventually they bought a farm up in Accord, New York. They had 116 acres, and it was beautiful. They had rented bungalows and they had chickens and some cows for fresh milk. My grandmother was a beautiful tall woman; she was loving and generous. After coming to this country and abandoning all her wealth on the other side, she ended up being a farmer's wife and struggling. I recall her on the farm many times milking cows and taking the milk and making cheese.

"Grandfather spoke at least three languages, but he spoke only Yiddish to the farm animals, who understood him very well. He was very assertive when he called the cows, and the cows came. He told them what to do and they did it. He was an enormous man. Probably the strongest man I ever saw in my life. On one Yom Kippur, I was sitting with him, and a young rabbi was given a *shofar*, which is the ram's horn, to blow. And he tried and tried and he really could not blow it. And so finally my grandfather said, 'Let me help you.' And he took the ram's horn and I thought he was going to knock the windows out. It sounded like a trumpet call.

"One of the nice things that I recall very vividly is when all the men would get together on a Saturday. Sometimes it was a prayer meeting and sometimes it was a social gathering. They were so happy. And they all agreed on one thing. As poor as they were here, they were so much better off than they were in the old country, where they were persecuted and had a very tough life. In this country, they came and went as they pleased. They settled where they liked. They worshipped where they pleased. We take it for granted. But it was something they cherished."

Top left: Mandolin brought by the Mirelowitz family when they came to America.

Top right: Two glass pitchers, each bearing a Star of David on the bottom.

Bottom right: Birth certificate for Harry Mirelowitz, witnessed by a government-appointed rabbi. The document is dated 1903 and indicates that the child was circumcised eight days after his birth.

Overleaf: Wheel and sign salvaged from the old Ellis Island ferry.

237

This Indenture made the Twenty seventh Day of November in the Year of our Lord one Thousand seven Hundred and sixty seven. Between Samuel Hunt of Middletown in the County of Monmouth in the Province of New Jersey Farmer, and Isabella his Wife of the one Part and John Beekman of the City of New York Merchant of the other Part. Witnesseth that the said Samuel Hunt and Isabella his Wife for and in Consideration of the Sum of Ten Shillings current Money of the Province of New York to them in Hand well and truly paid by the said John Beekman at or before the Execution hereof the Receipt whereof is hereby Acknowledged have and each of them hath granted, bargained and sold, And by these Presents do and each of them doth grant, bargain and sell unto the said John Beekman. All that certain Island, commonly known by the Name of Oyster Island situate lying and being in Hudsons River or the Bay of New York opposite the City of New York and between the said City and the Bergen Shore, in the Province of East New Jersey, and near to a certain Island called Bedloes Island. Together with all and singular the Houses, Buildings, Hereditaments, Improvements, Rights, Members, Priviledges, Advantages, Commodities, and Appurtenances whatsoever thereunto belonging or in any Wise Appertaining. And the Reversion and Reversions, Remainder and Remainders, Rents, Issues, and Profits thereof. To have and to Hold all and singular the said Premises hereby granted, bargained and sold with their and every of their Appurtenances unto the said John Beekman his Executors Administrators and Assigns, from the Day next before the Day of the Date of these Presents for and during and until the full End and

(Term)

Term of one whole Year thence next ensuing and fully to be compleat and ended. Yielding and Paying therefor the Rent of one Pepper Corn on the last Day of the said Term if demanded. To the Intent that by Virtue of these Presents and also by Force of the Statute made for Transferring Uses into Possession, he the said John Beekman may be in the actual Possession of all and singular the said Premises hereby granted, Bargained and sold with the Appurtenances. And thereby be enabled to accept and take a Grant and Release of the Fee Reversion and Inheritance thereof to him his Heirs and Assigns for ever. In Witness whereof the Parties to these Presents have hereunto interchangeably set their Hands and Seals the Day and Year first before written.

Sealed and Delivered in the Presence of us, by the before named Isabella Hunt.

mary Allaine

Cha: Morss

Sealed and delivered in the Presence of us, by the before named Samuel Hunt.

Joseph Price

Joseph Price Junr

Sam.l Hunt

Isabella Hunt

Deed of sale for "Oyster Island," 1767. John Beekman paid Samuel and Isabella Hunt 10 shillings for the island. The property was known by many names. Native Americans called it Kioshk, or Gull Island. Maps and historical accounts identify it as Dyre's Island, after one of its owners; Bucking Island, for unknown reasons; Gibbet Island, for a number of hangings that occurred there; and Anderson Island, for one of those hanged.

Island Chronicles

Though the histories of Ellis Island and of immigration to America were closely intertwined for three tumultuous decades, the island itself has a story all its own. About 10,000 years ago, it was part of the mainland and an ideal observation hill from which Native Americans could spot wild game. By 1,500 years ago, the rising seas had created an island surrounded by rich oyster beds. While this speck of land was never inhabited, Native Americans often went there to hunt small game, gather oysters, and fish for shad and striped bass. Later, American colonists visited the island for much the same reasons.

Over several hundred years, the island has been known by a succession of names, but its most descriptive was Oyster Island, used even by Samuel Ellis, who became owner by the 1780s. "That pleasant situated island," as Ellis called it in an advertisement for its sale, was a favorite spot for day-trippers who wanted to dig for oysters or enjoy the view of New York's busy harbor. Ellis failed to sell his island, which was inherited by his descendants.

In 1808, when the country was preparing for war with Great Britain, the U.S. War Department selected Ellis Island as a site for a fort. New York State bought the island, which by that time had several claimants, and then conveyed ownership to the federal government. The military fortified the island with a barracks, a powder magazine, and a battery of cannons. But like its counterparts around New York Harbor—Fort Wood on Bedloe's Island, Castle Williams on Governors Island, and Castle Clinton at the Battery—Ellis Island's Fort Gibson never saw action. During the War of 1812, the British navy blockaded the city but never attempted a direct attack.

After the war, Fort Gibson became a munitions dump, which during the Civil War accumulated large amounts of surplus gunpowder. When peace came, nothing was done to deplete the store of munitions, and the danger of an explosion alarmed neighboring communities in New Jersey and New York. One New Jersey congressman warned in 1876 that if the island were struck by lightning, "the shock would destroy Jersey City, Hoboken, and parts of New York." Not until 1890 did Congress adopt legislation directing the War Department to clear Ellis Island of its dangerous stockpile. Before the bill passed, however, it was amended to provide an initial appropriation of $75,000 to "improve Ellis Island for immigration purposes."

That same year, Castle Garden (formerly Castle Clinton), New York State's immigration depot located in Battery Park, had closed amid accusations that immigrants were being harassed and cheated

Samuel Ellis's advertisement for "Oyster Island," published in Loudon's New-York Packet, *January 20, 1785.*

By a Scale of Four Inches to a Mile

HUDSON's or NORTH RIVER.

City of New York

EAST RIVER

BROOKLYN

LONG ISLAND

WEST MUD FLAT

MUD FLAT

STATEN ISLAND

Robins Reef

The Kills

NARROWS

ENG DEP
U. STATES
TOP. BUREAU

A
Chart
of the
HARBOUR of NEW YORK
with the
Soundings between the Narrows and the City,
from an Actual Survey made under the direction of
Committees of the Corporation and the Military
By
Captain Isaac Kearney Marine and Charles Loss City Surveyor
in 1798.

The soundings are calculated for low Water mark and in fathoms, except
those marked f which are in feet.

Copied
By John S Hunn Street Commissioner
for the
Corporation of New-York
October
1807.

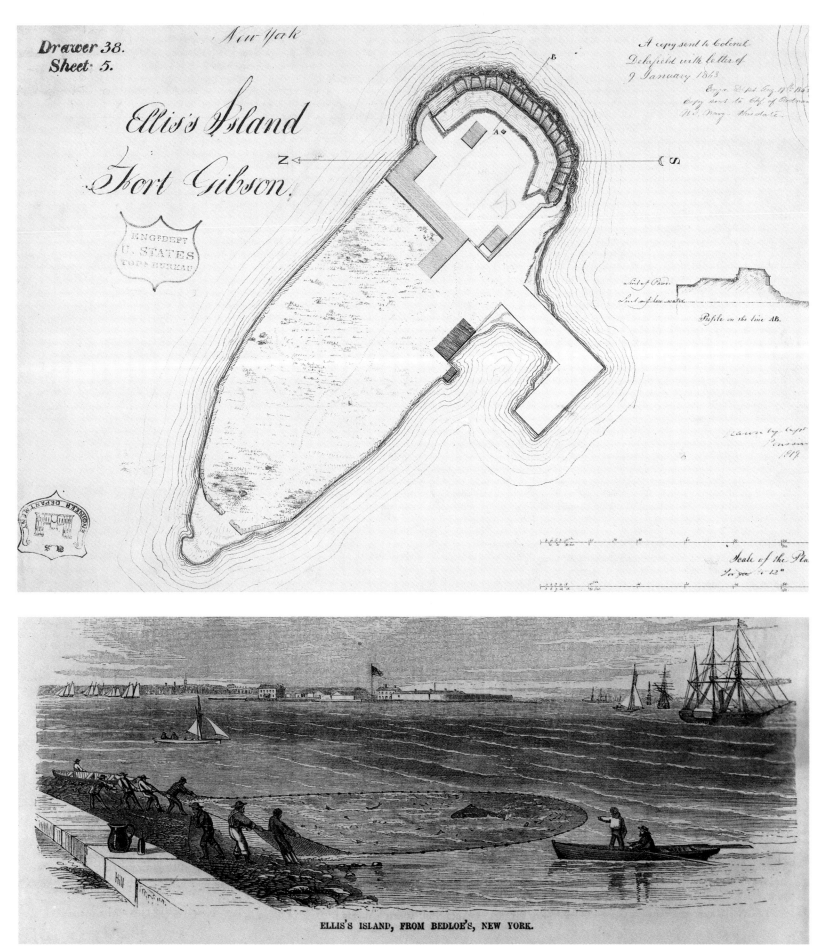

Opposite: An 1807 map of Upper New York Bay showing Ellis Island northeast of the "West Mud Flat."

Top: Military plan of Ellis Island's Fort Gibson, 1819.

Bottom: View of Ellis Island, ca. 1850.

District of the City of New York, Port of New York.

I, _____ Master of the s s "Nevada" do solemnly, sincerely and truly declare

that the following List or Manifest, subscribed by me, and now delivered by me to the Collector of the Customs of the Collection District of the City of New York, is a full and perfect list of all the passengers taken on board the said vessel at Liverpool & Queenstown from which port said vessel has now arrived; and that on said list is truly designated the age, the sex, and the calling of each of said passengers, the location of the compartment or space occupied by each during the passage, the country of citizenship of each, and also the destination or location intended by each; and that said List or Manifest truly sets forth the number of said passengers who have died on said voyage, and the dates and causes of death, and the names and ages of those who died; also of the pieces of baggage of each; also a true statement, so far as it can be ascertained, with reference to the intention of each alien passenger as to a protracted sojourn in this country. So help me God.

Sworn to this 7 January 1892.

List or Manifest OF ALL THE PASSENGERS taken on board the s. s. Nevada whereof John A Rhodberg is Master, from Great Britain & Ireland burthen 2354 tons

No.	NAMES.	AGE. Years	Mths	SEX.	CALLING.	The country of which they are citizens.	Intended destination or location.	Date and cause of death.		Location of compartment or space occupied.	Number of pieces of baggage.	Transient, or in transit, or intending protracted sojourn.
					Embarked at Queenstown							
1	Ellie King	21		F	Spinster	Ireland	Nebraska	yes	yes	After Steerage Start	1	Pro Soj
2	Annie Moore	13		"	"	"	New York		"	"		"
3	Anthony	11		M	Child	"	"		"	"		"
4	Phillip	7		"	"	"	"		"	"		"
5	John Ryne	24		"	Laborer	"	Minnesota		"	4-3 Forward "		"
6	Mary	30		F	Wife	"	"		"	"	2	"
7	Michael Connell	20		M	Laborer	"	Connecticut	No	No	After " Port	1	"
					Embarked at Liverpool							
8	Posich Knop	50		M	Smith	Russia	New York	yes	yes	After Steerage Port	1	Pro Soj
9	Morris Moss	20		"	Machinist	England	"	"	"	"	1	"
10	Charles Kelly	45		"	Tailor	Ud. States	Trenton N.J.	"	" 1—0	"	1	"

EWALD THIEL

by state officials. The federal government stepped in and took complete control of immigration, placing it under the jurisdiction of the Treasury Department. The government decided that New York needed a new immigrant landing station, far removed from the petty criminal activity that had stigmatized Castle Garden. After much searching for an available site, the government chose Ellis Island.

Soon after Congress appropriated money for a new station, Fort Gibson's munitions dump was removed. Landfill doubled the island's size to approximately six acres. After two years of construction, Ellis Island's first station, a two-story-high structure of Georgia pine, opened on January 1, 1892. *Harper's Weekly* reported that the new building looked like a "latter-day watering place hotel, presenting to the view a great many-windowed expanse of buff-painted wooden walls, of blue-slate roofing, and of light and picturesque towers."

On opening day, the new commissioner of immigration for the port of New York, Col. John B. Weber, presented a $10 gold piece to the first immigrant to set foot on Ellis Island. She was 15-year-old Annie Moore, from County Cork, Ireland. "It was the first United States coin she had ever seen," a New York journalist wrote. "She says she will never part with it, but will always keep it as a pleasant memento of the occasion." Annie Moore, traveling with her two younger brothers, was met by her parents, Mary and Matt Moore, who had been in New York for two years.

Because of an economic depression during the 1890s, immigration traffic was light over the next several years, and inspectors at Ellis Island easily processed the approximately 200,000 aliens who arrived annually. It was fortunate indeed that the island was not busy on June 15, 1897. Early that morning a fire broke out in one of the towers of the wooden complex and quickly swept through all the buildings. The *New York Sun* reported: "The flames were shooting a hundred feet in the air, and by their light hundreds of people could be seen on the island rushing hither and thither."

One hundred and forty immigrants and a large force of employees were on the island when the fire broke out. Miraculously there was no loss of life. Commissioner of Immigration Joseph H. Senner said later, "Ever since I have been in office, the fear of something like this fire has haunted me, and now that it has come and no lives were lost I am glad of it. A row of unsightly, ramshackle tinderboxes has been removed, and when the Government rebuilds we'll be forced to put up decent fireproof structures." A major casualty of the fire was a

vast store of immigration records that was completely destroyed.

The government announced almost immediately that Ellis Island would be rebuilt. The Treasury Department awarded the contract for designing Ellis Island's new complex to the New York architectural firm of William A. Boring and Edward L. Tilton. Their proposal was selected in a competition entered by five outstanding firms, including McKim, Mead & White and Carrère & Hastings. Boring wrote triumphantly that winning the commission was "a great victory, the biggest architects were in the contest."

Construction began in September 1898, and was scheduled to be completed within twelve months. But strikes, contract disputes, and lack of skilled workmen delayed the opening of the new, fireproof, brick and stone station until December 17, 1900. The completed main building was hailed as a "magnificent" structure with facilities for inspection "admirably arranged." The *New York Times* of December 3, 1900, described the station as "an imposing as well as a pleasing addition to the picturesque water front of the metropolis." The writer extolled the exterior design, "a conglomeration of several styles of architecture, the predominating style being that of the French Renaissance," as well as its interior arrangements. "The transportation, examining, medical, inquiry, and various quarters...are so arranged as to follow one after the other, according to its proper place in the department."

The following year, 1901, the kitchen and laundry were completed, and in March 1902, Ellis Island's hospital opened on a second island made of landfill and connected to the main island by a walkway. Despite initial praise for the new complex, officials working on Ellis Island soon complained not only about the building's construction (repairs were a constant necessity) but also its design, which compelled all immigrants, many lugging baggage and children, to climb up one staircase and then down another during the inspection routine. The station's principal fault, however, was its size. The new

Top: Exterior view of the first station, ca. 1897.

Opposite top: Ship's manifest from S.S. Nevada, *January 1, 1892. Listed are Annie Moore, the first immigrant to set foot on Ellis Island, and her brothers.*

Opposite bottom: Registry Room of Ellis Island's first station, an enormous wooden structure, 1897.

complex was designed at a time when arrivals averaged around 200,000 each year. By the time it opened, however, immigration was beginning a sharp upturn, and the island's capacity to handle 500,000 annual arrivals, thought more than ample, was soon overwhelmed. Immigration to New York increased steadily, most years numbering between 600,000 and 900,000. In 1907, it broke the one million mark.

To keep pace with the growing numbers, new wings and additions were periodically tacked on to various buildings, and for a time a row of wooden barracks provided temporary quarters for detainees. These firetraps, torn down in 1910, were replaced by a large baggage and dormitory building located next to the main building. Despite the additions and new construction, the island's space and resources could not meet the demands of the task at hand. "Totally inadequate" were two words frequently used by immigration commissioners when asked to describe Ellis Island's capacity for inspecting the enormous number of arrivals in New York.

Managing Ellis Island was a highly visible, high-pressure job, and the commissioner of immigration, the embattled man at the gate, generally lasted no more than four years. The exception was William Williams, whose long tenure and organizational ability loom large in Ellis Island's history. Williams served two separate terms, 1902 to 1905 and 1909 to 1913. The interim period was filled by Robert Watchorn, an immigrant himself, who was also an able administrator. During the peak years of immigration, these two men managed America's chief immigration station and coped with its complex amalgam of heartbreaking ordeals, overcrowded living conditions, and dishonest concessionaires.

They also had to defend themselves and their policies against sometimes scathing attacks in the press. Williams, because of his anti-immigration views and restrictionist policies, was a prime target for the pro-immigration foreign-language press. New York's *Staats-Zeitung* regularly ran stories about abuses on Ellis Island under headlines such as "Hell's Island," "Tyrannical Despotism," and "Disgrace for the Country." The attacks became so vitriolic that Williams asked President Theodore Roosevelt to appoint a committee to investigate the paper's allegations. On September 16, 1903, Roosevelt himself came to inspect the island and, according to a press clipping in William Williams's scrapbook, declared that "everything about the institution and its management was admirable."

As part of his tour, the President visited the Registry Room. "He began to ask questions at once," according to the article. "Rosa Klausner and her three-year-old boy from Germany were at the desk....She said her husband was a baker, earning a great deal of money in this city and that he had sent for her to come with the boy. Besides her German money, she had $15 in United States bills, which her husband had sent her. 'That's fine, fine!' exclaimed the President. 'The right sort.'"

In contrast to Williams, Robert Watchorn was seen as a "man with a heart," who was willing to give an immigrant a break. His kindly reputation, however, did not please everyone. Anti-immigration forces cited lenient inspection on Ellis Island as one of the

Top: Drawing of proposed main building, Boring & Tilton, Architects, 1898.

Bottom: Postcard showing the main building as it looked when the island opened for business in 1900. The canopy was not completed until 1903.

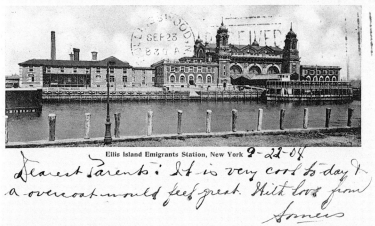

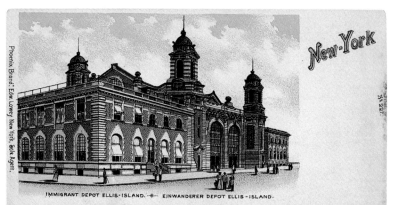

Top: View of Ellis Island against a smoky backdrop of New Jersey industry, ca. 1902. The kitchen and laundry building, immediately adjacent to the main building, was completed in 1901, while the 125-bed hospital, seen at left, opened in March 1902.

Bottom: Four postcards of Ellis Island, one of New York's major landmarks.

And Still They Come.
By J. Campbell Cory.

Top: President Theodore Roosevelt landing at Ellis Island on September 16, 1903. William Williams, commissioner of immigration, is on the right.

Bottom: Food counter in railroad ticket office, 1901. This photograph was included as evidence in a government investigation of corruption on Ellis Island. The food concession worker (labeled #1), wearing an official-looking uniform, allegedly threatened immigrants with deportation unless they bought a bag of lunch. Part of the immigration commissioner's job was to monitor the activities of the private concessions that provided services on Ellis Island—the money exchange, the food service, the baggage check, and the railroad pool. Keeping these businesses honest was a major challenge.

Right: Commissioner Robert Watchorn reports the latest arrival statistics to Uncle Sam in this Evening World *cartoon, April 17, 1906. Numbers continued to escalate into 1907, the busiest year at Ellis Island, with over one million arrivals.*

reasons behind the steadily rising number of admissions. They leveled relentless attacks on Watchorn, who finally resigned, forced out he said by "political exigency."

By the end of Williams's second term, Ellis Island's heyday was nearing its end. In 1914, Europe went to war, and because hostilities disrupted Atlantic shipping, immigration sharply declined. In 1915, the number of arrivals in New York fell to 178,416, and in 1916, to 141,390. With fewer people to care for, the new commissioner, Frederic C. Howe, was able to introduce a number of improvements. He set up classrooms, nurseries, and recreation rooms and organized concerts and other entertainments.

In 1916, the war seemed to invade Ellis Island itself when German saboteurs detonated fourteen munitions barges at New Jersey's Black Tom Wharf, less than a mile away. The exploding barges broke away from their moorings and drifted toward the island. Blasts shattered windows, collapsed roofs, and blew doors off their hinges. Though more than 500 persons were on the island at the time, no one was seriously injured. The ceiling of the Registry Room required major repair, which was carried out in 1917 with the installation of a Guastavino tile ceiling.

War changed life on Ellis Island in many ways. The closing of transatlantic shipping lanes meant deportations had to be suspended. The island began to fill up with excluded aliens who could not be admitted or deported. Following America's entry into the war in

A pristine and neatly landscaped Ellis Island, one of Commissioner
William Williams's proudest achievements, October 1, 1912. At the far end
of the building is a third-floor addition, which had detention rooms.

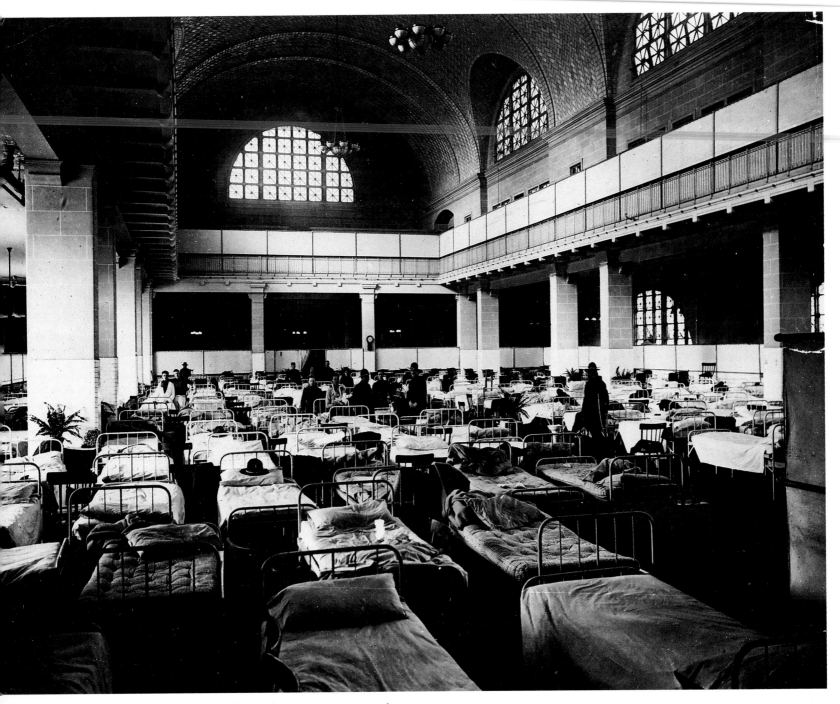

In March 1918, the U.S. Army transformed the Registry Room into the "largest ward in the world." Wounded servicemen returning from the war in Europe were cared for here and in Ellis Island's hospital buildings.

1917, Ellis Island also became a temporary detention center for over 1,800 merchant seamen who had been taken off German ships seized at various ports in the United States. As the war progressed, aliens suspected of sympathizing with the enemy, alleged spies, anarchists, and radicals added to the island's population. "I became a jailer," Howe wrote, "instead of a commissioner of immigration; a jailer not of convicted offenders but of suspected persons who had been arrested and railroaded to Ellis Island as the most available dumping-ground."

By 1918, most of the "enemy aliens" detained on Ellis Island had been shipped to detention camps in Hot Springs, North Carolina, or Fort Oglethorpe, Georgia. Their departure allowed the War and Navy Departments to take over much of the island. War casualties were treated in the Ellis Island hospital and in the main building's Registry Room, which was transformed into a giant ward. Sailors awaiting ship assignments stayed in the baggage and dormitory building.

The war heightened America's aversion to troublesome aliens. Following the war, widespread fear that Bolshevik agitators were infiltrating the U.S. labor movement fanned a wave of anti-immigrant hysteria, the "Red Scare." Violent strikes and a rash of bombings prompted the Department of Justice, under Attorney General A. Mitchell Palmer, to round up and arrest aliens suspected of subversive sympathies. Those caught in the Justice Department's net were sent to Ellis Island for deportation. By December 1919, hundreds of aliens were being held incommunicado on the island, including anarchists Emma Goldman, who had just been released from jail, and Alexander Berkman. On December 21, they and 247 alleged radicals were deported to Russia aboard the S.S. *Buford*, popularly known as the "Soviet Ark."

Once the Atlantic shipping lanes reopened after World War I, immigration began to rise. In 1920, almost a quarter of a million people, and in the next year, over half a million, arrived in New York. The postwar rush caught Ellis Island with its resources badly depleted. Experienced staff had been laid off during the war, and the buildings, which had received hard use by the U.S. Army and Navy, needed a thorough cleaning and extensive repairs.

Washington, meantime, watched with increasing alarm as growing numbers of refugees streamed to America's shores. It was estimated that between two and eight million persons in Germany alone wanted to come to the United States. To stanch the rising flow, Congress passed the First Quota Act, which took effect on June 3, 1921. It drastically reduced the number of admissions by setting low monthly quotas according to nationality. Excess-quota immigrants were automatically excluded. This last provision created a new phenomenon in New York, a monthly steamship race, with giant ships competing to land passengers before their quota was filled. On the night before the first of every month, sometimes as many as twenty ships waited outside the harbor for the stroke of midnight, the signal to race in. Immigration officers stationed at Fort Wadsworth and Fort Hamilton on either side of the Narrows judged the winners, whose passengers would be counted in the new monthly quota.

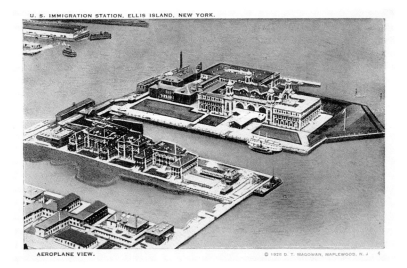

Top: Aerial view of Ellis Island, ca. 1925. The photograph shows the expanded hospital on the central island and a contagious disease hospital on a third island, at lower left.

Bottom: Leading anarchists Emma Goldman and Alexander Berkman were deported to Russia in December 1919, aboard S.S. Buford. *"The goal of the Federal agents," reported the* New York Times, *"was the capture of the leaders, the 'intellectuals' of agitation, and on the* Buford... *went the brains of the radical movement."*

Top: Dining room at lunch time, 1937. The wire-service caption reads: "{Ellis Island} is either the gateway to the promised land or a slough of despond." Most of those pictured here had entered the country illegally and were awaiting deportation.

Bottom left: Edward Laning and assistants working on Ellis Island dining-room mural, ca. 1936. Laning's mural, completed in 1938, was commissioned by the Works Progress Administration (WPA) as part of its program to decorate public buildings. Laning entitled the 110-foot-long work "The Role of the Immigrant in the Industrial Development of America." During the 1970s, the mural was transferred to the United States Courthouse in Brooklyn, where it remains today.

Bottom right: Detainees in Ellis Island dining room, 1947. Laning's mural appears in the background.

In 1924, the National Origins Act replaced the First Quota Act. Though the law increased restrictions, it also made one notable improvement by allowing prospective immigrants to undergo inspection before leaving their homeland. This made the trip through Ellis Island unnecessary. Shortly after the new law went into effect, one government official reported that Ellis Island "looked like a deserted village." By the 1930s, the island held only detainees whose papers or visas were not in order, foreign-born criminals awaiting deportation, and sick merchant mariners receiving treatment at the hospital.

During World War II, Ellis Island was used to detain "enemy aliens" and their families, and seamen from enemy ships that had been sequestered at American ports. The Coast Guard also took up residence in several buildings. After the war, the island returned to its usual routine of sorting out the papers of detained immigrants and deporting illegal aliens. Passage of the Internal Security Act in 1950, at the beginning of the Korean War, brought Ellis Island its last glimmer of notoriety. Reflecting the new politics of the Cold War, the law banned entry to the country by members of Communist organizations, and consequently arriving aliens were taken to Ellis Island for screening. The following year, 1,500 aliens suspected of illegal residence were rounded up in various raids and temporarily detained at the island. The furor soon passed, and by the following year the average daily population fell to about 250.

Ellis Island's days as a government facility were numbered. The high cost of maintaining the buildings finally persuaded the Immigration and Naturalization Service to move its New York operations from the island to Manhattan. In 1954, the Justice Department paroled all but a few detained aliens and announced the closing of all seaport detention centers, including Ellis Island. By that time, the island held only one inmate, a seaman who had overstayed his shore leave. He was released and ferried back to the mainland, a quiet finale for a government institution that had played a large and controversial role in immigration history.

Top: Aerial view of Ellis Island, ca. 1945. A last construction campaign in the 1930s brought the number of buildings to over thirty.

Bottom: Ellis Island ferry, 1934.

Silent Voices

After the government closed Ellis Island in 1954, the silent and empty immigration depot rapidly deteriorated into a ghostly complex of dilapidated buildings. Left in place were fixtures and furniture, papers, and other bureaucratic detritus, all quietly gathering dust, year after year. Roofs developed leaks that let in the harsh salt air, which considerably quickened the aging process. Occasional visitors came to the island to scavenge bits of ornamental copper, typewriters, fans—whatever they thought they could sell. Others came simply to look at the eerie landscape and search out clues to the past and explore a modern ruin.

Above: Abandoned office in the main building, 1957.

Opposite: Main building exterior, 1957. Fences were built during World War II, when the island served as a detention center for "enemy aliens."

Ellis Island ferry, 1968. In 1954, when Ellis Island closed, the ferry stayed in its slip in front of the main building. The waterlogged vessel finally sank in August 1968.

Overleaf: Baggage Room on ground floor of the main building, 1968.

Following overleaf: Abandoned bed in the new immigrant building, 1983.

Above: Exterior of the contagious disease hospital, 1984.　　　　　　　　*Opposite: Corridor in the baggage and dormitory building, 1987.*

Steam-cleaning limestone ornamentation on the front of the main building. Before restoration , the exterior was black with soot and other pollutants. The limestone trim with elaborately carved ornamentation was carefully cleaned with high-pressured jets of steam. The granite foundation, more durable than limestone, was cleaned with a solution of chemicals and water.

Restoring a Landmark

One of the four main towers. The new copper domes were installed on-site, piece by piece. Helicopters lowered the new spires, exact replicas of the originals, into place. All of the main building's copper ornamentation underwent a state-of-the-art reconstruction.

In 1965, President Lyndon B. Johnson signed a proclamation that recognized the historical significance of Ellis Island by incorporating it into the Statue of Liberty National Monument. Liberty's 1986 centennial sparked an ambitious project to repair and refurbish the statue and the main building on Ellis Island. The National Park Service and the Statue of Liberty/Ellis Island Foundation, with the generous help of the American people, spearheaded a restoration effort of unprecedented scale. Architects Beyer Blinder Belle and Notter Finegold & Alexander led a team that researched, planned, and designed the restoration of Ellis Island's main building.

A crucial first task was to dry out the interior of the building. Decades of exposure to the elements, leaking roofs, and condensation had saturated the walls with water. Several large generator-powered furnaces pumped warm air throughout the interior of the building. Once the structure was stabilized, work began. The most important area to undergo restoration was the Registry Room, the massive hall central to visitors' understanding of the immigration experience. This space was restored to its appearance between 1918 and 1924, the period when the room reached the height of its architectural development. Workers thoroughly inspected and cleaned the tile ceiling and restored the artificial Caen-stone plaster on the balcony walls. They scrubbed the exterior limestone, replaced roof tiles, and reconstructed the ornamental copper domes.

New construction included a staircase to the Registry Room and a canopy over the main entrance. Both were modern interpretations of vanished originals once used by millions of immigrants. In addition, exhibit galleries and two theatres were constructed in areas that had once served as offices, dormitories, and detention rooms. By 1990, after years of painstaking effort, the historic landmark building had been transformed from a decrepit ruin into a museum commemorating the immigrant experience.

Overleaf: An enormous freestanding scaffolding erected in the Registry Room enabled workers to clean the Guastavino tile ceiling, which was found to be in excellent condition. Of its 28,832 tiles, only 17 had to be replaced. The three-story-high scaffolding, constructed to rest only on the floor, needed no anchoring to the walls or ceiling.

A National Museum

The opening of the Ellis Island Immigration Museum in 1990 fulfills a dream shared by thousands of people who contributed to its creation. The museum is housed within Ellis Island's restored main building, a place that still evokes the presence and hopes of travelers who once walked its halls. Today's visitors can follow in the immigrants' footsteps from the ferry slip and into the main building, and they can try to imagine the feelings of the immigrants as they climbed the stairs to the Registry Room, the spacious hall where thousands were examined each day. This historic space marked a momentous point of departure in the lives of the immigrants, most just weeks away from the old country and about to enter the New World.

Within the museum, their story unfolds. The exhibits not only document Ellis Island's role in immigration history but also view it in the context of its time. Historic photographs, steamship tickets, a wall of passports, ethnic theatre posters, citizenship papers, clothing, and other personal items brought by the newcomers help convey a broad diversity of experiences. The immigration story is further expanded in an exhibit of three-dimensional graphics that explores the peopling of America and world migration trends over four centuries.

MetaForm Incorporated spent years conceptualizing, researching, curating, and designing the permanent exhibits for the museum. Its curators launched an ambitious effort, researching archives as well as libraries and historical societies, canvassing flea markets, contacting private collectors and dealers, and, most importantly, publishing appeals to the American public. The museum's outreach found a generous and constructive response. People from all over the country rummaged through attics and closets, looking for mementos that told their own family histories of passage to America, and they were willing to share those stories with others through the museum. Their contributions and words, incorporated into the exhibits, give individual identities to a subject often discussed in terms of masses, and impart a sense of history as human experience.

Top: Trunks and carpet bag typical of those brought through Ellis Island.

Bottom: The restored Registry Room, 1990. This historic place marked a great divide in the lives of millions of immigrants, their first stop in America. The enormous arched windows evoke the spirit of America's nineteenth-century railroad stations — the principal gateways of our cities. The room has been restored to its appearance in the early 1920s; the wooden benches are the original ones that provided weary immigrants with a place to rest.

Opposite: On the ground floor of the Ellis Island Immigration Museum, a platform heaped high with assorted trunks, wicker baskets, and suitcases occupies a space that, during the peak immigration years, was part of the baggage concession, where arriving immigrants checked their belongings.

Peak Immigration Years: 1880–1924 *presents the broad story of the immigrant experience, from the initial decision to leave, all the way to becoming American.*

Above: "Leaving the Homeland." A video monitor set in a large photomural of a Galician village shows archival film footage of men, women, and children packing up their belongings and starting the long trek to America.

Top left: "At Work in America." Under a row of signs showing typical wages around 1910, photographs depict the variety of immigrant jobs.

Top right: "Between Two Worlds." Large photomurals of immigrant families and neighborhoods convey the story of how the newcomers came to terms with their adopted homeland.

Bottom: "Passage to America." Visitors to the museum can search for their ancestors' immigrant ship among the hundreds of steamship postcards in the exhibit, or look at a model of R.M.S. Aquitania, which could accommodate 2,000 third-class passengers.

Overleaf: Four exhibits from Through America's Gate, which describes step-by-step what happened to immigrants on Ellis Island. "Arrival" (top left) describes landing on Ellis Island. "Medical Care" (bottom left) depicts the examination and treatment of sick immigrants. "Detention" (top right) shows immigrants slated for deportation, waiting behind a wire fence. "Food Service" (bottom right) describes the kitchen, dining room, meals, and snacks, which included an afternoon cup of milk for each detained child.

Treasures from Home *features a variety of belongings carried to America. Handmade clothes, delicate linens, trousseau items, musical instruments, personal documents, and photographs of loved ones create an intimate portrait of immigration.*

Right: Ellis Island Chronicles *documents the architectural and administrative history of the island. Scale models from five time periods describe the growth of the island from a 3.3-acre sand bank to a 27.5-acre complex of over thirty brick and stone buildings.*

Opposite: Silent Voices. *Furnishings and fixtures once part of the daily routine of processing and caring for new arrivals are displayed in the condition they were found in before the restoration of the main building began during the 1980s.*

The Peopling of America *is a statistical portrait that relates the Ellis Island story to American and world migration trends.*

Above: "Growth of a Nation" charts the ebb and flow of immigration to the United States, against a chronological series of photographs showing historic events from 1820 to 1990.

Below: "The Word Tree: Ethnic Americanisms." The rich stock of words and idioms in American English owes much of its variety and color to the nationalities that have settled in the United States. "The Word Tree" shows a selection of ethnic contributions to America's language: "stampede" and "lariat" (Spanish), "raccoon" and "hickory" (Native American), "hunky-dory" and "Yankee" (Dutch), and many others.

"A Changing Pattern: Male/Female Immigration Trends." Though until World War I most immigrants were male, this is no longer the case. By the 1930s, legislation that restricted immigration but allowed continued admission for family members had dramatically changed the trend in women's favor. Today, about two-thirds of the immigrants are women and children. Men, however, still dominate the flow from Africa and the Middle East.

"Millions on the Move: Worldwide Migrations." Immigration to the
United States is part of a larger pattern of people moving to new lands all
over the world. A large globe, crisscrossed with paths of lights, shows the
most common migrations in different time periods: Africans, in bondage,
to the east coast of North and South America as well as the Caribbean,
Chinese and Indians to various places in Southeast Asia and Oceania;
and Europeans to the United States, Canada, South America, Australia,
and Africa.

"Where We Came From: Sources of Immigration." This three-dimensional graph, divided into twenty-year intervals, shows the number of people who immigrated to the United States from each of seven major areas of the world. The graph shows the shift in immigration sources, from northwestern Europe in the nineteenth century to southern and eastern Europe in the early twentieth century. In recent times, another important shift has occurred, with most immigrants coming from Asia and the Americas.

"A Two-Way Street: Immigration vs. Emigration." Not all immigrants stayed in America; many went home again. The blue signs show arrivals (in millions), while the red show departures. During the twentieth century, for example, 36 million immigrants entered the United States, but an estimated 12 million people exited.

"The American Flag" is a mosaic of faces of over 750 Americans from all
ethnic backgrounds. The United States continues to attract new arrivals.
Like those who came before them, they seek new freedom and opportunities for
themselves and their children.

References

Abbreviations:

NPS: National Park Service Collection, Statue of Liberty National Monument, Ellis Island Immigration Museum.

WWP: William Williams Papers, Rare Books and Manuscripts Division, New York Public Library

Quotations not listed below are from oral histories (conducted 1985–87) in the National Park Service Collection, Statue of Liberty National Monument, Ellis Island Immigration Museum.

Introduction

p. 17   "Well, we're off": Sholom Aleichem, "Off for America," *New York World*, January 1916, quoted by Irving Howe and Kenneth Libo, eds., *How We Lived: A Documentary History of Jews in America 1880–1930* (New York: New American Library, 1981), p. 20.

p. 17   "By preserving their": Letter from Darlene Smith-Ash to MetaForm, December 1991, courtesy NPS.

p. 18   "You just did": Interview with Emanuel Steen in "Treasures of Ellis Island" segment of "Sunday Morning," CBS Inc. 1990. All rights reserved. Originally broadcast on September 9, 1990, over CBS Television Network.

Peak Immigration Years: 1880–1924

p. 22   "I left Barbados": Lyle Small quoted by Barbara Strauch, "An Often-Forgotten Passage/Ellis I. a Stop for W. Indians," *Newsday*, June 1, 1986, p. 7.

p. 24   "My boyish imagination": Louis Adamic, *Laughing in the Jungle: The Autobiography of an Immigrant in America* (New York: Harper Brothers, 1932), p. 6.

p. 24   "There was never": "Various Paths by Immigrants in U.S., Illustrated," *New York Times*, February 13, 1910.

p. 26   "I can remember": Golda Meir, *My Life* (New York: Dell Publishing Co., Inc., 1975), p. 25.

p. 26   "I wish you": Letter from Adam Raczkowski to Teofil Wolski, August 6, 1906, quoted by William I. Thomas and Florian Znaniecki, *The Polish Peasant in Europe and America: Monograph of an Immigrant Group* (Boston: Richard G. Badger/The Gorham Press, 1918), vol. 2, p. 193.

p. 26   "When someone returns": Adolfo Rossi, "Vantaggi e danni dell'emigrazione," *Bollettino dell'emigrazione* 13 (1908): 11, quoted by Michael La Sorte, *La Merica: Images of Italian Greenhorn Experience* (Philadelphia: Temple University Press, 1985), p. 4.

p. 29   "The day I": Julia Goniprow quoted by Joan Morrison and Charlotte Fox Zabusky, *American Mosaic* (New York: E.P. Dutton, 1980), p. 68.

p. 34   "We were stationed": Ludwig Hofmeister, ibid., p. 70.

p. 36   "Many immigrants had": Luciano De Crescenzo, "Il Gomitolo di Lana," in Paola Cresci and Luciano Guidobaldi, *Partono i bastimenti* (Milano: Mondadori, 1980), p. 21. Quoted by La Sorte, *La Merica*, p. 202.

p. 39   "Neither cleanliness, decency": *Report of Conditions Existing in Europe and Mexico Affecting Emigration and Immigration, Being a Compilation, in Digested Form, of Reports Submitted by the Following Named Officers*, ca. 1907, pp. 105–106. Typescript, RG85:51411/1, National Archives.

p. 39   "There is neither": Edward A. Steiner, *On the Trail of the Immigrant* (New York: Fleming H. Revell Company, 1906), p. 35.

p. 42   "Disgusting and demoralizing": "Abstract of the [1909] Report on Steerage Conditions," in *Reports of the United States Immigration Commission*, vol. 2, 1911, pp. 291–303.

p. 42   "Dismal, damp, dirty": "Steerage Conditions," *Reports of the United States Immigration Commission*, vol. 37, 1911, quoted by Edith Abbott, *Immigration: Select Documents and Case Records* (Chicago: The University of Chicago Press, 1924), p. 91.

p. 43   "I felt grateful": Stella Petrakis quoted by Harry Mark Petrakis, "A Portrait of a Miracle," *Chicago Tribune*, July 4, 1986.

p. 44   "The perils of": Mary Antin, *The Promised Land* (Boston: Houghton Mifflin Co., 1912), p. 178.

p. 45   "It is magnificent": Diary of Karl Puffe, November 19, 1892 (translated from German by Denise Heller), lent to NPS by Laurie Klemarczyk.

p. 45   "Furtive sunshine": M. Antin, *Promised Land*, p. 178.

p. 48   "A thousand sorrows": Him Mark Lai, Genny Lim, and Judy Yung, *Island: Poetry and History of Chinese Immigrants on Angel Island 1910–1940* (San Francisco: Chinese Culture Foundation of San Francisco, 1980), p. 162.

p. 51   "One immense empire": *Minnesota as It Is*, 1889, p. 4. Great Northern Railway Company Records, Minnesota Historical Society.

p. 51   "Go and see": B.&M.R.R. lands poster, reproduced in Peter C. Marzio, ed., *A Nation of Nations: The People Who Came to America as Seen through Objects and Documents at the Smithsonian Institution* (New York: Harper & Row, Publishers, 1976), p. 190.

pp. 51–53   "We left on": Diary of Marius Larsen, May 30, 1912 (translated from Danish by Carl G. Larsen), donated to NPS by Elna S. and Carl G. Larsen.

p. 53   "Knoxville feels that": Knoxville Board of Trade, *Knoxville Tennessee: The Queen City of the Mountains*, ca. 1906, p. 23. RG85:51411/29, National Archives.

p. 53   "TEXAS is an": Broadside distributed by Karesch & Stotskzy in Bremen, 1906. German original and translation, RG85:51411/54, National Archives.

p. 56   "Well, I came": Old Italian story quoted by Elly Shodell, *Particles of the Past: Sandmining on Long Island, 1870's–1980's* (Port Washington, New York: Port Washington Public Library, 1985), p. 11.

p. 59   "All those bridges": Joseph Baccardo quoted by Morrison and Zabusky, *American Mosaic*, p. 67.

p. 62   "He who can": Peter Sørensen, April 14, 1885, letter quoted by Frederick Hale, ed., *Danes in North America* (Seattle: University of Washington Press, 1984), pp. 101–102.

p. 64   "I started at": Adelard Janelle quoted by Dyke Hendrickson, *Quiet Presence/Histoire de Franco-Américains en New England* (Portland, Maine: Guy Gannett Publishing Co., 1980), p. 1.

p. 67   "The coal you": John Mitchell quoted in Leslie Allen, *Liberty: The Statue and the American Dream* ([New York:] The Statue of Liberty–Ellis Island Foundation, Inc. , 1985), p. 236.

p. 70   "Rivington Street was": Alfred Kazin, *A Walker in the City* (New York: Harcourt Brace Jovanovich, Inc., 1951), p. 151.

p. 70   "The architecture seemed": Arnold Bennett, *Your United States* (New York: Harper and Brothers, 1912), p. 187.

p. 70   "A sociable Southern": Bernardine Kielty, *The Sidewalks of New York* (New York: Little Leather Library Corporation, 1923), p. 77.

p. 73   "Little coffins are": Jacob A. Riis, *How the Other Half Lives* (New York: Charles Scribner's Sons, 1890). Reprint of 1901 ed. (New York: Dover Publications, Inc., 1971), p. 129.

p. 74   "While I am": Stoyan Christowe, "Half an American," quoted by Marzio, *Nation of Nations*, p. 276.

p. 75   "Many Swedes are": Carl and Fred, January 23, 1896, letter quoted by H. Arnold Barton, ed., *Letters from the Promised Land: Swedes in America, 1840–1914* (Minneapolis: University of Minnesota Press for the Swedish Pioneer Historical Society, 1975), p. 242.

p. 77   "My brother and": Matthew Murray quoted by Morrison and Zabusky, *American Mosaic*, pp. 61–62.

p. 79   "I myself rarely": Gim Chang quoted in Victor G. and Brett de Bary Nee, *Longtime Californ': A Documentary Study of an American Chinatown* (Stanford: Stanford University Press, 1972), p. 72.

p. 88   "All the distinguishing": Commissioner of Common Schools in New York City quoted by Marzio, *Nation of Nations*, p. 309.

p. 92   "There is no": Theodore Roosevelt, ibid., p. 308.

p. 93   "For our own": Frank B. Lenz, "The Education of the Immigrant," *Educational Review* 51 (1916), ibid., p. 323.

pp. 94–96   "Are you a bigamist?": Son of Moses Kirshblum quoted in Maldwyn A. Jones, *Destination America* (New York: Holt, Rinehart and Winston, 1976), p. 171.

p. 96   "We allow the": Henry H. Curran, "Fewer and Better, or None," *Saturday Evening Post*, April 26, 1924: 8.

p. 96   "Tony, Tony, where's": Cermak and adversary quoted by John M. Allswang, *A House for All Peoples: Ethnic Politics in Chicago, 1890–1936* (Lexington, Kentucky: University Press of Kentucky, 1971), pp. 105–107.

p. 98   "The influence upon": Francis A. Walker, *Discussions in Economics and Statistics*, ed. Davis R. Dewey (New York: Lenox Hill Publishers & Distributors [Burt Franklin], 1899), vol. 2, p. 448.

p. 99   "The present predominating": William Williams quoted by the *New York Times*, May 24, 1903.

p. 99   "Gradually supplanting the": "Report of the Immigration Investigation Committee to the Honorable Secretary of Treasury" (Washington, D.C.:1895), p. 53.

p. 101   "The new immigration": Madison Grant, *The Passing of the Great Race or the Racial Basis of European History*, rev. ed. (New York: Charles Scribner's Sons, 1918). Reprint ed. (New York: Arno Press and The New York Times, 1970), pp. 89–90.

p. 101   "Those who are": New Immigrants' Protective League, *Bulletin No. 1*, November 16, 1906. RG85:51480/2, National Archives.

p. 102   "Voluntary emigration always": Mary Antin, *They Who Knock at Our Gates* (Boston: Houghton Mifflin Co., 1914), p. 64.

p. 102   "Where would your": Rep. Samuel McMillan quoted by National Liberal Immigration League, *Immigration in the Sixtieth Congress. Extracts from Speeches Delivered in January 1908 by Representatives Murphy, Sabath, Cockran, O'Connell, Goulden and McMillan* (New York: 1908), p. 17.

p. 102   "I welcome this": Rep. Bourke Cockran, ibid., p. 13.

p. 102   "Very fabric of": Sen. Henry Cabot Lodge, *Congressional Record* (March 16, 1896), 54th Congress, 1st session.

p. 104   "The melting pot": Dr. George B. Cutten quoted by Henry A. Wise Wood, *Who Shall Inherit the Land of Our Fathers?* (New York: The American Defense Society, 1923), p. 6.

p. 104   "America of the Melting Pot Comes to End": *New York Times*, April 27, 1904, p. 3.

p. 105   "The welfare of": Rep. Albert Johnson quoted in "To Halt the European Invasion," *The Literary Digest* 67 (December 25, 1920): 14.

p. 105   "Jews dominate the": Ku Klux Klan, *The Fiery Cross*, quoted by Ann Novotny, *Strangers at the Door: Ellis Island, Castle Garden, and the Great Migration to America* (Riverside, Connecticut: The Chatham Press, Inc., 1971), p. 119.

Through America's Gate

p. 110   "A floating waiting": Stephen Graham, *With Poor Immigrants to America* (New York: The Macmillan Company, 1914), p. 43.

p. 110   "All were thinking": Ibid., p. 43.

p. 114   "The good old": Oral history with Dr. Grover A. Kempf, 1977, NPS.

p. 117   "The nearest earthly": Graham, *Poor Immigrants*, p. 41.

p. 118   "Had we known": *Jewish Daily Forward*, n.d., clipping in William Williams's scrapbook no. 2, WWP.

p. 121   "I remember my": Letter from Rosanne Welch to MetaForm, August 11, 1987, courtesy NPS.

p. 122   "The Italian kisses": Maud Mosher, "Ellis Island as the Matron Sees It," 1910, typescript, Maud Mosher Papers, NPS, gift of Diane Kokes.

p. 125   "Instructions received as": *Comedies and Tragedies at Ellis Island*, ca. 1913, typescript, RG85, National Archives, Suitland, Maryland.

p. 125   "A new era": *Evening Post*, W. Williams's scrapbook no.1, WWP.

p. 125   "During other administrations": W. Williams's scrapbook no.2, WWP.

p. 133   "They wanted to": Abraham Cahan, "Two Love Stories," *New York Commercial Advertiser*, August 18, 1900, in Moses Rischin, ed., *Grandma Never Lived in America: The New Journalism of Abraham Cahan* (Bloomington: Indiana University Press, 1985), p. 189.

p. 134   "One case haunted": Fiorello H. La Guardia, *The Making of an Insurgent: An Autobiography, 1882–1919* (Philadelphia: J.B. Lippincott Co., 1948), p. 65.

p. 137   "Walter took sick": Interview with Martha Strahm, May 14, 1988, sent to MetaForm, courtesy NPS.

pp. 137–139   "If an Englishman": E.H. Mullan, "Mental Examination of Immigrants. Administration and Line Inspection at Ellis Island," *Public Health Reports*, May 18, 1917: 737-738.

p. 139   "Always haphazard": Kempf, NPS.

p. 142   "Very heart of": A.C. Geddes, *Despatch from H.M. Ambassador at Washington Reporting on Conditions at Ellis Island Immigration Station* (London: 1923), unpaginated.

p. 143   "Ask them why": Edward Steiner, *Trail*, pp. 87–88.

p. 144   "Men can work": "Woman in Male Garb Gains Her Freedom," *New York Times*, October 6, 1908.

p. 145   "Those days we": Frank Martocci, inspector at Ellis Island, discussing conditions at Ellis Island in 1907. Quoted by Edward Corsi, *In the Shadow of Liberty: The Chronicle of Ellis Island* (New York: The Macmillan Company, 1935), p. 78.

p. 145   "Were being improperly": Theodore Roosevelt quoted by Thomas M. Pitkin. *Keepers of the Gate: A History of Ellis Island* (New York: New York University Press, 1975), pp. 35–36.

p. 145   "Immigrants were hustled": William Williams, *Annual Report of the Commissioner of Immigration for the Port of New York*, September 24, 1902.

p. 145   "That is not": W. Williams's scrapbook no. 2, WWP.

p. 150   "They are arranged": Geddes, *Despatch*.

p. 150   "I have seen": Henry C. Curran, *Pillar to Post* (New York: Charles Scribner's Sons, 1941), p. 294.

p. 151   "The first night": Adamic, *Laughing*, pp. 41–42.

p. 154   "The kitchen methods": Williams, *Annual Report*.

p. 154   "The food is": Geddes, *Despatch*.

p. 159   "They tell us": Ludmila K. Foxlee, "The World through Ellis Island— Immigrants and Emigrants," n.d., typescript, Ludmila K. Foxlee Papers, NPS, gift of Joyce Pratt.

p.159   "A great many": Robert Watchorn, 1908, quoted by Pitkin, *Keepers*, p. 80.

Treasures from Home

p. 169   "I arrived in": Letter of Abraham Burstein, 1985.

p. 173   "Most dear to": Letter from Birgitta Hedman Fichter to MetaForm, 1987, courtesy NPS.

p. 174   "Became teachers, supervisors": Rose Ishmael [Brown] Tully, ca. 1985, typescript, courtesy NPS.

p. 192   "When I was": Joel Greenberg, statement in *Silent Voices* exhibit, Ellis Island Immigration Museum.

p. 193   "I remember": Irma Busch quoted by David M. Brownstone, Irene Franck, and Douglas L. Brownstone, *Island of Hope, Island of Tears* (New York: Rawson, Wade Publishers, Inc. 1979), p. 189.

p. 193   "He loved books!": Letter from Alcina Morais to MetaForm, December 8, 1987, courtesy NPS.

p. 199   "I have a": Letter from Evellyn S. Huyser to MetaForm, August 13, 1987, courtesy NPS.

p. 211   "Since our departure": Letter from Pauline Baum Nismann, ca. 1987, courtesy NPS.

p. 214   "He was the": Fichter letter.

p. 215   "All of my": Petrakis, "Portrait."

p. 222   "It took mother": Letter from William B. Solyom to MetaForm, July 24, 1986, courtesy NPS.

p. 226   "I was born": Nathan Solomon, *The Last and Only Survivor of Flora*, 1983, courtesy NPS.

p. 226   "The physician": Nathan Solomon quoted in Bethany Kandel, "A Dream of a New Life Come True," *USA Today*, September 7, 1990, p. 8A.

p. 226   "My father is": Solomon S. Solomon, ibid.

p. 231   "I became the": Letter from Mary Kudrna Garba to MetaForm, February 7, 1987, courtesy NPS.

p. 232   "There were separate": Alice Semerjian, letter to the editor, *The Philadelphia Inquirer*, July 13, 1986, p. 6–F.

p. 233   "On our last": Ibid.

Island Chronicles

p. 241   "The shock would": *New York Sun*, May 26, 1876.

p. 241   "Improve Ellis Island": Quoted by Pitkin, *Keepers*, p. 12.

p. 245   "Latter-day watering": *Harper's Weekly*, October 24, 1891, p. 821.

p. 245   "It was first": *New York Times*, January 2, 1892.

p. 245   "The flames were": *New York Sun*, June 15, 1897.

p. 245   "Ever since I": *New York Daily Tribune*, June 16, 1897.

p. 245   "A great victory": William Alciphron Boring, *Memories of the Life of William Alciphron Boring*, unpublished manuscript, Boring Collection, Avery Architectural and Fine Arts Library, Columbia University.

p. 246   "Hell's Island": W. Williams's scrapbook no. 1, WWP.

p. 246   "Everything about the": W. Williams's scrapbook no. 1, WWP.

p. 246   "He began to": Ibid.

p. 246   "A man with": obituary for Robert Watchorn, *New York Times*, April 15, 1944.

p. 251   "I became a": Frederic C. Howe, *The Confessions of a Reformer* (New York: Charles Scribner's Sons, 1925) p. 267.

p. 251   "The goal of": *New York Times*, December 22, 1919.

p. 253   "Looked like a": *New York Times*, July 20, 1924.

Picture Credits

Abbreviations:

(t) top, (m) middle, (b) bottom, (l) left, (r) right

MF: MetaForm Incorporated.

MF/NPS: Photographs taken by MetaForm Incorporated / Karen Yamauchi of artifacts in the National Park Service Collection, Statue of Liberty National Monument, Ellis Island Immigration Museum.

NPS: National Park Service Collection, Statue of Liberty National Monument, Ellis Island Immigration Museum.

Front Matter and Introduction

2–3 Photo by A. Loeffler, LC-USZ62-37784, Library of Congress. 4 Augustus F. Sherman Collection, NPS. 8–9 Koch Collection, Michigan Historical Collections, Bentley Historical Library, University of Michigan. 10–11 Alland Collection, Culver Pictures. 14 Lewis W. Hine Collection, New York Public Library. 16, 19 Augustus F. Sherman Collection, NPS. 20–21 Bildarchiv der Österreichischen Nationalbibliothek, Vienna.

Peak Immigration: 1880–1924

22(tl) Culver Pictures; (tr) Photo by Armin T. Wegner, Deutsches Literaturarchiv, Marbach am Neckar, Germany, courtesy U.S. Holocaust Memorial Museum; (bl) Albert J. Carcieri Collection; (br) FPG International. 23 YIVO Institute for Jewish Research. 24(l) MF/NPS; (r) Lot 8080, Library of Congress. 25 MF/NPS. 26(t) Photo by Anders B. Wilse, Norsk Folkemuseum, Oslo; (b) YIVO Institute for Jewish Research. 27 Touring Club Italiano, Milan. 28 Photo by Lewis W. Hine, International Museum of Photography at George Eastman House. 29 Alland Collection, Culver Pictures. 30(tl) MF/NPS, gift of Helen P. Psaras; (tr) MF/NPS, gift of Yolanda Talbot; (ml) MF/NPS, gift of Jeanne A. Bisignano; (mr) MF/NPS, gift of Sheldon Marcus; (br) MF/NPS, gift of Heinz L. Herz. 31(tl) MF/NPS, lent by Joshua D. Lowenfish family; (tr) MF/NPS, lent by Birgitta Hedman Fichter; (ml) MF/NPS, gift of Victoria Sarfatti Fernández; (mr) MF/NPS, lent by Olga Pojani; (br) MF/NPS, lent by Rando family. 32(tl) MF/NPS, gift of Doris L. Codner; (tr) MF/NPS, gift of Margaret Flinck Moulton; (mr) MF/NPS, lent by Bir B. Singh; (bl) MF/NPS, lent by Catherine Izumi and descendants of Walter Tokusaburo and Chiyoto Sakai Matsumoto; (br) MF/NPS, lent by Sylvia Stolarz. 33(tl) MF/NPS, gift of Helen Suknaich Alexander; (tr) MF/NPS, lent by Lucy LaCugna Yakowenko; (mr) MF/NPS, gift of Rose Ishmael Tully and Grace Ishmael Robins; (bl) MF/NPS, gift of Arthur Klein.

Passage to America

34(t) Photo by Johann Hamann, Bildarchiv Preussischer Kulturbesitz, Berlin; (b) 90-G-60-1, National Archives. 35(t) Touring Club Italiano, Milan; (bl) MF/NPS, gift of Mrs. William Podgett; (br) MF/NPS, gift of Claire F. Judin. 36(l) MF/NPS; (r) RG85: 51411/53 oversize, National Archives. 37(l) RG85: 51411/53 oversize, National Archives; (r) MF/NPS. 38 Norsk Folkemuseum, Oslo. 39(l) MF/NPS; (tr) UPI/Bettmann Newsphotos; (br) Photo by William H. Rau, LC-USZ62-7307, Library of Congress. 40–41 MF/NPS. 42(l) RG85: 51411/53 oversize, National Archives; (r) Edwin Levick Collection, Mariners' Museum. 43 Photo by Edwin Levick, LC-USZ62-11202, Library of Congress. 44 American Jewish Joint Distribution Committee. 45(tl) MF/NPS, gift of Theresa A. Thomas and John L. Thomas; (tr) MF/NPS, gift of Greg Steffon; (bl), (br) MF/NPS, lent by Balch Institute for Ethnic Studies.

Ports of Entry

47(t) New-York Historical Society; (b) Boston Public Library. 48 RG85, Immigration and Naturalization Services, San Francisco District Files, Box 6, Densmore Investigation, 1914–18, National Archives. 49(t) California Department of Parks and Recreation; (b) New Bedford Whaling Museum.

Across the Land

50 New-York Historical Society. 51 Nebraska State Historical Society. 52(l),(tr) RG85: 51411/29, National Archives; (br) Minnesota Historical Society. 53 Union Pacific Railroad Museum Collection. 54(t) Boston Athenaeum; (bl) MF/NPS, gifts of Edwin L. Dunbaugh; (br) MF/NPS. 55(t) #49764, National Museum of American History, Smithsonian Institution; (b) MF/NPS.

At Work in America

56 Brown Brothers. 57(t) Minnesota Historical Society; (b) Photo by K. S. Melikian, Project SAVE, courtesy Alice Gulanian Papazian. 58(t) LC-USZ62-28403, Pinchot Collection, Library of Congress; (b) Photo by Anders B. Wilse, Special Collections Division, University of Washington Libraries. 59(t) LC-D4-19055, Library of Congress; (b) State Historical Society of Wisconsin. 60–61 Photo by Boulanger et Frères, Instructional Services, Dimond Library, University of New Hampshire. 62(tl) Beck Archives of Rocky Mountain Jewish History, Center for Judaic Studies, University of Denver; (tr) UPI/Bettmann Newsphotos; (bl) Photo by Clifford W. Ashley, New Bedford Whaling Museum; (br) Minnesota Historical Society. 63 Brown Brothers. 64(t) National Child Labor Committee, courtesy PhotoCollect Gallery; (b) Lewis W. Hine Collection, New York Public Library. 65 Photo by Lewis W. Hine, LC-M5-2704, Library of Congress. 66 Photo by Lewis W. Hine, International Museum of Photography at George Eastman House. 67(t) Photo by Charles Heinrichs, Paterson Museum; (b) Brown Brothers. 68 LC-USZ62-22198, Bain Collection, Library of Congress. 69(t), (bl) Brown Brothers; (br) Urban Archives, Temple University.

Between Two Worlds

70–71 LC-D401-12683, Library of Congress. 72 Cincinnati Historical Society. 73(t) MF/NPS; (m) Photo by Jessie Tarbox Beals, Museum of the City of New York; (b) Photo by Lewis W. Hine, Photography Archive, Carpenter Center for the Visual Arts, Harvard University. 74 Solomon D. Butcher Collection, Nebraska State Historical Society. 75 Ukrainian Cultural Institute, Dickinson State College, North Dakota, courtesy Ukrainian Museum, New York. 76(tl) Photography Archive, Carpenter Center for the Visual Arts, Harvard University; (tr) Historical Association of Southern Florida; (bl) Western Reserve Historical Society; (br) Utah State Historical Society. 77(t) Minnesota Historical Society; (m) Visual Communications Archive, Los Angeles; (b) Nassif family, courtesy NPS. 78–79 Photo by Arnold Genthe, LC-USZ62-41901, Library of Congress. 79(r) LC-USZ62-48502, Library of Congress. 80–81 Photo by Annie Sievers Schildhauer, State Historical Society of Wisconsin. 82–85 MF/NPS. 86(l) *The Big Stick*, New York, May 27, 1910, p.15, Jewish Division, New York Public Library; (tr) *Il Grido del Popolo*, Denver, October 30, 1907, Immigration History Research Center, University of Minnesota; (br) *The Big Stick*, New York, November 18, 1910, p.13, Jewish Division, New York Public Library. 87(l) *Katolik Cesko-Americky Kalendar*, Chicago, 1916, Immigration History Research Center, University of Minnesota; (tr) *Kalenteri Amerikan Suomalaiselle Tyovaelle*, Fitchburg, Massachusetts, 1921, Immigration History Research Center, University of Minnesota; (br) *Hospodar*, Omaha, March 1, 1896, p.23, Immigration History Research Center, University of Minnesota. 88(t) Atlantis Records Photographs, Balch Institute for Ethnic Studies; (b) Minnesota Historical Society. 89 Schlesinger Library, Radcliffe College.

New Americans

90(t) MF/NPS, lent by Immigration History Research Center, University of Minnesota; (b) MF/NPS. 91(t) Michigan Historical Collections, Bentley Historical Library, University of Michigan; (b) Brown Brothers. 92(tl) Encyclopaedia Britannica, Inc.; (tr), (bl), (br) MF/NPS. 93 MF/NPS. 94(t) FPG International; (b) MF/NPS, gift of Mary Abdnour. 95 MF/NPS. 96 MF/NPS. 97 Portfolio 131, #17a, Broadside Collection, Rare Book and Special Collections Division, Library of Congress.

The Closing Door

98(l) MF/NPS; (r) #76–9638, National Museum of American History, Smithsonian Institution. 99 #88-8676, Archives Center, National Museum of American History, Smithsonian Institution. 100, 101 MF/NPS. 102 B'nai B'rith Archives. 103 MF/NPS. 104(l) MF/NPS; (r) UPI/Bettmann Newsphotos. 105(l) MF/NPS; (r) Library of Congress. 106–107 Photography Archive, Carpenter Center for the Visual Arts, Harvard University.

Through America's Gate

108 Brown Brothers. 109(tl) MF/NPS, gift of Angelo E. Forgione in memory of Antoinette Cammarata Forgione and Mary Cammarata Forgione; (bl) MF/NPS, lent by Joshua D. Lowenfish family; (r) MF/NPS, gift of Theodore Anderson. 110 Brown Brothers. 111(t) Culver Pictures; (b) Brown Brothers.

The Inspection Maze

112(t) MF/NPS, gift of Lillian Ziebell; (m) MF/NPS, gift of Albert and Aida Slabotzky; (b) MF/NPS, lent by Evelyn Silberman. 113 Alland Collection, Culver Pictures. 114(l) Brown Brothers; (tr) MF/NPS; (br) State Historical Society of Wisconsin. 115 MF. 116(t) MF/NPS; (b) William Williams Collection, New York

Public Library. 117(t) MF/NPS; (b) LC-USZ62-26543, Library of Congress.
118(t) Culver Pictures; (b) William Williams Collection, New York Public Library.
119 Temple University-Balch Institute Center for Immigration Research.
120 MF/NPS, gift of Joseph H. Mintzer. 121 Augustus F. Sherman Collection, NPS.

Free to Land
122(l) NPS, gift of Helen Goldflus; r) State Historical Society of Wisconsin.
123 Culver Pictures. 124 MF/NPS, gifts of Terry Kaplan, Sylvia Zide, lent by Anna
Schiller Griasch. 125(t) MF/NPS; (b) State Historical Society of Wisconsin.
126(t) Alland Collection, Culver Pictures; (b) Lewis Hine Memorial Collection,
courtesy PhotoCollect Gallery. 127 State Historical Society of Wisconsin. 128–131
Robert Watchorn Collection, Watchorn Methodist Church, Alfreton, England.

Held for Investigation
132 RG85: 52706/4, National Archives. 133 Photo by J.H. Adams, Photography
Archive, Carpenter Center for the Visual Arts, Harvard University. 134(l) Brown
Brothers; (tr) MF/NPS, lent by Museum of Opthalmology, The Foundation of the
American Academy of Opthalmology; (br) LC-USZ62-22339, Library of Congress.
135(t) Culver Pictures; (b) MF/NPS, gift of Louisa Hayter Gordon. 136 Brown
Brothers. 137(t) Rosi Edythe Flamm, courtesy NPS; (b) NPS, gift of Eric R. Moberg.
138 Culver Pictures. 139 *New York Medical Journal*, September 3, 1913, New York
Academy of Medicine. 140 MF/NPS, lent by Archives of the History of American
Psychology, University of Akron. 141(t) MF/NPS, gift of Knox family; (bl) *Manual
for the Testing of Immigrant Aliens*, p.110, RG90: Box 36, File 219, National Archives;
(br) Brown Brothers. 143 Photo by Lewis W. Hine, General Board of Global
Ministries, United Methodist Church.

Day In and Day Out
144(t) Augustus F. Sherman Collection, NPS; (b) Alland Collection, Culver Pictures.
145 Photo by J.H. Adams, Photography Archive, Carpenter Center for the Visual
Arts, Harvard University. 146, 147 MF/NPS. 148 Photo by J.H. Adams, Photography Archive, Carpenter Center for the Visual Arts, Harvard University.
149 Augustus F. Sherman Collection, NPS. 150(t) Alland Collection, Culver
Pictures; (b) Albert J. Carcieri Collection. 151 *Leslie's Weekly*, October 14, 1907,
NPS. 152–153 Alland Collection, Culver Pictures. 154 RG85: 51462/4, National
Archives. 155(l) MF/NPS, fork gift of Stanley E. Ufier; (r) UPI/Bettmann Newsphotos.

Immigrant Aid Societies
156(l) UPI/Bettmann Newsphotos; (r) YIVO Institute for Jewish Research. 157 State
Historical Society of Wisconsin. 158 LC-USZ62-20622, Library of Congress. 159 *The
NEA Service*, January 26, 1926, Ludmila K. Foxlee Papers, NPS, gift of Joyce Pratt.

Isle of Hope/Isle of Tears
160, 161 Photos by J.H. Adams, Photography Archive, Carpenter Center for the
Visual Arts, Harvard University. 162–163 Alland Collection, Culver Pictures.

Treasures from Home
164 MF/NPS, gift of Mary Simonelli. 165 Photo by Norman McGrath.
166 MF/NPS, gift of Theresa A. and John L. Thomas. 167 MF/NPS, gift of Mr. and
Mrs. Frank Joch. 168(l) MF/NPS, gift of Virginia Macaluso; (r) MF/NPS, lent by
Japanese American National Museum. 169 MF/NPS, gift of Mary Lelet, Regional
Council in New Jersey, Ukrainian National Women's League of America, Inc.
170(t) MF/NPS, gift of Virginia G. Ciocco; (b) MF/NPS, gift of Ellen Whaite Pierce.
171(t) MF/NPS, gift of Juan Ramirez-Muñoz; (b) MF/NPS, gift of Mr. and Mrs.
Frank Joch. 172 MF/NPS, gift of Antoinette J. Zulli. 173 MF/NPS, gift of Birgitta
Hedman Fichter. 174 MF/NPS, gift of Henry A. Witt. 175 MF/NPS, gift of Anna
Schiller Griasch. 176 MF/NPS, gift of William Linczer. 177 MF/NPS, gift of
Jennette Pyne. 178 MF/NPS, lent by Joshua D. Lowenfish family. 179 Lori Hanley
Moody, courtesy MF. 180 (tl) MF/NPS, gift of Elizabeth Smith Nimmo; (tr)
MF/NPS, lent by Lucy LaCugna Yakowenko; (bl) MF/NPS, gift of Rose Ishmael
Tully and Grace Ishmael Robins; (br) MF/NPS, lent by Flora Sutton Chambers and
Helen Sutton Wolf. 181 MF/NPS, gift of George H. Cook. 182(t) Photo by Norman
McGrath; (b) MF/NPS, gift of Josephine E. Nadeau. 183(l) MF/NPS, gift of Mary
Proodian; (r) MF/NPS, gift of Margaret Mudri Smyers. 184 MF/NPS, gift of Jean C.
Osajda. 185 MF/NPS, gift of B. Jean Oline. 186(l) MF/NPS, gift of Tessie Argianas;
(tr) MF/NPS, gift of Nina Stetzky Yasdick; (br) MF/NPS, gift of The Jewish
Museum. 187 MF/NPS, gift of Anna Popkin. 188(tl) MF/NPS, gift of Martin H.
Hofstetter; (tr) MF/NPS, lent by Louise Segota Niemi; (bl) MF/NPS, gift of Mary T.
Rutherford; (br) MF/NPS, lent by Florence Ercolano. 189(tl), (bl) MF/NPS, gift of
Jean C. Osajda; (tr) MF/NPS, gift of Priscilla Christine Burroughs; (br) MF/NPS, gift
of Thomas A. Michalski. 190 MF/NPS, gift of George and Georgia Kadlec.

191 MF/NPS, lent by Charlotte Weinkle Chazin. 192 Photo by Norman McGrath.
193 MF/NPS, gift of Lily T. Lowe. 194 MF/NPS, lent by Lottie Y. Alto.
195 MF/NPS, gift of Martha Marie Petersen Snyder. 196 MF/NPS, gift of Mary Jue.
197 MF/NPS, gift of Erna Henges Hays. 198 MF/NPS, gift of Rae Orlov Ginsberg.
199(l) MF/NPS, gift of Lena and Henry J. Asendorf; (tr) MF/NPS, gift of Larsine
Jensen Bogelund; (br) MF/NPS, gift of Anna Popkin. 200(tl) MF/NPS, gift of Pearl
Pohrille; (tr) MF/NPS, lent by Luther College Collection, Vesterheim, The
Norwegian-American Museum, Decorah, Iowa; (bl) MF/NPS, gift of Barbara
Voichick Kulicke; (br) MF/NPS, lent by Kathleen Ann Magill. 201(t) MF/NPS, gift
of Alice and Marjorie Semerjian; (m) MF/NPS, gift of Franklin R. Fitz; (b) MF/NPS,
lent by Vesterheim, The Norwegian-American Museum, Decorah, Iowa.
202 MF/NPS, lent by Alcina de Jesús Silva Morais. 203 MF/NPS, lent by Leonora
Butler. 204(l) MF/NPS, gift of Edward A. Schmidt; (r) MF/NPS, lent by Rose
Weber. 205 MF/NPS, lent by Craig Anthony Bannister. 206–207 MF/NPS, lent by
Jeanne d'Arc Chénard. 208 Martha Marie Petersen Snyder, courtesy NPS. 209 Muriel
M. Petioni, courtesy NPS. 210(l) Ingrid Sjöman Alhfors, courtesy NPS; (r) Gertrude
Itak Decker, courtesy NPS. 211(l) Mimi Vang Olsen, courtesy NPS; (r) MF/NPS, gift
of Pauline Baum Nismann. 212(t) Beiser family Photographs, Balch Institute for
Ethnic Studies; (b) Watka Family Photographs, Balch Institute for Ethnic Studies.
213 Sonia Podell, courtesy NPS. 214(l) NPS, lent by Birgitta Hedman Fichter;
(r) Paul and Evelyn Burlant, courtesy NPS. 215(l) family of the Rev. Mark E.
Petrakis, courtesy NPS; (r) Ralph G. Martin family, courtesy NPS. 216(l) Esko J.
Koskinen, courtesy NPS; (m) MF/NPS, lent by Alan M. Olswing and family of
Michel Dorogoi; (r) Frederick C. Wolf, courtesy NPS. 217 NPS, lent by Elizabeth
Ricca. 218(t) Vartan Hartunian, courtesy NPS; (b) Isayo Kiyonaga Yoshida, courtesy
NPS. 219(t) Mimi Vang Olsen, courtesy NPS; (b) MF/NPS, gift of Erna Henges
Hays. 220 Wai Murata Konishi and Bessie Konishi, courtesy NPS. 221 MF/NPS,
gift of Celia Adler. 222(l) William Bela Solyom, courtesy NPS; (r) Juliet Halpern,
courtesy NPS. 223(l) Maljan Chavoor, courtesy NPS; (r) MF/NPS, gift of Edmund
Frank and Ruth Harris Goussé. 224, 225 MF/NPS, gifts of Gertrude Schneider
Smith. 226 (l) MF/NPS, gift of Nathan Solomon; (r) Nathan Solomon, courtesy MF.
227 MF/NPS, gifts of Nathan Solomon. 228, 229 MF/NPS, gifts of Louis Vukan
Zauneker. 230(l) and (tr) MF/NPS, gifts of Alba Stramesi Fiorentino; (br) Joseph and
Rita Zucchino, courtesy NPS. 231 MF/NPS, gifts of Mary Kudrna Garba.
232, 233 MF/NPS, gifts of Alice and Marjorie Semerjian. 234, 235 MF/NPS, gifts of
Harold A. Perris. 236, 237 MF/NPS, lent by Stanley Mirel. 238–239 Photo by James
Nubile.

Island Chronicles
240 MF/NPS. 241 *Loudon's New-York Packet*, January 20, 1785, New-York Historical
Society. 242 RG77: Map D1, Cartographic Branch, National Archives. 243(t) RG77:
Drawer 38, Sheet 5, Cartographic Branch, National Archives; (b) NPS. 244(t) Temple
University-Balch Institute Center for Immigration Research; (b) Bildarchiv
Preussischer Kulturbesitz, Berlin. 245 New-York Historical Society. 246(t) Avery
Architectural and Fine Arts Library, Columbia University; (b) MF/NPS.
247(t) Keystone-Mast Collection, California Museum of Photography, University of
California, Riverside; (ml), (bl), (br) MF/NPS; (mr) Fred Wasserman Collection.
248(tl) William Williams Papers, New York Public Library; (bl) Powderly Collec-
tion, Catholic University of America; (r) Robert Watchorn Collection, Watchorn
Methodist Church, Alfreton, England. 249 George R. Rinhart Collection. 250 FPG
International 251(t) Fred Wasserman Collection; (b) Bettmann Archives. 252 NPS.
253(t) Frederic Lewis Stock Photos; (b) Eagle Collection, Brooklyn Public Library.

Silent Voices
254(t) Photo by Nir Bareket. (b) Photo by Shirley Burden ©1981. 255 Photo by
Shirley Burden ©1981. 256–257 Photo by Nir Bareket. 258–259 Photo by Eleni
Mylonas. 260 Photo by Joel Greenberg. 261 Photo by David Wasserman.

Restoring a Landmark
262 Photo by Beth Leahy, Beyer Blinder Belle/Notter, Finegold & Alexander, Inc.
263 Photo by Christopher Barnes. 264–265 Photo by Dan Cornish/Esto.

A National Museum
266, 267 Photos by Norman McGrath. 268 Photo by Gilles Peress/Magnum.
269(tl) Photo by Norman McGrath; (tr), (b) Photos by Gilles Peress/Magnum.
270 Photos by Gilles Peress/Magnum. 271 Photos by James Nubile. 272(t) Photo by
James Nubile; (b) Photo by Norman McGrath. 273 Photo by Norman McGrath.
274(t), (br) Photos by James Nubile; (bl) Photo by Gilles Peress/Magnum. 275 Photo
by Gilles Peress/Magnum. 276(l) Photo by Norman McGrath; (r) Photo by James
Nubile. 277 Photo by Norman McGrath (flag portraits by Pablo Delano).

Further Reading

Peak Immigration Years: 1880–1924

Abbott, Edith. *Immigration: Select Documents and Case Records.* Chicago: The University of Chicago Press, 1924. Reprint. New York: Arno Press and The New York Times, 1969.

Adamic, Louis. *Laughing in the Jungle: The Autobiography of an Immigrant in America.* New York: Harper & Brothers, 1932.

Allen, Leslie. *Liberty: The Statue and the American Dream.* [New York:] The Statue of Liberty-Ellis Island Foundation, Inc., 1985.

Antin, Mary. *The Promised Land.* Boston: Houghton Mifflin Co., 1912. 2nd ed. with a foreword by Oscar Handlin. Princeton: Princeton University Press, 1985.

Bodnar, John. *The Transplanted: A History of Immigrants in Urban America.* Bloomington: Indiana University Press, 1985.

Brandenburg, Broughton. *Imported Americans: The Story of the Experiences of a Disguised American and His Wife Studying the Immigration Question.* New York: S.A. Stokes Company, 1904.

Daniels, Roger. *Coming to America: A History of Immigration and Ethnicity in American Life.* New York: Harper Collins Publishers, 1990.

Graham, Stephen. *With Poor Immigrants to America.* New York: The Macmillan Company, 1914.

Handlin, Oscar. *A Pictorial History of Immigration.* New York: Crown Publishers, 1972.

Higham, John. *Strangers in the Land: Patterns of American Nativism, 1860-1925.* New Brunswick, New Jersey: Rutgers University Press, 1955.

Jones, Maldwyn A. *Destination America.* New York: Holt, Rinehart and Winston, 1976.

Kraut, Alan. *The Huddled Masses: The Immigrant in American Society, 1880-1921.* Arlington Heights, Illinois: Harlan Davidson, Inc., 1982.

Lai, Him Mark, Genny Lim, and Judy Yung. *Island: Poetry and History of Chinese Immigrants on Angel Island 1910–1940.* San Francisco: HOC DOI (History of Chinese Detained on Island), a project of the Chinese Culture Foundation of San Francisco, 1980.

Marzio, Peter C., ed. *A Nation of Nations: The People Who Came to America as Seen through Objects and Documents at the Smithsonian Institution.* New York: Harper & Row, Publishers, 1976.

Morrison, Joan, and Charlotte Fox Zabusky. *American Mosaic: The Immigrant Experience in the Words of Those Who Lived It.* New York: E.P. Dutton, 1980.

Morton Allan Directory of European Passenger Steamship Arrivals. Baltimore: Genealogical Publishing Co., Inc., 1987.

Novotny, Ann. *Strangers at the Door: Ellis Island, Castle Garden, and the Great Migration to America.* Riverside, Connecticut: The Chatham Press, Inc., 1971. Abridged ed. New York: Bantam Pathfinder Editions, 1974.

Steiner, Edward A. *On the Trail of the Immigrant.* New York: Fleming H. Revell Company, 1906. Reprint. New York: Arno Press and the New York Times, 1969.

Stern, Gail F. *Freedom's Doors: Immigrant Ports of Entry to the United States.* Philadelphia: The Balch Institute for Ethnic Studies, 1986.

Taylor, Philip. *The Distant Magnet: European Emigration to the U.S.A.* London: Eyre and Spottiswoode, 1971. Paperback ed. New York: Harper Torchbooks, 1972.

Thernstrom, Stephan. *Harvard Encyclopedia of American Ethnic Groups.* Cambridge: The Belknap Press of Harvard University Press, 1980.

U.S. Department of Commerce/Bureau of the Census. *Historical Statistics of the United States: Colonial Times to 1970.* New York: Basic Books, 1976.

Through America's Gate and Island Chronicles

Benton, Barbara. *Ellis Island: A Pictorial History.* New York: Facts On File Publications, 1985.

Beyer Blinder Belle/Anderson Notter Finegold. *Ellis Island. Statue of Liberty National Monument. Historic Structure Report: The Main Building,* vol. 1; *Unit One Buildings,* vol. 2; *Powerhouse,* vol. 3; *Units 2, 3, and 4,* vol. 4. Washington, D.C.: U.S. Department of the Interior/National Park Service, 1988.

Brownstone, David M., Irene Franck, and Douglas L. Brownstone. *Island of Hope, Island of Tears.* New York: Rawson, Wade Publishers, Inc., 1979.

Corsi, Edward. *In the Shadow of Liberty: The Chronicle of Ellis Island.* New York: The Macmillan Co., 1935. Reprint. New York: Arno Press and The New York Times, 1969.

Cowen, Philip. *Memories of an American Jew.* New York: International Press, 1932. Reprint. New York: Arno Press, 1975.

Curran, Henry H. *Pillar to Post.* New York: Charles Scribner's Sons, 1941.

Hardwick, Mary-Angela. "Guardians at the Golden Door." *Seaport* 25, nos.1&2, 1991: 30–37.

Howe, Frederic C. *The Confessions of a Reformer.* New York: Charles Scribner's Sons, 1925. Reprint. New York: Quadrangle/The New York Times Book Co., 1967.

Jonas, Susan, ed. *Ellis Island: Echoes from a Nation's Past.* New York: Aperture, 1989.

La Guardia, Fiorello H. *The Making of an Insurgent: An Autobiography, 1882–1919.* Philadelphia: J.B. Lippincott Co., 1948.

Pitkin, Thomas M. *Keepers of the Gate: A History of Ellis Island.* New York: New York University Press, 1975.

Pousson, John F. *An Overview and Assessment of Archeological Resources on Ellis Island. Statue of Liberty National Monument. New York.* Rockville, Maryland: U.S. Department of the Interior/National Park Service, Denver Service Center, Eastern Team, 1986.

Safford, Victor. *Immigration Problems. Personal Experiences of an Official.* New York: Dodd, Mead and Company, 1925.

Shapiro, Mary J. *Gateway to Liberty: The Story of the Statue of Liberty and Ellis Island.* New York: Vintage Books, 1986.

Tifft, Wilton S. *Ellis Island.* New York: W.W. Norton, 1971.

_____. *Ellis Island.* Chicago: Contemporary Books, 1990.

Unrau, Harlan D. *Historic Resource Study (Historical Component). Ellis Island. Statue of Liberty National Monument. New York-New Jersey.* 3 vols. Washington, D.C.: U.S. Department of the Interior/National Park Service, 1984.

_____. *Historic Structure Report. Ellis Island. Historical Data. Statue of Liberty National Monument. New York/New Jersey.* Washington, D.C.: U.S. Department of the Interior/National Park Service, Denver Service Center, 1981.

West, Herbert Faulkner, ed. *The Autobiography of Robert Watchorn.* Oklahoma City: Robert Watchorn Charities, 1958.

Index

Note: Page numbers in *italics* refer to illustrations or captions